S0-AJC-772

SCRIPTURE IN CONTEXT II

MORE ESSAYS ON
THE COMPARATIVE METHOD

SCRIPTURE IN CONTEXT II

MORE ESSAYS ON
THE COMPARATIVE METHOD

Edited by

WILLIAM W. HALLO
JAMES C. MOYER
LEO G. PERDUE

WINONA LAKE, INDIANA
EISENBRAUNS

Copyright ©1983 Eisenbrauns

All rights reserved

Printed in the United States of America

Library of Congress Cataloging in Publication Data

Scripture in context II.

   Includes bibliographical references and index.
   1. Bible. O.T.—Criticism, interpretation, etc.—Addresses, essays, lectures. 2. Bible. O.T.—Comparative studies—Addresses, essays, lectures. I. Hallo, William W. II. Moyer, James C. III. Perdue, Leo G. IV. Title: Scripture in context two.
BS1171.2.S35 1982   221.6   82-13868
ISBN 0-931464-14-5

CONTENTS

ABBREVIATIONS

AASOR	Annual of the American Schools of Oriental Research
AB	Anchor Bible
AfO	*Archiv für Orientforschung*
AHR	*American Historical Review*
AHW	W. von Soden, *Akkadisches Handwörterbuch*
AJSL	*American Journal of Semitic Languages and Literatures*
ANEH	W. W. Hallo and W. K. Simpson, *The Ancient Near East: A History*
ANEP	James B. Pritchard (ed.), *The Ancient Near East in Pictures*
ANET	J. B. Pritchard (ed.), *Ancient Near Eastern Texts*
AOAT	Alter Orient und Altes Testament
AOS	American Oriental Series
ARW	*Archiv für Religionswissenschaft*
AS	Assyriological Studies
ASOR	American Schools of Oriental Research
ASTI	*Annual of the Swedish Theological Institute*
ATD	Das Alte Testament Deutsch
ATR	*Anglican Theological Review*
BAR	*Biblical Archaeologist Reader*
BARev	*Biblical Archaeology Review*
BASOR	*Bulletin of the American Schools of Oriental Research*
BHT	Beiträge zur historischen Theologie
Bib	*Biblica*
BiOr	*Bibliotheca Orientalis*
BJRL	*Bulletin of the John Rylands University Library of Manchester*
BKAT	Biblischer Kommentar: Altes Testament
BO	*Bibliotheca Orientalis*
BR	*Biblical Research*
BTB	*Biblical Theology Bulletin*
BZAW	Beihefte zur *ZAW*
CAD	The Assyrian Dictionary of the Oriental Institute of the University of Chicago
CAH	Cambridge Ancient History
CBQ	*Catholic Biblical Quarterly*
CQR	*Church Quarterly Review*
Enc Jud	*Encyclopaedia Judaica*
Exp Tim	*Expository Times*
HSS	Harvard Semitic Series
HTR	Harvard Theological Review

HUCA	*Hebrew Union College Annual*
ICC	International Critical Commentary
IEJ	*Israel Exploration Journal*
JANESCU	*Journal of the Ancient Near Eastern Society of Columbia University*
JAOS	*Journal of the American Oriental Society*
JBL	*Journal of Biblical Literature*
JCS	*Journal of Cuneiform Studies*
JEA	*Journal of Egyptian Archaeology*
JNES	*Journal of Near Eastern Studies*
JQR	*Jewish Quarterly Review*
JSOT Sup	Journal for the Study of the Old Testament, Supplements
JSS	*Journal of Semitic Studies*
JTS	*Journal of Theological Studies*
KAT	E. Sellin (ed.), Kommentar zum A.T.
MSL	Materialien zum Sumerischen Lexikon
MVAG	Mitteilungen der vorderasiatisch-ägyptischen Gesellschaft
NICOT	New International Commentary on the Old Testament
OIP	Oriental Institute Publications
Or	*Orientalia* (Rome)
OrAnt	*Oriens antiquus*
OTL	Old Testament Library
OTS	*Oudtestamentische Studiën*
RA	*Revue d'assyriologie et d'archéologie orientale*
RB	*Revue Biblique*
REg	*Revue d'égyptologie*
RLA	*Reallexikon der Assyriologie*
RSR	*Recherches de science religieuse*
SACT	S. T. Kang, *Sumerian and Akkadian Cuneiform Texts*
SANE	Sources from the Ancient Near East
SBLMS	Society of Biblical Literature Monograph Series
SBS	Stuttgarter Bibelstudien
SBT	Studies in Biblical Theology
Sem	*Semitica*
StudOr	Studia Orientalia
TDOT	Theological Dictionary of the Old Testament
TLZ	*Theologische Literaturzeitung*
TynBul	*Tyndale Bulletin*
UF	*Ugarit-Forschungen*
VT	*Vetus Testamentum*
VTSup	Vetus Testamentum, Supplements
WMANT	Wissenschaftliche Monographien zum Alten und Neuen Testament

WO	*Die Welt des Orients*
YNER	Yale Near Eastern Researches
ZA	*Zeitschrift für Assyriologie*
ZÄS	*Zeitschrift für Ägyptische Sprache und Altertumskunde*
ZAW	*Zeitschrift für die alttestamentliche Wissenschaft*
ZDPV	*Zeitschrift des deutschen Palästina-Vereins*

PREFACE

In the summers of 1978 and 1980, William W. Hallo directed two National Endowment for the Humanities Summer Seminars, both of which had the title: "Biblical History in its Near Eastern Setting." These seminars, conducted at Yale University, have now resulted in two related collections of essays. The first collection, originating in the 1978 seminar, was

Carl D. Evans, William W. Hallo, and John B. White, eds. *Scripture in Context: Essays on the Comparative Method* (Pittsburgh Theological Monograph Series 34; Pittsburgh: Pickwick, 1980).

This second collection, *Scripture in Context II*, had its origins in the 1980 seminar. The essays that follow, with the exceptions of those by Carl D. Evans and William W. Hallo, were originally presented as seminar papers.

Both seminars investigated in chronological sequence the major phases of ancient Near Eastern history and focused on the history, literary traditions, and religion of ancient Israel within the context of her cultural environs. A major concern was to recognize and explore the implications of the ways in which the native biblical and extra-biblical literary traditions rendered account of themselves. The methodology followed in both the seminars and the resulting essays for the two collections is the contextual approach. This approach to the study of biblical history, literature, and religion is concerned not only to discover illuminating and insightful parallels between biblical and extrabiblical sources, but also to note and recognize the implications of significant and important differences. The methodological essay that explores the rationale and dynamics of this approach is the one by Professor Hallo, published in the 1978 volume: "Biblical History in its Near Eastern Setting: the Contextual Approach" (pp. 1-26). This article should serve as an introduction to both volumes. (Spellings of proper names generally follow *ANEH*.)

The editors of this volume wish to express their thanks to the National Endowment for the Humanities which provided the grants and stipends that funded the work of these two seminars and supported in part the preparation of both manuscripts for publication. For this second volume, special thanks are due James Eisenbraun for his congenial and able assistance in seeing this volume through to publication. We are also indebted to Dikran Y. Hadidian, general editor of the Pittsburgh Theological Monograph Series, for his kind permission to use the same title for this subsequent volume. Finally, thanks also go to Anthony Spalinger who provided some helpful suggestions for the essays by Nelson and Perdue that involve Egyptian sources.

WWH
JCM
LGP

CONTRIBUTORS

R. G. Albertson, Ph.D. (Claremont University), Professor of Religion, University of Puget Sound, Tacoma, Washington

Henry E. Chambers, Ph.D. (Indiana University), Professor of History, California State University, Sacramento, California

Carl D. Evans, Ph.D. (University of Chicago), Associate Professor of Religious Studies, University of South Carolina, Columbia, South Carolina

William E. Evans, Ph.D. (Ohio State University), Assistant Professor of English, Kansas State University, Manhattan, Kansas

W. C. Gwaltney, Jr. Ph.D. (Hebrew Union College), Professor of Bible, Milligan College, Johnson City, Tennessee

William W. Hallo, Ph. D. (University of Chicago), Laffan Professor of Assyriology and Babylonian Literature, Curator of the Babylonian Collection, and Chairman of the Department of Near Eastern Languages and Literatures, Yale University, New Haven, Connecticut

W. Robert McFadden, Ph.D. (Boston University), Professor of Religion, Bridgewater College, Bridgewater, Virginia

James C. Moyer, Ph.D. (Brandeis University), Professor of Religious Studies, Southwest Missouri State University, Springfield, Missouri

Richard D. Nelson, Th.D. (Union Theological Seminary in Virginia), Assistant Professor of Old Testament, Lutheran Theological Seminary, Gettysburg, Pennsylvania

Leo G. Perdue, Ph.D. (Vanderbilt University), Associate Professor of Old Testament, The Graduate Seminary, Phillips University, Enid, Oklahoma

Stephen Stohlmann, Ph.D. (Brandeis University), Associate Professor of Religion, Concordia College, St. Paul, Minnesota

CULT STATUE AND DIVINE IMAGE: A PRELIMINARY STUDY

WILLIAM W. HALLO

Yale University

I. NO GRAVEN IMAGE?

The startling finds at Kuntillet ꜥAjrud in the northeastern Sinai peninsula include votive inscriptions and prayers on pottery, stone jars and walls, in association with drawings, all dated by the excavator to approximately 800 B.C.E.[1] They have raised anew the perennial question whether Israel's God could be represented in art during the biblical period.[2] The very notion would strike most scholars as improbable. Not only is biblical legislation explicitly aniconic and anti-iconic, but even the non-legal descriptions of the divine attributes in the biblical texts are so thoroughly and deliberately aphysical that it would be impossible to translate them into representational, artistic terms. Excavations in Israel have yielded thousands of icons and cultic figurines, but to suggest that even a single one of them represents the God of Israel is to operate in the realm of pure hypothesis.

The attempt has been made nonetheless, most recently by G. W. Ahlström, who contends that a cult-figurine from Hazor, since it comes from an Israelite stratum, may represent an "Israelite God Figurine."[3] And he holds out for that possibility in spite of the cogent criticisms of O. Keel,[4] which he considers.[5] M. Haran finds "mention of a statue of

---

[1]Z. Meshel, *Kuntillet ꜥAjrud: a religious center from the time of the Judaean monarchy on the border of Sinai* (= Israel Museum Cat. No. 175, 1978); Z. Meshel and C. Meyers, "The name of God in the wilderness of Zin," *BA* 39/1 (1976) 6-10.

[2]Meshel, "Did Yahweh have a consort? The new religious inscriptions from the Sinai," *BARev* 5/2 (1979) 24-35; cf. M. H. Pope, "Response to Sasson on the Sublime Song," *Maarav* 2 (1979-80) 207-14, esp. pp. 210f.

[3]G. W. Ahlström, "An Israelite God figurine from Hazor," *Orientalia Suecana* 19-20 (1970-71) 54-62. See photos also in *ANEP* fig. 833 and Y. Yadin, *Hazor* (Schweich Lectures 1972) pl. xxiv b, c.

[4]O. Keel, "Das Vergraben der 'fremden Götter' in Genesis XXXV 4b," *VT* 23 (1973) 305-36, esp. pp. 325f.

[5]Ahlström, "An Israelite God figurine, once more," *VT* 25 (1975) 106-9.

Yahweh" in the story of Micah and the Danites (Judges 17-18)[6] and, for a
later period, Morton Smith refers to "seals on which Hebrew, and
sometimes Yahwist, names are combined with figures of deities some of
[which] deities may be representations of Yahweh."[7] He even cites the
Wisdom of Solomon, which attacks the application of the name Yahweh
to statues, as attesting the existence of the practice.[8]

But the weight of the evidence is overwhelmingly on the other side.
Linguistically, it is true, the biblical text necessarily treats God in
human terms, i.e., invariably in the masculine gender, generally in
singular number, and frequently in idioms compounded with parts of
the (human) body—a common characteristic of the Semitic vocabulary.[9]
But the Aramaic versions (Targumim) dispose of many of these anthro-
pomorphisms, innocent of theological implications though they may
appear to us. And beyond this there is nothing to suggest what Yahweh
would have looked like, how an ancient Israelite should have proceeded
to make a "Yahweh-idol," or a modern archaeologist to identify one. All
that we know of the biblical image of God ($selem$ $^el\bar{o}h\hat{\imath}m$) is that man
was created according to it or in imitation of it (bid^emut $^el\bar{o}h\hat{\imath}m$),[10] and
that the prohibition enshrined in the Second Commandment—albeit
honored in the breach more often than in the observance[11]—was presumably intended to discourage all experimentation to arrive at a more
precise depiction of the deity. The divine presence was adequately
symbolized by the cloud, the ark and certain other natural phenomena,
cult-objects and standards.[12] And it was left for post-biblical times to

---

[6]Menahem Haran, *Temples and Temple-Service in Ancient Israel* (Oxford:
Clarendon, 1978) 35 and note 39; cf. *idem,* "The divine presence in the Israelite
cult and the cultic institutions," *Bib* 50 (1969) 251-67, esp. p. 264.

[7]M. Smith, *Palestinian Parties and Politics that Shaped the Old Testament*
(New York and London: Columbia U.P., 1971) 24f. Cf. *Bib* 50 (1969) 178.

[8]*Bib* 50 (1969) 216 n. 78. Earlier studies by Smith had dealt with other aspects
of the same question; see especially "The image of God: notes on the Hellenization
of Judaism . . . ," *BJRL* 40 (1958) 473-512, and "On the shape of God and the
humanity of Gentiles," in Jacob Neusner, ed., *Religions in Antiquity*: Essays in
Memory of Erwin Ramsdell Goodenough (Leiden: Brill, 1968) 315-26.

[9]E. Dhorme, *L'emploi métaphorique des noms de parties du corps en
hébreu et en accadien* (Paris: Gabalda, 1923); A. L. Oppenheim, "Idiomatic
Akkadian," *JAOS* 61 (1941) 251-71.

[10]Gen 1:26f.; 5:1-3; 9:6. Out of a vast literature one may cite here J. M.
Miller, "In the 'image' and 'likeness' of God," *JBL* 91 (1972) 289-304. Cf. also
note 8 above.

[11]J. Gutmann, "The 'Second Commandment' and the image in Judaism,"
HUCA 32 (1961) 161-74.

[12]See T. W. Mann, *Divine Presence and Guidance in Israelite Traditions: the
Typology of Exaltation* (= Johns Hopkins Near Eastern Studies 9, 1977).

speculate about the divine image in mysticism or somehow to capture it in art.

The situation here described is generally held to be in diametric contrast to that prevailing in the rest of the biblical world. The polytheistic religions of the Asiatic Near East, not to mention Egypt, have left abundant evidence, both textual and artifactual, to their iconodulic attitudes. We possess elaborate (albeit late) treatises on the fabrication of specific divine statues and figurines,[13] detailed descriptions of the characteristic features and attributes distinguishing each,[14] and elaborate rituals for breathing life into the image by opening and washing its mouth,[15] and then maintaining it alive by an elaborate cult aptly described by A. L. Oppenheim as "the care and feeding of the gods."[16] The excavations have turned up innumerable representations, both in the round and on two-dimensional surfaces,[17] which often enough correlate with the textual descriptions or come provided with their own captions and permit a specific identification of the divine image and its particular iconography, especially in the Mesopotamian case.

It is specifically the Mesopotamian divine image, and more particularly its sculptural manifestation, which is to be considered here, in part because its very name (*ṣalam ili/ilāni*) is the precise cognate of the biblical *ṣelem ᵉlōhîm*,[18] in part because it has recently been the subject of several insightful treatments. With their help, one can hope to show that the contrast between Israelite and Mesopotamian attitudes in this regard is less absolute at some times than at others, and thus to illustrate once

[13]See especially F. Köcher, "Der babylonische Göttertypentext," *Mitteilungen des Instituts für Orientforschung* 1 (1953) 57-107. The deities involved here are mainly minor ones. Cf. also C. G. von Brandenstein, *Hethitische Götter nach Bildbeschreibungen in Keilschrifttexten* (= MVAG 46/2 [1943]).

[14]See T. Jacobsen, *The Treasures of Darkness: a History of Mesopotamian Religion* (New Haven and London: Yale U.P., 1976) ch. 4 for an example of descriptions of the major deities drawn from the texts; J.-R. Kupper, *L'iconographie du dieu Amurru dans la glyptique de la Iʳᵉ dynastie babylonienne* (=Académie royale de Belgique, Classe des Lettres, Mémoires 55/1, 1961), for a monographic treatment of a single deity.

[15]G. Meier, "Die Ritualtafel der Serie 'Mundwaschung'," *AfO* 12 (1937-39) 40-45 and pls. i-ii. M. Civil, *JNES* 26 (1967) 211.

[16]A. L. Oppenheim, *Ancient Mesopotamia: Portrait of a Dead Civilization* (University of Chicago Press, 1964) 183-98.

[17]For examples from Canaan and Syria, see especially O. Negbi, *Canaanite Gods in Metal: an Archaeological Study of Ancient Syro-Palestinian Figurines* (Tel Aviv: Institute of Archaeology, 1976); cf. also R. Merhav and T. Orman, "The attire of a Canaanite goddess," *The Israel Museum News* (1979) 90-97.

[18]Cf. my earlier remarks in "Problems in Sumerian Hermeneutics," *Perspectives in Jewish Learning* 5 (ed. B. L. Sherwin, 1973) 2 and 11 n. 4.

more the importance of both contrast and comparison in the contextual approach to biblical history.[19]

II. EMERGENCE OF A MESOPOTAMIAN CULT STATUE

The cult and culture of Mesopotamia were notoriously free of a principal biblical inhibition: sculpture in the round as proscribed in the Decalogue. The human figure in general was the most prized form of votive offering,[20] and the figure of the king, in particular, was a frequent subject of plastic art. From late Early Dynastic times to the end of the Old Babylonian period (ca. 2500-1600 B.C.E.), it is possible to trace the evolution of such statuary and to correlate it with epigraphic evidence, whether inscribed onto the statue itself, or on its pedestal, or contained in late copies, date formulas and a variety of other textual genres.[21] At the same time early Mesopotamia evinced no monotheistic or even henotheistic qualms about the multiplication of deities. Hence the question raised above with respect to alleged "Yahweh-idols"—i.e., how would we know one if we found one—would not at first blush seem to have to bother the archaeologist of Mesopotamia. But matters are not so simple even here.

The common distinctive criteria of the divine in the representational art of ancient Mesopotamia were at one time thought to be such features as size of the figure (absolutely or relative to the surrounding figures), size of eyes, and decoration of the pedestal.[22] More recently, they have been identified as the horned crown and the flounced skirt or garment (respectively the pleated skirt or garment).[23] To these may be added the

[19]Hallo, "Biblical history in its Near Eastern setting: the contextual approach," in C. D. Evans, W. W. Hallo, and J. B. White, eds., *Scripture in Context: Essays on the Comparative Method* (= Pittsburgh Theological Monograph Series 34, 1980) 1-26.

[20]Below, n. 50. See in detail E. Strommenger, "Das Menschenbild in der altmesopotamischen Rundplastik von Mesilim bis Hammurapi," *Baghdader Mitteilungen* 1 (1960) 1-103, pls. 1-22, tables 1-19, maps 1-2; E. A. Braun-Holzinger, *Frühdynastische Beterstatuetten* (= Abhandlungen der deutschen Orientgesellschaft 19, 1977).

[21]See the exhaustive survey by M.-Th. Barrelet, "La 'figure du roi' dans l'iconographie et dans les textes . . . ," in P. Garelli, ed., *Le Palais et la royauté (Archéologie et civilisation)* (=Rencontre Assyriologique Internationale 19, 1974) 27-138, figs. 1-6, and pls. I-III.

[22]H. Frankfort, *The Art and Architecture of the Ancient Orient* (London: Penguin, 1954) 24. Cf. below, n. 53.

[23]R. M. Boehmer, "Götterdarstellungen in der Bildkunst," *Reallexikon der Assyriologie* 3 (1969) 466-69; *idem*, "Die Entwicklung der Hörnerkrone von ihren Anfängen bis zum Ende der Akkadzeit," *Berliner Jahrbuch für Vor- und Frühgeschichte* 7 (1967) 273-91; *idem*, "Hörnerkrone," *RLA* 4 (1975) 431-34.

particular weapon or other symbol associated with various major deities and distinguishing them from each other.[24] But by these criteria, explicit representations of divinity are not attested before Early Dynastic II times (ca. 2700-2500 B.C.E.) at the earliest, and even then only in two-dimensional form, i.e., relief and glyptic. Indeed a votive plaque from Level VII (the latest phase) of the so-called Nintu-temple at Tutub (Khafaje) in the Diyala valley, dated by the excavators to the beginning of the Early Dynastic III period, is described by Eva Strommenger as "one of the earliest unmistakable representations of a god in ancient Western Asia."[25] The first sculptures in the round that may be said to represent deities are the Early Dynastic III foundation figurines such as those from Lagash (El-Hiba); on the testimony of the stone inscriptions juxtaposed with them, these represent the personal deity of the royal builder (Enannatum I)—but with their limited size and function they cannot yet be said to constitute cult statues.[26]

The first monumental (i.e. more or less life-size) sculpture in the round for which this claim can be and has been made dates from the succeeding Sargonic period (ca. 2300-2150 B.C.E.). In 1968, Agnes Spycket was able to rejoin a head wearing a crown featuring three tiers of horns with a headless statue wearing a flounced garment.[27] Both had been found at Susa; together they formed the seated cult-statue of a goddess—Inanna according to Parrot,[28] Narunte according to Hinz[29] and Orthmann[30]—dedicated, according to the inscription,[31] by Puzur-Inshushinak (Kutik-

[24]U. Seidl, "Göttersymbole und -attribute. A. Archäologisch. - I. Mesopotamien," *RLA* 3 (1969) 483-90; earlier: E. D. van Buren, *Symbols of the Gods in Mesopotamian Art* (= Analecta Orientalia 23, 1945).

[25]E. Strommenger, *5000 Years of the Art of Mesopotamia* (New York: N. Abrams, 1964); translation of *Fünf Jahrtausende Mesopotamien . . .* (Munich, 1962) fig. 65. The German original calls it "eine der ältesten gesicherten bildlichen Wiedergaben eines Gottes in Altvorderasien" (reference courtesy H. el-Safadi).

[26]D. P. Hansen, "Al-Hiba, 1968-1969, a preliminary report," *Artibus Asiae* 32 (1970) 243-50, figs. 1-18, and *apud* Orthmann, *Der alte Orient*, 168 *ad* fig. 33a.

[27]A. Spycket, "Une grande déesse élamite retrouve son visage," *Syria* 45 (1968) 67-73.

[28]A. Parrot, *Sumer: the Dawn of Art*, tr. by S. Gilbert and J. Emmons (New York: Golden Press, 1961) (= A. Malraux and G. Salles, eds., *The Arts of Mankind* 1) fig. 203.

[29]W. Hinz, *The Lost World of Elam*, tr. by J. Barnes (New York U.P., 1973) 48f. and pl. 4.

[30]W. Orthmann, *Der alte Orient* (= Propyläen Kunstgeschichte 14, 1975) fig. 50.

[31]G. A. Barton, *The Royal Inscriptions of Sumer and Akkad* (New Haven: Yale U.P., 1929) 158f. No. 7 (= MDP 14:17ff.).

Inshushinak).[32] But this example comes from outside Mesopotamia, and Spycket herself went on to consider the entire phenomenon of the cult statue within Mesopotamia.[33]

III. THE SPYCKET HYPOTHESIS

Within Mesopotamia itself, the Sargonic period has nothing comparable to offer. It does, however, witness the first deification of the reigning monarch, and the iconography duly reflects this abrupt innovation. The king and other members of the royal family are now depicted wearing either the flounced garment (Naram Sin's Stele A, from Diarbekir;[34] Enheduanna's disc[35]) or the horned crown (Naram-Sin's Stele B, from Susa)[36] but not both. Only "real" gods are represented with both.[37]

This occurs first in the late Sargonic or early neo-Sumerian period (ca. 2150-2100 B.C.E.). The outstanding example is the stele of Gudea, showing the ruler of Lagash (clearly identified by the cartouche on his garment) being led before a great deity by the god Ningizzida, "recognizable by the dragon heads rising from his shoulders."[38] Ningizzida in turn is preceded by another deity, presumably his vizier Alla.[39] For it is apparently the same minor deity who is the subject of the first Mesopotamian sculpture that may lay claim to being a cult statue: it is inscribed with the name and title of Alla, but unfortunately its head and with it its headdress is lost.[40]

---

[32]For his date see R. M. Boehmer, "Die Datierung des Puzur/Kutik-Inšušinak ...," *Or* 35 (1966) 345-76.

[33]A Spycket, *Les statues de culte dans les textes Mésopotamiens des origines à la Ire dynastie de Babylone* (= Cahiers de la Revue Biblique 9, 1968).

[34]Parrot, *Sumer*, fig. 211; Orthmann, *Der alte Orient*, fig. 105.

[35]Orthmann, *Der alte Orient*, fig. 101; W. W. Hallo and J. J. A. van Dijk, *The Exaltation of Inanna* (= YNER 3, 1968) frontispiece and ch. 1: "Enheduanna: her life and works." Cf. E. Sollberger, *RA* 63 (1969) 180.

[36]Parrot, *Sumer*, figs. 212f.; Orthmann, *Der alte Orient*, fig. 104; Strommenger, *5000 Years*, figs. 122f.

[37]Boehmer, *RLA* 3, p. 467.

[38]Parrot, *Sumer*, fig. 284 and p. 230; cf. Spycket, *RLA* 6 (1980) 36, fig. 18. Cf. also the fragmentary stele in Parrot, *Tello. Vingt campagnes de fouilles (1877-1933)* (Paris: Albin Michel, 1948) 183 fig. 38a which identifies both Gudea and Ningizzida by name though the deity is shown without any headdress, only wearing the flounced garment. Differently J. Börker-Klähn *apud* Orthmann, *Der alte Orient*, 206 *ad* fig. 117a.

[39]Cf. An = Anum (ed. Litke, MS) V: 262f.: ^{d}Ib-bu = sukkal [^{d}nin-giš-zi]-da-ke₄, ^{d}Al-^{r}x-x^1 = ŠU.

[40]Spycket, *Les Statues*, pp. 17 and 57f., based on Strommenger, *ZA* 53 (1959) 47-50. Cf. Orthmann, *Der alte Orient*, 176 and fig. 52.

With the advent of the Ur III dynasty and the neo-Sumerian period proper (ca. 2100-2000 B.C.E.), there occurred a dramatic change in temple architecture from the bent-axis approach to one in which the worshipper confronted the cella at the far end of the temple immediately upon entering it from the opposite end of its longer axis.[41] This cella, like the throne-room of a palace, would logically suggest the concomitant emergence of a proper cult statue, seated or standing on a throne-dais like a king. But for the Ur III period itself, the excavations have provided only tantalizing glimpses of sculptured heads without torsos and vice versa.[42]

The Early Old Babylonian period (ca. 2000-1800 B.C.E.) introduces a new variation—and a new ambiguity: seated feminine figures in flounced garments and lacking the horned crown, but featuring holes which may have served for the attachment of such crowns.[43] These may then represent either goddesses or priestesses or even, conceivably, both, according as such a crown, of which separate examples are known,[44] was or was not attached.[45]

The first clear examples of the horned crown on a standing figure of more or less life-size dimensions come from Mari. In the case of the famous goddess with the flowing vase, we are probably dealing with a monument from the period of Mari's independence (ca. 1800-1750 B.C.E.).[46] In the case of Puzur-Ishtar's statue, we are in the period of the "šakkanakku's," somewhere in the twentieth century.[47] Here the successful rejoining of head and torso show that the divine headdress is combined with the non-divine garment; hence the statue represents the royal donor, not the divine beneficiary.[48] This was already pointed out by Nagel in 1959, who derived from it the more general conclusion that

[41]Spycket, *Les statues*, pp. 9-11. Cf. E. Heinrich *apud* Orthmann, *Der alte Orient*, 138f.

[42]Spycket, *Les statues*, pp. 16f.

[43]Spycket, *Les statues*, pp. 17-19, fig. 6; Parrot, *Sumer*, fig. 328; Orthmann, *Der alte Orient*, fig. 164c; Strommenger, *5000 Years*, fig. 142.

[44]E. Borowski, "Eine Hörnerkrone aus Bronze," *Or* 17 (1948) 294-98 and pls. XXV—XXVIII; D. J. Wiseman, "The goddess Lama at Ur," *Iraq* 22 (1960) pl. xxiia.

[45]Hallo, "Women of Sumer," *Bibliotheca Mesopotamica* 4 (1976) 33f. and 136 fig. 16; *idem*, "The birth of kings," forthcoming, n. 44.

[46]Parrot, *Sumer*, figs. 339f.; Orthmann, *Der alte Orient*, fig. 160b; Strommenger, *5000 Years*, figs. 162f.

[47]H. Limet, *Textes administratifs de l'époque des šakkanakku* (= ARMT 19, 1976) 8.

[48]Parrot, *Sumer*, figs. 334f.; Orthmann, *Der alte Orient*, figs. 159-60a; Strommenger, *5000 Years*, figs. 152f.

inscribed statues represent the donor (or conceivably his princely but
still mortal beneficiary), but never demonstrably the divine recipient.[49]
    The rule was generalized even more in 1968, when I first pointed to
"the fact that the most expensive type of votive, the statue, clearly depicts
the worshipper, not the deity" in ancient Mesopotamia.[50] The point was
reiterated in 1970,[51] this time buttressed by appeal to the comprehensive
study of both the archaeological and textual evidence by Spycket, who
concluded that before the neo-Sumerian period, divine cult statues are
attested neither in the excavations from Mesopotamia nor in the texts. If
the deity was conceived in anthropomorphic terms in third millennium
Mesopotamia, this was confined to representations in glyptic, relief, and
wall painting, or in statuettes and figurines far smaller than life-size, or
perhaps in the substitution of humans for deities in rites such as the
sacred marriage. The primary medium for figurative, three-dimensional
representation of the deity in the cult was apparently, at this time, the
symbol or totem.[52]

IV. CRITIQUES OF THE HYPOTHESIS

    On the archaeological side Spycket's argument has not been refuted.
True, Jacobsen, following Frankfort and Lloyd, continues to regard a
pair of Early Dynastic II statues found in their Diyala excavations as
representing deities. The larger of them is described as "a statue of
Ninurta,"[53] presumably on the basis of its greater size, enormous eyes,
and decorated base. But there is nothing else to distinguish it from all
the other statues found buried together beneath the floor of the Temple
of Abu at Eshnunna (Tell Asmar).[54] The same is true of the "cult statue
of a goddess"[55] found in the same buried hoard. Certainly the mere fact
of their being buried, or the location of their burial place next to the
altar, does not qualify the statues as divine, for they were clearly interred
together with statues which by common consent are non-divine votive
statues. Moreover, one of them shares with the smaller statues (and with
Early Dynastic statuary generally) the typical attitude of veneration with

---

[49]W. Nagel, "Die Statue eines neusumerischen Gottkönigs," ZA 53 (1959)
261-65, esp. p. 265 and n. 21.
    [50]Hallo, "Individual prayer in Sumerian: the continuity of a tradition,"
JAOS 88/1 (= AOS 53, 1968) 75.
    [51]Hallo, "The cultic setting of Sumerian poetry," in A. Finet, ed., Actes de la
XVIIe Rencontre Assyriologique Internationale (1970) 134.
    [52]Cf. Spycket, Les statues, pp. 99-105 for most of these points.
    [53]Jacobsen, Treasures of Darkness, frontispiece.
    [54]See the "group picture" in Parrot, Sumer, fig. 129; P. Delougaz and
S. Lloyd, Pre-Sargonid Temples in the Diyala Region (= OIP 58, 1942) 188 fig. 149.
    [55]So Lloyd, ibid., p. 190.

hands clasped at the chest. Seton Lloyd's own reconstruction of a cult statue is utterly different, as witness his drawing[56] and his remark that "the appearance of the cult statue . . . was based on fragments from other contemporary excavations."[57]

And indeed, Jacobsen himself argues repeatedly that "the earliest (cult) images would seem to have shown the gods in their nonhuman forms; later on images in human form became prevalent and the older nonhuman images were considered mere 'emblems' though . . . they were still the form under which the gods accompanied the army in battle and the form under which they validated oaths."[58] He dates the non-human forms to the fourth millennium, while "with the beginning of the third millennium, from Early Dynastic onward, the human form came to dominate almost completely, leaving to the older forms the somewhat ambiguous role of divine 'emblems' only."[59] Although he thus differs from Spycket in the dating of the process, he agrees with her sequence, and speaks of a "protracted contest between anthropomorphic and nonanthropomorphic shapes" which ended only in the first millennium, in Ninurta's case with the "god in human form, but still winged. Significantly he is throwing thunderbolts at his own older form. . . ."[60]

More fundamental objections can be raised against Spycket's view on textual grounds. Sollberger, for one, continues to translate the Early Dynastic III references from Lagash as "Ur-Nanše a façonné (la statue

---

[56]Ibid., p. 198 fig. 159.

[57]Ibid., p. 197. Cf. Parrot, *Sumer*, 106; Hansen *apud* Orthmann, *Der alte Orient*, 163f.

[58]*Treasures of Darkness*, p. 14. For the oath by the weapon of Ninurta see also *ana ittišu* VI iii 37-46, edited by B. Landsberger, *MSL* 1 (1937) 84f., and Hallo, "The slandered bride," *Studies . . . Oppenheim* (1964) 95.

[59]*Treasures of Darkness*, p. 9. Perhaps this development is only a special case of the general priority of symbolic over representational forms, already illustrated by the painted pottery of the late sixth millennium, especially from Samarra; see the illustrations in B. L. Goff, *Symbols of Prehistoric Mesopotamia* (New Haven and London: Yale U.P., 1963) figs. 32-41 and her discussion, pp. 3-9. Earlier, Jacobsen defended a comparable if less explicitly dated evolution towards anthropomorphism in "Formative tendencies in Sumerian religion," in G. E. Wright, ed., *The Bible and the Ancient Near East: Essays in Honor of William Foxwell Albright* (1961) 267-78, reprinted in his *Toward the Image of Tammuz* (= HSS 21, 1970) 1-15. Cf. also Parrot, *Sumer*, 102.

[60]*Treasures of Darkness*, p. 128 and note 201 (correct to *Sculptures*, pl. XXXVII and *Stones*, p. 138). For the role of Ninurta's weapons in the myth of his return to Nippur (Angim) and in lawsuits of the second millennium, see Hallo, Review of J. S. Cooper, *The Return of Ninurta to Nippur*, *JAOS* 101 (1981) 253-57 and above, n. 58, respectively.

de) Nanše" etc.[61] where Spycket translates "Ur-Nanše sculpta (sa statue) pour Nanše"[62] on the analogy of the votive statue of Entemena.[63] Sauren notes that texts (and seal designs) testify to the practice of divine travels well before neo-Sumerian times. The practice (quite distinct from the later "journeys of the divine weapon" for the purpose of administering oaths)[64] could well have demanded statues of wood and other reasonably portable but at the same time perishable materials.[65] (For the late second millennium, the use of *mēsu*-wood as the "flesh of the gods," i.e., the body of the divine statues, is attested by the Erra Epic along with other precious and semiprecious materials;[66] for the first millennium, the "Göttertypentext" makes the corresponding point.)[67] Pettinato adds the evidence of early month names as well as numerous references to offerings for deities (as distinct from their emblems) which fail to specify their statues only because the statues were equated with the deity; by contrast, offerings to the statues of (living) kings and other mortals were so identified.[68]

Additional, if ambiguous, evidence could be cited from the letter-prayers and divine hymns. The former were typically deposited at the feet of the divine statue,[69] or placed in its mouth,[70] but are not known in their classical form and function before neo-Sumerian times.[71] The latter can on various grounds be said to have their cultic setting in "the dedication of a cult statue of the relevant deity."[72] But the divine hymn,

---

[61]E. Sollberger and J.-R. Kupper, *Inscriptions royales sumériennes et akkadiennes* (= Littératures anciennes du Proche-Orient 3, 1971) 46. So also most recently J. S. Cooper, "Studies in Mesopotamian lapidary inscriptions II," *RA* 74 (1980) 101-10, esp. p. 108.

[62]*Les statues*, p. 38.

[63]Ibid., p. 31.

[64]R. Harris, "The journey of the divine weapon," in H. G. Güterbock and Th. Jacobsen, eds., *Studies in Honor of Benno Landsberger* . . . (= AS 16, 1965) 217-24.

[65]H. Sauren, review of Spycket, *Les statues, JSS* 14 (1969) 116-19.

[66]L. Cagni, *L'Epopea di Erra* (= Studi Semitici 34, 1969) and "The poem of Erra," *SANE* 1 (1977) 61-119, I 150.

[67]See above, n. 13.

[68]G. Pettinato, review of Spycket, *Les statues* in *BiOr* 26 (1969) 212-16. (1969) 212-16.

[69]Hallo, "Individual prayer" (above, n. 50), esp. p. 79 and n. 74.

[70]Hallo, "The expansion of cuneiform literature," *Proceedings of the American Academy for Jewish Research* 46-47 (1980) 307-22, esp. p. 318.

[71]Hallo, "Letters, prayers and letter-prayers," *Proceedings of the 7th World Congress of Jewish Studies (1977)* vol. 1 (1981) 101-11.

[72]Hallo, "Cultic setting," p. 120; cf. R. Kutscher, *Kramer Anniversary Volume* (= AOAT 25, 1976) 305 n. 3 and 307 *ad* line 3.

too, achieves its classical Sumerian form only in the early second millennium; the hymns which demonstrably antedate Old Babylonian and even Ur III times tend rather to be in honor of temples. They are thus largely lacking in the prominent allusions to the physical attributes and emanations of the divine image which characterize many of the later divine hymns.[73]

V. THE LATER EVIDENCE

Thus the thesis of Spycket remains a hypothesis, still awaiting decisive confirmation but meantime challenging easy generalizations about polytheism in general and the early Mesopotamian cult in particular.[73a] But even if the worship of the deity in the form of an anthropomorphic cult statue should eventually prove to antedate the dramatic change in temple architecture at the end of the third millennium in Mesopotamia, there can be no doubt of the growing and pervasive role of the divine statue there in the second and first millennia. This assertion could easily be documented by a systematic survey of the references gathered in the lexica under such translations as "image of a deity,"[74] "statue . . . of a deity,"[75] "statue of a goddess,"[76] "representation (of the *lamassu*-spirit) in human shape,"[77] or "figural representation of a goddess or (female) divine being."[78] Here only a handful of particularly telling examples, selected mainly from the long cult-history of the city of Babylon, can be adduced by way of illustration.

A curious letter from Hammurapi[79] (ca. 1792-1750 B.C.E.) concerns itself in great detail with the transport of the goddesses (*ištarātu*) of Emutbal from Emutbal to Babylon by boat. The goddesses were to be provided with food for the journey and with *kezertu*-women whose specific duties included dressing their hair.[80] A related letter[81] concerns

---

[73]For the Sumerian evidence see especially W. H. Ph. Römer, "Beiträge zum Lexikon des Sumerischen," *BiOr* 32 (1975) 145-62, 296-308.

[73a]Her major new work, *La Statuaire du Proche-Orient* (= Handbuch der Orientalistik 7/1/2B2, 1981) reaffirms the hypothesis; see e.g., pp. 77-83, 144-46.

[74]*CAD* s.v. *ilu* 7; cf. Ibid. s.v. *iltu* d.

[75]Ibid. s.v. *ṣalmu* a 1'.

[76]Ibid. s.v. *ištaru* 3.

[77]Ibid. s.v. *lamassu* 3.

[78]Ibid. s.v. *lamassatu* 2.

[79]LIH I 34, last edited by R. Frankena, *Altbabylonische Briefe* 2 (1966) 34.

[80]Cf. most recently M. L. Gallery, "Service obligations of the *kezertu*-women," *Or* 49 (1980) 333-38, esp. p. 337 and n. 19. Differently: *CAD* s.v.

[81]LIH I 45, last edited by F. R. Kraus, *Altbabylonische Briefe* 5 (1972) 135.

itself with the return of the same goddesses, now referred to as *ilātu*.[82] That statues are involved seems to go without saying. For the long interval from the fall of the First (Hammurapi) Dynasty of Babylon (ca. 1595 B.C.E.) to that of the Fourth (Isin II) Dynasty (ca. 1027 B.C.E.),[83] the fortunes of its most prominent cult-statue are rehearsed in the "Prophecy of Marduk," a unique document newly reconstructed by Borger from numerous fragments of a single large tablet from Nineveh and a duplicate from Assur.[84] Combining features of "pseudo-autobiography" and "prophecy,"[85] the document describes the successive deportations of the statue of Marduk by Hittites, Assyrians, and Elamites as self-imposed exiles ordained by the deity himself, and foretells a definitive restoration, presumably under Nebuchadnezzar I (ca. 1126-1105 B.C.E.).

A period of Babylonian weakness followed, from the Fifth (Sealand II) Dynasty to the Eighth ("E") Dynasty (ca. 1026-732 B.C.E.). From some point during this period dates the Erra Epic and its explicit allusions to our theme.[86] Indeed, it has rightly been said that one of the most important features of this epic "is the light it throws on religious concepts, and in particular the 'theology' of the divine statue."[87] In this connection, W. G. Lambert cites a boundary-stone[88] which records the loss of the statue of Shamash of Sippar to Sutian invaders under Simbar-Shipak (ca. 1026-1009 B.C.E.). This loss was provisionally made good by substituting a sun-disc as a symbolic equivalent.[89] But it was only in the

---

[82]Spycket, *Les Statues*, p. 84; cf. M. Stol, *Studies in Old Babylonian History* (1976) 67f.

[83]See simply W. W. Hallo and W. K. Simpson, *The Ancient Near East: a History* (New York: Harcourt Brace Jovanovich, Inc., 1971) 107, fig. 20.

[84]R. Borger, "Gott Marduk und Gott-König Šulgi als Propheten: Zwei prophetische Texte," *BiOr* 28 (1971) 3-24. For the significance of the text in literary history, see Hallo, "The expansion of cuneiform literature," *Proceedings of the American Academy for Jewish Research* 46-47 (1979-80) 314.

[85]For both genres, see A. K. Grayson, *Babylonian Historical-Literary Texts* (Toronto Semitic Texts and Studies 3, 1975), pp. 4-22. A dissertation by Tremper Longman will clarify their mutual relationship.

[86]See above, note 66.

[87]W. G. Lambert, Review of F. Gössmann, *Das Era-Epos*, *AfO* 18 (1957-58) 398. Lambert provides an excellent summary of the epic's evidence on the subject (pp. 398f.).

[88]L. W. King, *Babylonian Boundary-Stones and Memorial Tablets in the British Museum* (London, 1912) No. 36.

[89]J. A. Brinkman, "A note on the Shamash cult at Sippar in the eleventh century B.C.," *RA* 70 (1976) 183f.; previously *idem, A Political History of Post-Kassite Babylonia, 1158-722 B.C.* (= Analecta Orientalia 43, 1968) 152, n. 917. For sun discs see also Hallo, *BiOr* 20 (1963) 141f.

reign of Nabu-apla-iddina (ca. 887-855 B.C.E.) that the fortuitous discovery of a clay-model, or a "baked clay drawing"[90] or "a colored reproduction of his statue of baked clay (i.e., a reproduction on a colored clay plaque)"[91] or "a kiln-fired clay mold showing a relief with his (Šamaš') likeness"[92] made it possible to fashion a proper new statue. Whether or not the inscription is a "pious fraud" in whole or in part,[93] it shows that the loss of the cult-statue was no small matter. It involved the inexorable disruption of the cult and implied the withdrawal of divine favors (and, incidentally, of royal emoluments), even as the restoration of the statue was "the palpable sign that the deity had taken up his dwelling (in the temple) once more."[94]

During the period of Assyrian ascendancy and hegemony (the so-called Ninth Dynasty, 732-626 B.C.E.), the deportation of cult statues became a regular element of state policy, as Cogan has shown.[95] So far from imposing her cults on subjugated peoples, Assyria symbolized her victory by carrying the cult and the cult-statue of the defeated people back to Assyria. (If the vanquished replaced the lost native cult with the conqueror's, it was at his own option; whether Manasseh of Judah chose to do so, as sometimes argued,[96] or whether he was innocent of the charges levelled against him by prophetic and Deuteronomic historiography,[97] is another question.)[98] Babylon itself was not spared in this respect: when Sennaherib sacked the holy city in 689 B.C.E., he carried the statue of Marduk off to Assur, where it remained until restored to its rightful home by Assurbanipal in 668 B.C.E.[99]

[90]Cogan, *op. cit.* (below, n. 95) p. 34, n. 76.

[91]*CAD* Ḫ (1956) 132.

[92]*CAD* Ṣ (1962) 209.

[93]Lambert, *loc. cit.* (above, n. 87); Brinkman, *op. cit.* (above, n. 89) 189f., note 115.

[94]Yochanan Muffs, "Joy and Love . . . : divine investitures . . . in the light of neo-Babylonian royal grants," in Jacob Neusner, ed., *Christianity, Judaism, and other Greco-Roman Cults: Studies for Morton Smith at Sixty* (= Studies in Judaism in Late Antiquity 12) 3 (1975), p. 17, n. 27.

[95]Morton Cogan, *Imperialism and Religion: Assyria, Judah, and Israel in the Eighth and Seventh Centuries B.C.E.* (= SBL Monograph Series 19, 1974) ch. 2: "Assyrian spoliation of divine images."

[96]M. Greenberg, *Prolegomenon* to *Pseudo-Ezekiel and the Original Prophecy,* by C. C. Torrey (New York, KTAV, 1970).

[97]Morton Smith, "The veracity of Ezekiel, the sins of Manasseh, and Jeremiah 44:18," *ZAW* 87 (1975) 11-16.

[98]Carl D. Evans, "Judah's foreign policy from Hezekiah to Josiah," in Evans, Hallo, and White, eds., *Scripture in Context: Essays on the Comparative Method* (= Pittsburgh Theological Monograph Series 34, 1980) 157-78.

[99]Cogan, p. 30.

This restoration is duly recorded in the Babylonian Chronicle,[100] a genre which shows unusual interest in the comings and goings of divine statues,[101] particularly under Babylon's Tenth and last (Chaldaean) Dynasty (625-538 B.C.E.). Already in 626 B.C.E., on the eve of the accession of its first king Nabopolassar, "the gods of Kish went to Babylon,"[102] presumably for safekeeping, followed a year later by those of Shapazzu and Sippar,[103] of which the former had already suffered capture by Tiglat-pileser III in 745 B.C.E.[104]

Such capture was described in the Chronicle by verbs for "lead (away),"[105] "rob,"[106] "take away (by force),"[107] or "take away by force under threat."[108] When therefore under the very last Chaldaean king Nabonidus (555-539 B.C.E.), the chronicle reports that the gods of Kish and Marada "entered" Babylon,[109] it seems once again a move designed as a safeguard against the imminent approach of Cyrus, the more so as the gods of Sippar, Kutha, and Borsippa did not participate in it. The notion that Nabonidus forced the move on the cities and thereby angered their gods[110] or Marduk[111] seems rather a biased, later judgment from circles friendly to Cyrus. The modern concept that the move represented an analogy to the cult-centralization advocated by Deuteronomy seems even less likely.[112] Other Biblical analogies, however, virtually impose themselves.

VI. SOME BIBLICAL IMPLICATIONS

That is not to say, in other words, that Nabonidus' move went unnoticed by his Biblical contemporaries. Deutero-Isaiah, for one,

[100]Chronicle I iv 34-36, last edited by Grayson, *Assyrian and Babylonian Chronicles* (= Texts from Cuneiform Sources 5, 1975) p. 86 (hereafter: ABC).

[101]Cf. I ii 4' f (Grayson, ABC p. 76) for the return of the gods of the Sealand under Sargon II (707 B.C.E.).

[102]Chronicle 2: 6 (Grayson, ABC p. 88).

[103]Chronicle 2: 19 (Grayson, ABC p. 89).

[104]Chronicle 1: 5 (Grayson, ABC p. 71).

[105]Ibid. and Chronicle 2: 16f. and 3:8 (Grayson, ABC pp. 88 and 91); cf. *CAD* s.v. *abāku* A 3b.

[106]Chronicle 1 iii 1 (ibid., p. 79); cf. *CAD* s.v. *ḫabātu*.

[107]Chronicle 1 iii 3 (Grayson, ABC p. 79); cf. *CAD* s.v. *ekēmu* (d). The return of these statues is duly recorded in Chronicle 1 iii 29 (Grayson p. 81).

[108]Chronicle 3:9 (Grayson, ABC p. 91); cf. *CAD* s.v. *lequ* 4.

[109]Chronicle 7 iii 8-12 (Grayson, ABC p. 109). The verb used is *erēbu*, as in the restoration noted above, note 107.

[110]So according to "Verse Account of Nabonidus" vi 12f.; cf. *ANET*, p. 315.

[111]So according to the Cyrus Cylinder 11. 9f. and 33f.; cf. most recently P.-R. Berger, "Der Kyros-Zylinder ...," *ZA* 64 (1975) 192-234.

[112]M. Weinfeld, "Cult centralization in Israel in the light of a neo-Babylonian analogy," *JNES* 23 (1964) 202-12. For a critique of this position, see Cogan, p. 33, n. 67.

marked it by alluding to the frantic attempts to carry the gods of Babylonia to safety, and, failing that, their going into captivity, and their worshippers' elaborate exertions to make new cult-statues to replace them.[113] And already the earliest literary prophets had castigated Israelite imitation of the almost obsessive concern of the Babylonians for the cult-statues of their deities.[114] But it would not be surprising if knowledge and even sharing of the concern went still further back in Israel, for there is considerable and in part early evidence for cult-statues on the Mesopotamian periphery, not only at Susa in the (south)east as pointed out above,[115] but more particularly at Mari[116] and further to the (north)west. Mari even knew the profession of image-maker,[117] probably sculptors of divine images in light of later evidence.[118] The practice of offering sacrifices to the images of long-deceased Sargonic kings, notably Sargon and Naram-Sin, has long been known from Babylonia;[119] now it is attested for Old Babylonian Mari by a recently published text in which *lamassu* (fem. *lamassatu*) has become a virtual synonym for *ṣalmu*, according to M. Birot.[120] This in turn suggests that comparable veneration may have been accorded to the statue of the deceased ruler at Ugarit as well.[121]

Another feature of earlier Mesopotamian usage, possibly related to the cultic function of both royal and divine statues, that becomes particularly prevalent in Syria-Palestine, is their ritual burial. The example of the statue of King Idrimi of Late Bronze Alalakh is most familiar but, as D. Ussishkin has shown, analogous examples can be identified at Zinjirli (royal or divine statue and gate-lions), Arslantepe

[113]Isaiah 46:1-7 (cf. 40:19f. + 41:6f.); 44:9-20.

[114]Cf. e.g. Amos 5:26 on which see most recently Hallo, *HUCA* 48 (1977) 15, and Charles D. Isbell, "Another Look at Amos 5:26," *JBL* 97 (1978) 97-99.

[115]See above, notes 27-33.

[116]See above, notes 46-49.

[117]*CAD* s.v. *ēpiš ṣalmi*.

[118]Sennaherib describes himself as *epiš ṣalam Anšar u ṣalam ilāni rabūti*; cf. H. Tadmor, "The 'sin of Sargon,' " *Eretz-Israel* 5 (1958) p. 93* (English) and 160 (Hebrew).

[119]For evidence of their cult in Mesopotamia proper, see Hallo, "Royal titles from the Mesopotamian periphery," *Anatolian Studies* 30 (1980) 190 note 15.

[120]M. Birot, "Fragment de rituel de Mari relatif au *kispum*," *Rencontre Assyriologique Internationale* 26 (= *Mesopotamia* 8, 1980) 139-50, esp. pp. 146f. For the iconography of the corresponding Sumerian goddess, see Spycket, "La déesse Lamma," *RA* 54 (1960) 73-84; Wiseman, *loc. cit.* (above, n. 44); below, n. 130. For other synonyms of "image," note especially *lānu, maṭṭalātu, zikru*.

[121]M. Dietrich - O. Loretz, "Totenverehrung in Māri (12803) und Ugarit (KTU 1.161)," *UF* 12 (1980) 381f.

(royal statue), and Hazor (gate-lions).[122] Additional examples of the practice are collected by Keel who, however, hesitates to regard the burial of cult statues and other cult objects as a specifically Western (Syro-Hittite) ritual.[123] Keel's survey further includes objects of precious metal, which were also buried, at least on some occasions. According to a recent interpretation of an Old Babylonian text from Alalakh, however, practical considerations might lead to the reuse rather than the burial of a divine statue when it was made of silver.[124]

It is Keel's contention that the archaeologically attested burial of cult statues has a direct bearing on the story of Jacob's burial of the alien gods and earrings near Shechem (Gen 35:4). He considers it a possible aetiology for an actual burial of such a type which accidentally came to light in antiquity and was, like other features of the Shechem landscape, brought into association with Jacob.[125] At the same time it introduces a theophany ("a terror from God," 35:5) which enables Jacob and his party to escape Shechem for Bethel.

A somewhat different conclusion is reached when the earrings of the passage are emphasized. Then one is reminded of Gideon who, while refusing the offer of kingship,[126] instead accepted earrings to make an *ephod* which became a snare to him and his house. As in the story of Jacob, then, "the earrings are somehow the counterpart of idols whose influence must be disposed of."[127] In this connection it may be noted that earrings have been identified in the newly discovered texts from Ebla as early as the middle of the third millennium B.C.E. both in the native Semitic language (*ne-zi-mu*)[128] and in Sumerian logography if *giš-geštug-lá*[129] may be so interpreted. They were certainly among the typical accoutrements of cult statues by neo-Sumerian times at the end of the millennium if we may so interpret *níg-geštug* (literally: ear-thing).[130]

---

[122]D. Ussishkin, "The Syro-Hittite ritual burial of monuments," *JNES* 29 (1970) 124-28 and pl. V. Cf. also G. H. Oller, "A note on lines 102-104 of the Idrimi inscription," *JCS* 29 (1977) 167f.

[123]*Op. cit.* (above, note 4) 315-26, esp. p. 334.

[124]Nadav Na³aman, "The recycling of a silver statue," *JNES* 40 (1981) 47f.

[125]*Op. cit.* (above, note 4) 332.

[126]See especially M. Buber, *Kingship of God* (3rd ed., New York: Harper and Row, 1967) ch. 1: "The Gideon passage."

[127]E. C. Kingsbury, "He set Ephraim before Manasseh," *HUCA* 38 (1967) 136.

[128]L. Milano, "Due reconditi di metalli da Ebla," *Studi Eblaiti* 3 (1980) 1-21, esp. pp. 15f. *ad* obv. iii 10.

[129]G. Pettinato, *Testi Administrativi della Biblioteca L. 2769* (= Materiali Epigrafici di Ebla 2, 1980) p. 29 *ad* 2 obv. iii 3.

[130]Cf. e.g. David I. Owen, *The John Frederick Lewis Collection* (= Materiali per il Vocabulario Neosumerico 3, 1975) No. 152, ll. 27, 29: ornaments of Annunitum; Shin T. Kang, *Sumerian Economic Texts from the Umma Archive*

An actual earring, complete with an inscription dedicating it to the goddess[131] (or the deified and deceased queen-mother)[132] has also been found from this period.[133]

There are, then, a host of paths along which Mesopotamian conceptions of the divine image may have impinged on biblical ones. It must be left for future investigations to pursue these paths. Our purpose here was only to forestall facile contrasts and comparisons that overlook the inherent problems of interpretation on the Mesopotamian side of the equation.[134]

(= SACT 2, 1973) 119: for the cult statue ([d]Lamma) of the (living) king Amar-Suena. Other terms for earring or pendant are: Sumerian a-gúg-geštug for which see H. Limet, *Le travail du métal au pays de Sumer au temps de la IIIe dynastie d'Ur* (Paris: "Les Belles Lettres," 1960) 198f.; Akkadian anṣabtu, ḫuppu (D), and lulmû; Hittite ištamaḫura- and ašuša- for which see H. Otten, *ZA* 54 (1961) 150.

[131]Pierre Amiet and Maurice Lambert, "Objets inscrits de la Collection Foroughi," *Revue d'Assyriologie* 67 (1973) 157-62.

[132]Piotr Steinkeller, "More on the Ur III royal wives," *Acta Sumerologica* 3 (1981) 77-92, esp. p. 78.

[133]For later periods see W. F. Leemanns, *Ishtar of Lagaba and her Dress* (= Studia . . . de Liagre Böhl 1/1, 1952) and A. L. Oppenheim, "The golden garments of the gods," *JNES* 8 (1949) 172-93. John F. X. McKeon, "Achaemenian cloisonné-inlay jewelry: an important new example," *AOAT* 22 (1973) 109-17.

[134]Abbreviations follow SBL Guidelines. Note in addition the following:
AS = Assyriological Studies
BiOr = Bibliotheca Orientalis
MSL = Materialien zum Sumerischen Lexikon
RLA = Reallexikon der Assyriologie . . .
YNER = Yale Near Eastern Researches

HITTITE AND ISRAELITE CULTIC PRACTICES: A SELECTED COMPARISON

JAMES C. MOYER

Southwest Missouri State University

I. INTRODUCTION

Many ancient Near Eastern texts have been used to help illuminate the OT and study it in its original context, but the value of Hittite[1] texts for this purpose is less widely known. There have been specialized studies on a limited topic, and a few brief surveys that compare and contrast the Hittite and Old Testament texts.[2] Our purpose in this paper is to fill this gap by taking up more than a limited topic, yet avoiding the brevity of surveys. We will compare and contrast a selected number of Israelite and Hittite cultic or religious practices.[3] A significant degree

[1]The term "Hittite" can be applied to at least four distinct groups which may be conveniently summarized as follows:

    I. Hattians occupying Anatolia before 2000 B.C.E.

    II. Indo-European invaders of Anatolia, after 2000 B.C.E., who eventually developed a great empire lasting until about 1200 B.C.E.

    III. Neo-Hittites who lived in Syria after 1200 B.C.E.

    IV. Hittites mentioned in the OT.

For further discussion of these groups see H. A. Hoffner, "Some Contributions of Hittitology to Old Testament Study," *TynBul* 20 (1969) 27-55, esp. pp. 28-37. All references to "Hittite" in this paper will be to the Hittites of category II unless otherwise indicated.

[2]Examples of surveys would be Hoffner, "Some Contributions," and *idem*, "The Hittites and Hurrians," *Peoples of Old Testament Times* (ed. D. J. Wiseman; Oxford: Clarendon, 1973) 197-228. Examples of specialized studies can be found in the nn. which follow.

[3]The original motivation to concentrate on cultic or religious practices was due to a suggestion by J. Van Seters ("The Terms 'Amorite' and 'Hittite' in the Old Testament," *VT* 22 [1972] 64-81 and *idem, Abraham in History and Tradition* [New Haven: Yale University Press, 1975]) that the term Hittite was always used pejoratively in the OT. We hypothesized that if Van Seters were correct this might reflect itself in a condemnation by the OT of Hittite cultic or religious practices. But the more we worked with Van Seters' suggestion the more weaknesses we discovered in his position. At least three significant problems can be raised: 1. Not all usages of "Hittite" in the OT can be shown to have the pejorative sense as he maintains. 2. He has not made a convincing case for

of difference and/or similarity may help illuminate both OT and Hittite texts though our emphasis here is to illuminate the OT. Space limits our discussion to six of the most significant comparisons. Four of these show a significant degree of difference: divination by consulting the dead, Deut 18:9-11, 1 Sam 28; bestiality, Lev 18:23, 24; rites of transformation relating to symbols of masculinity and femininity, Deut 22:5; and the ritual uncleanness of the pig and the dog, Lev 11:7, 27. Two show a significant degree of similarity: the scapegoat ritual, Lev 16; and the custody and policing of religious sanctuaries, Num 3:7, etc.

Before proceeding any further we must consider a possible objection concerning the validity of the comparative approach which we propose to make. It is generally agreed that the Hittite empire never extended into Canaan. At most it reached as far as Damascus. In addition, Hoffner and others see the early Hittites mentioned in the OT as being a native Semitic tribe who have nothing to do with the Hittites of Anatolia.[4] These alternate views, while they should keep our conclusions cautious, do not invalidate drawing comparisons between the OT and the Hittite cuneiform texts. Hoffner himself draws such comparisons, and gives the following justification.

> Hittite cultural influence, reaching the Israelites indirectly via the Canaanite and Aramaean kingdoms and only after the passage of time, can be detected in many instances. But it should not be assumed that the vehicle for such influence was a Hittite enclave existing in Palestine since the time of the Patriarchs. Assyriology as a discipline would have profound relevance to Old Testament studies, even if Abraham had not migrated from Ur or the Assyrian and Neo-Babylonian rulers had not led their armies westward into the land of Israel. The significance of Assyro-Babylonian literature (as of Hittite literature) to Old Testament scholars lies rather in its contribution to one's understanding of the way men lived and thought during the era of the Old Testament revelation. When similarities are found between ancient Israelite laws and customs and those of the Sumerians, Babylonians, Egyptians, or Hittites, one does not always conclude that there has been direct influence of one society upon the other. If further evidence points in that direction, one may indeed be justified in seeking to determine precisely the time and manner of the transfer. But far more frequently scholars are left with the similarity alone.[5]

---

dating all references to the Hittites in the OT to the first millennium B.C.E. 3. Therefore, he treats all Hittites in the OT as Neo-Hittites and never discusses, and shows no awareness of, other views regarding the identity of the Hittites in the OT. He is successful in showing that many times the term Hittite in the OT is used pejoratively, but our study is not designed to prove or disprove this.

[4]Hoffner, "Some Contributions," 28-37.
[5]Hoffner, "Hittites and Hurrians," 214.

To this we can add that there is a small but growing amount of archaeological evidence indicating there were some Hittite contacts with Palestine before 1200 B.C.E.[6]

II. DIVINATION BY CONSULTING THE DEAD

Divination by consulting the dead is condemned as something Israel's neighbors practice (Deut 18:9-11). In ancient Israel there were both legitimate and illegitimate methods of getting divine information.[7] Naturally their own information about their legitimate means is more complete, and our limited knowledge of illegitimate means comes primarily from prohibitions in legal material, or from ridicule and scorn preserved in historical or prophetic material.

The story of Saul and the "witch" of Endor in 1 Samuel 28 gives us some information about consulting the dead for which the Hittite texts provide further illumination. Near the end of Saul's life, after Samuel had died, the Philistines massed their forces at Shunem to fight against Saul. The latter countered by assembling his forces at Gilboa (1 Sam 28).

---

[6]Aharon Kempinski, "Hittites in the Bible—What Does Archaeology Say?," *BARev* 5 (1979) 20-45, gives the following evidence of cultural influence reaching northern Palestine before 1200 B.C.E.

(1) Two Hittite jugs imported from Anatolia were found in a Megiddo tomb dating from 1650 B.C.E.

(2) Hieroglyphic Hittite seals, Syro-Hittite ivories, jewelry, etc. have been found in Palestine dating to the Late Bronze age and coming from either Anatolia or Syria.

(3) Hittite influence can be seen in the 14th-13th century lion orthostats from Hazor and Syro-Hittite influence can be demonstrated on the columns of the Hazor temple portico from the same time period.

(4) A Hittite bulla fragment dating to the 13th century with an inscription "son of the king" was found at Aphek. In the same context a letter from a high official at Ugarit (under Hittite influence) was found. For further information see D. I. Owen, "An Akkadian Letter from Ugarit at Tel Aphek," *Tel Aviv* 8 (1981) 1-17.

(5) A krater with hollow piping running around the rim and used for ritual purposes was found at Khirbet Raddana and, dating from the late 13th century, has its closest functional analogues to the early Hittite Old Kingdom.

[7]Another illegitimate method of divination using the *tĕrāphîm* has also been connected with Hittite practice. See H. A. Hoffner, "Hittite *Tarpiš* and Hebrew *Terāphîm*," *JNES* 27 (1968) 61-68. Because of space limitations and doubt cast by F. Josephson ("Anatolian *Tarpa/i-*," *Florilegium Anatolicum* [E. Laroche Anniversary Volume; Paris: De Boccard, 1979] 177-84) on the linguistic connections of the Hittite and Hebrew terms, we will omit discussion of this topic here.

In accord with the requirements of holy war Saul sought divine information through three approved means of divination: dreams, ꜣûrîm, and prophets (28:6). However, the text says in verse 7, "The Lord did not answer him." It was unthinkable to go into holy war without a word from the Lord. So in desperation Saul sought the Lord through a medium (ba῾ălat ꜣôb, a feminine term meaning "owner of a pit") who brought up Samuel in the form of a spirit from the ground through the pit. The OT does not describe how the medium prepared her pit or any of the ritual she used to gain information. Several Hittite texts, however, describe precisely these things and enable us to understand why consulting the dead was condemned in Israel. Harry Hoffner has written the definitive article on this, and we can do no better than to summarize his work.[8]

We begin by selecting and quoting only three of the relevant Hittite texts, and we number them for ease of reference in the discussion which follows.

1. Relocation of the Black Goddess, KUB XXIX 4 rev iv 31-36.

When at night on the second day (of the ritual) a star leaps, the offerer comes to the temple and bows to the deity. The two daggers which were made along with the (statue of) the new deity they take, and (with them) dig a pit for the deity in front of the table. They offer one sheep to the deity for *enumaššiya* and slaughter it down in the pit.[9]

2. Ritual drawing paths for ^{d}MAḪ^{MEŠ} and ^{d}Gulšeš, KUB XV 31, obv. ii 6-26.

When they furnish (it) with nine paths, they pick up the tables and take them to the place of the pit. This is the way in which we determined the matter (place and number?) of the pit by the gods: they open up seven pits. (Result:) Unfavorable. Then eight pits they open up. (Result:) Favorable. Then nine pits they open up. When they bring them (images) to the place of the pit, they put the gods down and open up the nine pits. Quickly he takes a hoe and digs. Next he takes a pectoral ornament and digs with that. Then he takes a *šatta*, a shovel, and a *hupparaš*-vessel, and gathers up (the loose soil?). Then he pours in(to the pits) wine and oil. He breaks up "thin loaves" and puts them around (the mouths of the pits) on this side and that side. Next he puts down into the first pit a silver ladder and a silver pectoral ornament. On the pectoral he places a silver ear and hangs them down into the first pit. To the last of the ears a *kurešš ar*-headdress is

---

[8]H. A. Hoffner, "Second Millennim Antecedents to the Hebrew ꜣOB" *JBL* 86 (1967) 385-401. See also Hoffner's article on ꜣôbh in *TDOT* 1 (1977) 130-34. These articles go into much greater detail than we have.

[9]Translation by Hoffner, "Second Millennium," 389.

bound. When he finishes, he offers one bird to all for *enumašši* and *itkalzi*. He smears the nine pits with blood. Then for the nine pits (there are) nine birds and one lamb. For *ambašši* and *keldi* he offers nine birds and one lamb. He puts one bird in each pit, but the lamb they cut up and put it at the first pit.[10]

3. Ritual and Prayer to Ishtar of Nineveh, KBo II 9 iv 9-16.

The diviner says these words, and when they draw him/her/it with 'thick bread,' they fill a *kukūbu*-vessel[11] with water besides. Then in that place they open up pits (text has misspelling: *a-pé-e*), and the diviner with ear-shaped loaves (alt. reading: with four ears) draws the deity up from thence seven times, and says: 'If anyone—king, queen (or) princes— has done something and has buried it, I am now drawing it forth from the ground.' Then he proceeds to speak other words of similar import, and they perform this action just so in that place.[12]

The use of the pit and the rituals associated with it can be derived from these three passages, and others not listed here, and summarized as follows.

1. The goal of the ritual was to bring up the spirits of the dead, and this was accomplished only when it was dark. So the ritual was performed at night or in the dark (text 1 and 1 Sam 28:8).

2. The pit had to be located at a propitious spot (text 2). Undoubtedly the medium of Endor had had previous success at her pit and reused it again and again.[13]

3. The pit had to be dug with an appropriate instrument (text 1 and 2).

4. Into the pit several kinds of offerings were lowered to entice the spirits of the dead to come up and eat (text 2).

5. The food offerings included liquids used for libations. Text 2 mentions wine and oil; other texts include honeyed milk and water.

6. Especially important was the blood of sacrificial animals. In text 1 it ran down into the pit, while in text 2 it was smeared around the mouth of the pits. This blood was what gave the spirits of the dead special power to communicate, etc.

---

[10]Ibid., 390. In this quotation we have substituted "pit(s)" where Hoffner has the Hittite spelling *a-a-bi*.

[11]A. Salonen (*Die Hausgeräte der Alten Mesopotamier* [Helsinki: Suoma-lainen Tiedeakatemia, 1966] 2.218) suggests that a *kukkubu*-vessel is a pitcher with a long neck and spout.

[12]Hoffner, "Second Millennium," 392.

[13]Despite illegal activities her reputation seems to be well known, since Saul's men immediately suggest her when Saul asks them to find him a medium (1 Sam 28:7).

7. Other gifts were lowered into the pit to entice the spirits of the dead up from the netherworld.[14]

8. The object of the ritual was to lure the spirit up out of the pit to get the desired information.

9. The spirit was apparently recognizable to the medium but not to the client (1 Sam 28:12-14). The spirit made sounds variously described as something like the chirping of birds or whispering (Isa 8:19, 29:4).

10. After the information was attained, the pit had to be sealed up properly to prevent the spirits from entering the land of the living and wreaking havoc.

This *modus operandi* contrasts with the orthodox approach of Israel which, for the most part, can be described as not bypassing Yahweh.[15] It is easy, therefore, to understand this condemnation in Isa 8:19: "When men tell you to consult mediums and spiritists, who whisper and mutter, should not a people inquire of their God? Why consult the dead on behalf of the living?"[16] The statement in Isa 29:4 is less direct but still negative: "Brought low you will speak from the ground; your speech will mumble out of the dust. Your voice will come ghostlike from the earth; out of the dust your speech will whisper." What better way, then, could the biblical writer portray Saul in the most negative light than to have him seek out a medium which he himself had condemned (1 Sam 28:3)?[17] Saul had reached the nadir of his life by doing this, and his death followed immediately in the battle with the Philistines.

This comparison of divination by consulting the dead has shown that the OT condemned the practice and was silent about the details of the ritual. The Hittite texts describe the ritual with sufficient detail that we can develop a *modus operandi* that *might* have been used in Israel. The *modus operandi* also makes it clear why this ritual was condemned in Israel since it completely bypassed Yahweh.

---

[14]Hoffner ("Second Millennium," 395) points out the prominence of silver and connects this with European superstition. This is uncertain at best. Another possibility is that metals were associated with the gods. In Mesopotamia gold corresponds to Enlil, silver to Anu, and copper to Ea (CT 24:49). M. Eliáde (*A History of Religious Ideas* [Chicago: University of Chicago Press, 1978] 1.83) points out that ritual manipulation of a metal object brought the manipulator under the protection of the god symbolized by the metal.

[15]J. J. M. Roberts ("Divine Freedom and Cultic Manipulation in Israel and Mesopotamia," *Unity and Diversity* [ed. H. Goedicke and J. J. M. Roberts; Baltimore: Johns Hopkins Press, 1975] 181-90) provides a necessary caution in drawing the distinction between Israel and her neighbors too sharply.

[16]All Biblical quotations in this paper are taken from the *New International Version*.

[17]Compare also the condemnation in 1 Chr 10:13-14.

III. BESTIALITY

We turn next to bestiality. At first glance this might not appear to have any cultic significance. However, bestiality was linked to cultic practice at Ugarit. In the Baal cycle, Baal mated with a heifer, and this was probably reenacted annually by priests of Baal substituting for Baal.[18] Also, *if* one assumes a totemic heritage, gods and animals are interchangeable. Thus such intercourse could even be sacramental.

The biblical prohibition in Lev 18:23, 24 reads: "Do not have sexual relations with an animal and defile yourself with it. A woman must not present herself to an animal to have sexual relations with it; that is a perversion. Do not defile yourselves in any of these ways because this is how the nations that I am going to drive out before you became defiled." Here again the appeal is made to a negative practice of Israel's neighbors. Again Hittite texts provide illumination for this passage. This time it is primarily the Hittite laws which contain the contrasting information. The relevant laws follow.

187: If a man does evil with a head of cattle, it is a capital crime and he shall be killed. They bring him to the king's court. Whether the king orders him killed, or whether the king spares his life, he must not appeal to the king.[19]

188: If a man does evil with a sheep, it is a capital crime and he shall be killed. They bring him to the king's court. Whether the king orders him killed , or whether the king spares his life, he must not appeal to the king.

199: If anyone does evil with a pig, he shall die. They will bring them to the gate of the palace and the king may order them killed, the king may spare their lives; but he must not appeal to the king. If an ox leaps at a man, the ox shall die, but the man shall not die. A sheep may be proffered in the man's stead and they shall kill that. If a pig leaps at a man, there shall be no punishment.

200 (A): If a man does evil with a horse or a mule, there shall be no punishment. He must not appeal to the king nor shall he become a case

---

[18]See H. L. Ginsberg's translation of the Ugaritic "Poems about Baal and Anath," *ANET*, 129-42, esp. pp. 139 and 142.

[19]H. A. Hoffner ("Incest, Sodomy and Bestiality in the Ancient Near East," *Orient and Occident*, AOAT 22 [ed. H. A. Hoffner, Butzon & Bercker Kevelaer, 1973] 85, n. 21) thinks the translation "he must not appeal to the king" is unlikely. The person committing the act of bestiality would have been considered ritually impure, and the sacred person of the king needed to be protected from anyone bearing impurity. A translation like "He must not approach the king" better indicates this. For further discussion of purity and the king see J. C. Moyer, *The Concept of Ritual Purity Among the Hittites* (Ph.D. dissertation, Brandeis University; Ann Arbor: University Microfilms, 1969) 79-93, esp. p. 84.

for the priest.[20] If anyone sleeps with a foreign (woman) and (also) with her mother or [her] si[ster], there will be no punishment.[21]

These laws appear in the context of forbidden sexual relations, and Hoffner has argued that *ḫurkel*, which Goetze translates "does evil with" (first verb in each of the laws quoted above), really means "having sexual relations of a forbidden type."[22] In laws 187, 188, and 199 (first part) sexual relations with oxen, sheep, or pigs are forbidden on pain of death. But the punishment apparently could be lessened by the king, who could substitute banishment instead of death. In these laws no punishment is indicated for the animals since it was apparently a person and not the animal that initiated the sexual relations.[23] But in the second part of law 199 the ox and pig apparently make the sexual advances. Here the person is not punished but the ox is killed (presumably because such a large animal's attacks are too dangerous) while the pig is not punished at all. This contrasts with Lev 20:15, 16 where we are informed that *both* the person *and* the animal engaging in sexual relations are put to death.[24] Law 200 A permits sexual relations with a horse or mule. This is the most direct statement of the permissibility of certain types of bestiality known to us, though the function or purpose is never explained.[25]

[20]Hoffner ("Incest," 85, n. 22) corrects the translation "nor shall he become a case for the priest" to "he shall not become a priest." The law means that a person committing bestiality with a horse or mule was not punished, but his impurity did not allow him to approach the king nor ever after become a priest.

[21]Translation by A. Goetze, *ANET*, 196-97.

[22]Hoffner, "Incest," 90. However, this translation may be too strong in light of what is permitted in 200 (A).

[23]However, Hoffner ("Incest," 83) says, "There is no indication in the Hittite laws that the life of the animal was ever spared when the human was executed." This is possible but not certain since the texts never say that when the human was executed the animal was also executed.

[24]In Leviticus 20 the laws pertaining to bestiality occur in a list of forbidden sexual unions similar to Hittite laws 187-200.

[25]It is hard to explain why bestiality is prohibited with some animals, but permissible with the horse and mule. Hoffner ("Incest," 82-83) gives two suggestions. The first is a varying degree of kinship felt by the ancients to the animals, and the second is the more recent domestication of the horse and mule. He is not satisfied by either of these suggestions and neither are we. Since the horse and the mule are the most valuable of the animals (Hoffner, "Hittites and Hurrians," 207) it may have something to do with their value. Alternatively, the horse and the mule were the animals most often taken along on trips away from home; e.g., military campaigns, trade, etc. Since opportunities for normal sexual relations were impossible on such trips it might have been considered permissible to engage in sexual relations with the horse and mule.

Other Hittite texts provide some additional information. In the case of the banishment of the offender the townsfolk must afterward engage in purification rites.[26] The banished man would take his impurity with him away from the city in a fashion similar to the scapegoat in Lev 16:20-28. At a later time period the offender was permitted to pay a fine and purify himself while the animal involved could be sent away from the city.[27]

In the Hittite texts bestiality can result in death, banishment, or, at a later time period, payment of a fine and purification. On the other hand sexual relations with a horse or mule were permissible though the person at least became impure. The animal was sent away and killed or suffered no punishment. In Israel all bestiality was prohibited and both the person and the animal guilty of bestiality were always killed.

IV. RITES OF TRANSFORMATION RELATING TO MASCULINITY AND FEMININITY

The distinction between the sexes was clearly defined in the ancient Near East. Ideal men were capable warriors or hunters who could sire many children. Ideal women bore many children and did domestic work in the home. Consequently these roles were often symbolized in the literature. Weapons of war or the hunt such as bows, arrows, shields, and swords symbolized masculinity, e.g., 2 Sam 22:35-36 and 1:21-22. The mirror and distaff or spindle frequently symbolized femininity, e.g., Prov 31:19. In Israel one sex was prohibited from using (wearing) the things that symbolized the other sex according to Deut 22:5. It reads: "A woman must not wear men's clothing,[28] nor a man wear women's clothing, for the Lord your God detests anyone who does this." No explanation is given for this prohibition here or elsewhere in the OT. But the Hittite rituals are illuminating. They show that implements and dress of one sex are used to bestow the sexual attributes of that sex on the opposite sex. This is accomplished by a rite of transformation.[29] Let us turn to the relevant Hittite information.

The first text describes a ritual by Paskuwatti, the Arzawa woman, in which a man is sterile or possesses no desire for women. Among the many ritual acts she performs is the following from KUB IX 27 obv 19ff.

[26]KUB XIII, 2 iii 14-15; translation by Goetze, *ANET*, 211.

[27]Hoffner ("Incest," 85-90) goes into further detail, and gives a transliteration and partial translation of KUB XLI 11.

[28]The Hebrew term *kĕlî* translated here as "clothing" can mean the equipment of a warrior (*BDB*, 749), a translation supported by the Hittite texts.

[29]H. A. Hoffner ("Symbols for Masculinity and Femininity," *JBL* 85 [1966] 326-34) prefers the term "sympathetic magic rituals." It should be recognized that the term magic immediately carries negative connotations. We prefer to use "rite of transformation" since it is a more neutral term.

> I shall twine together [a cord] of red wool (and) of white wool. I shall place a mirror (and) a distaff in the sacrificer's [hand]. He will pass under the gate. When he comes [for]th through the gate, I shall take the mirror (and) the distaff away from him. I shall [gi]ve him a bow [and arrows] and while doing so I shall speak as follows: "See! I have taken womanliness away from thee and given thee manliness. Thou hast cast off the ways of a woman, now [show] the ways of a man!"[30]

The mirror and distaff are clearly female symbols, and by a rite of transformation Paskuwatti is taking womanliness away from the sacrificer and replacing it with manliness symbolized by bow and arrows.

In the Soldiers' Oath, KBo vi 34 ii 43ff., the soldiers must take a self-maledictory oath as follows:

> They bring the garments of a woman, a distaff and a mirror, they break an arrow and you speak as follows: "Is not this that you see here garments of a woman? We have them here for (the ceremony of taking) the oath. Whoever breaks these oaths and does evil to the king (and) the queen (and) the princes, let these oaths change him from a man into a woman! Let them change his troops into women, let them dress them in the fashion of women and cover their heads with a length of cloth! Let them break the bows, arrows (and) clubs in their hands and (iii) [let them put] in their hands distaff and mirror!"[31]

The situation is reversed this time, but the symbolism is identical. By a rite of transformation feminine dress and implements will bring feminine ways to soldiers not doing what they were supposed to do. Similarly, the prayer of the practitioner which follows is designed to destroy the masculinity and military capability of the enemy troops. The text is from the Ritual and Prayer to Ishtar of Nineveh, KBo II 9 i 25-30.

> Take from (their) men masculinity, prowess, robust health, swords(?), battle-axes, bows, arrows, and dagger(s)! And bring them to Hatti! Place in their hands the spindle and mirror of a woman! Dress them as women! Put on their (heads) the kuressar! And take away from them your favor![32]

In both of these last two cases the use of feminine dress and implements has its effects in the rite of transformation described in the first text.

Returning to Deut 22:5 we can ask why one sex would want to wear the attire or implements of the other sex. There are three possibilities. (1) It could be a sexual perversion such as homosexuality, except that other passages (Lev 18:22) directly refer to homosexuality. (2) It could be veneration of a bisexual deity, but the evidence used to support this

---

[30]Translation by A. Goetze, *ANET*, 349.
[31]Translation by A. Goetze, *ANET*, 354.
[32]Translation by Hoffner, "Symbols," 331.

tends to be late.[33] (3) Most likely, in light of the above Hittite rituals, it was a (magical) way of maintaining, increasing, or restoring the sexual potency of oneself or of eradicating that of one's enemy. Such (magical) rituals were prohibited in Israel because these kinds of rites (magic) were designed to manipulate the deity.[34] These rituals were an invasion of Yahweh's personal liberties and actions and therefore considered detestable.[35]

V. RITUAL UNCLEANNESS OF THE PIG AND THE DOG

It is well known that the pig and the dog were unclean animals in ancient Israel. Lev 11:7 and Deut 14:8 directly state that the pig was unclean, but the only explanation offered is that it does not chew the cud. Nowhere is there a direct statement that dogs were unclean, but Lev 11:27 implies this with a simple statement that animals that walked on all four paws (kap) were unclean. No explanation is offered. Such cryptic statements invite additional comment. Four main explanations have been advanced for these and other laws distinguishing clean and unclean animals, birds, etc. They are that the laws are simply arbitrary; that Israel is reacting to cultic usage of her neighbors; that they have a hygienic basis; or that they are of symbolic value. It is beyond the scope of this paper to discuss each of these explanations and their merits,[36] but the Hittite evidence cited below tends to support the cultic explanation. However, we are not implying that this evidence necessarily precludes other explanations.[37] What is most significant is that the Hittite evidence seems to be relatively unknown and/or unused, especially in the commentaries.[38]

[33]Hoffner, "Symbols," 333.

[34]The cautions of J. J. M. Roberts ("Divine Freedom," 181-90) are again necessary though they do not invalidate the force of the argument.

[35]Hoffner, "Symbols," 334. See also W. H. Ph. Römer, "Randbemerkungen zur Travestie von Deut 22, 5," Travels in the World of the Old Testament (M. A. Beek Anniversary Volume; Assen: van Gorcum, 1974) 217-22.

[36]See G. J. Wenham (The Book of Leviticus [NICOT; Grand Rapids: Eerdmans, 1979] 166ff.) for fuller discussion and evaluation of the merits of each explanation. A variation on the symbolic explanation has recently been given by Jean Soler ("The Dietary Prohibitions of the Hebrews," The New York Review of Books 26 [June 14, 1979] 24-30).

[37]We are convinced that there is value to explanations other than the cultic explanation and that no single explanation is entirely satisfactory.

[38]M. Noth (Leviticus: A Commentary [OTL; rev. ed.; Phila.: Westminster, 1977] 92) gives the cultic explanation though he offers little support and nothing from Hittite cultic practices. On the other hand, P. Craigie (The Book of Deuteronomy [NICOT; Grand Rapids: Eerdmans, 1976] 231) does mention Hittite evidence.

The term for pig (*ḥazîr*) occurs only five additional times (to the two mentioned above) in the Hebrew Bible. In Ps 80:14 it is used as a figure of destruction, while in Prov 11:22 a beautiful woman without discretion is likened to a gold ring in a pig's snout. The other three occurrences are in the later part of Isaiah and describe unorthodox cultic practices. In 65:4 and 66:17 the ritual includes eating the flesh of pigs and in 66:3 the sacrifice includes presenting pig's blood. The implication is that some Israelites were doing these negative things, but the larger question of where these practices originated will be discussed later.

The term for dog (*keleb*) occurs 31 times in the Hebrew Bible, and space only permits a survey of these usages. The scavenging nature of the dog is frequently mentioned, 1 Kgs 21:23, 24, and its frequent contact with corpses would make it ritually unclean. It follows, then, that there is a general aversion to the dog, especially as indicated in figurative usages. It is a term for contempt when applied to a man, 1 Sam 17:43; an enemy may be called a dog, Ps 22:16, 20 (Heb 17, 21); the wicked are referred to as dogs; and in Deut 23:18 (Heb 19) it is used as a euphemism for temple prostitutes. In Isa 66:3 an unorthodox cultic act of sacrificing a dog is connected with the sacrifice of the pig mentioned previously. This combination of the pig and the dog calls forth similar Hittite evidence.

In Hittite laws 81-90 there are several prescriptions about pigs and dogs clearly indicating their value to farmers or herdsmen.[39] It is fair to conclude that dogs and pigs were quite common in Hittite households.[40] Still, both were considered unclean animals, and "swineherd" applied to the Kaskaeans is probably a disparaging expression.[41] Temple officials were warned that everything in the temple, and associated with it, was to be kept meticulously clean. This meant exclusion of pigs and dogs as the next two quotations indicate.

> Furthermore, let a pig or a dog not stay at the door of the place where the loaves are broken. Are the minds of men and of the gods generally different? No! With regard to the matter with which we are dealing? No! Their minds are exactly alike.[42]

Later in the same text these regulations are reiterated and the following is added:

> If a pig (or) a dog somehow approaches the implements of wood or bitumen which you have, and the kitchen servant does not discard it, but

[39]For a translation of these laws by A. Goetze see *ANET*, 193.

[40]Einar von Schuler, *Die Kaškäer: Ein Beitrag zur Ethnographie des alten Kleinasien* (Berlin: Walter de Gruyter, 1965) 77, 80, 149-51.

[41]Hoffner, review of von Schuler, *Die Kaškäer* in *JAOS* 87 (1967) 183.

[42]KUB XIII 4 i 20ff., translation by A. Goetze, *ANET*, 207.

gives the god to eat from an unclean (vessel), to such a man the gods will give dung (and) urine to eat (and) to drink.[43]

In the ritual of Tunnawi one small black dog and one small black pig were to be included in the ritual equipment used to remove impurities.[44] Later in the ritual the pig and the dog were waved over the worshippers while the proper charms were recited. The evil or uncleanness was transferred to these unclean animals which were thought to be able to "absorb" the impurities. Then the animals were burned. Since both animals were black (the appropriate color for the chthonic deities), it is likely that they were being "sacrificed" to the deities in the dark earth.

Other rituals mention either the dog or the pig, and we take them up in the order listed.[45] In the ritual of Pupuwanni the sacrifice is designed to appeal to the netherworld and includes a black puppy, black lamb, and black goat. Another ritual against family quarrel describes how the sacrificers who are troubled with quarreling spit into a dog's mouth. Then the practitioner performing the ritual says, "You have spit out the curses of that day." Then the dog, full of curses, is killed and buried, probably as a gift to the netherworld.[46]

In the ritual of Huwarlu, KBo IV 2 ii 5ff., a live puppy carries away evil.

> They take a live puppy and wave it over the king and queen, also in the palace the Old Woman waves it about, and she says: 'Whatever evil thing is in the body of the king and queen and in the palace, now see! . . . It has vanquished it. Let it carry away the evil thing and bring it to the place that the gods have appointed.' Then they take away the live puppy.[47]

There are two rituals which make use of the pig. In the first, Mastiggas, the woman from Kizzuwatna, is dealing with domestic quarrels.

> The Old Woman takes a small pig, she presents it to them and speaks as follows: "See! It has been fattened with grass (and) grain. Just as this

---

[43]KUB XIII 4 iii 65ff., translation by A. Goetze, ANET, 209.

[44]For translation and commentary see A. Goetze, The Hittite Ritual of Tunnawi (New Haven: American Oriental Society, 1938).

[45]For a summary of the role of the dog see M. Pope, "A Divine Banquet at Ugarit," The Use of the Old Testament in the New and Other Essays (W. F. Stinespring Anniversary Volume; ed. J. M. Efird; Durham, N.C.: Duke University Press, 1972) 183-89.

[46]D. Englehard, Hittite Magical Practices: An Analysis (Ph.D. dissertation, Brandeis University; Ann Arbor: University Microfilms, 1970) 167.

[47]Translation by O. R. Gurney, Some Aspects of Hittite Religion (Oxford: Oxford Univ. Press, 1977) 50.

one shall not see the sky and shall not see the (other) small pigs again, (ii) even so let the evil curses not see these sacrificers either!"

   She waves the small pig over them, and then they kill it. They dig a hole in the ground and put it down into it. They put a sacrificial loaf down with it, she also pours out a libation of wine and they level the ground.[48]

Evidently the small pig is used to absorb the impurities and then offered to the deities that reside in the ground. In another ritual designed to produce a fertile vine, a sow figures prominently. After evil spells against the vineyard are removed, nine holes are dug at various places in the vineyard. Some bread is thrown into one of the holes and the text continues, "They cut off the female genitals of a pig and I throw them down secretly." By analogy, since the sow is fertile so should the vineyard be fertile and bear much fruit; the reproductive organs implanted in the soil are probably designed to produce fertility. Less likely, these organs may be an offering to the deities inhabiting the earth under the vineyard.[49]

   It is readily apparent from this survey that pigs and dogs figured prominently in Hittite rituals, and especially in those involving the chthonic deities. Did the Israelites consider the pig and the dog to be negative because of their prominence in Hittite rituals? Striking support for this thesis has come recently from an article by Jack Sasson on Isa 66:3-4a.[50] He translates these verses as follows:

He who slaughtered an ox	(would now) slay a man,
who sacrificed a lamb	(would now) break a dog's neck,
who presented cereal offering	(would now present) the blood, of a swine
who burnt commemorative incense	(would now) worship an idol
for, although they had chosen their (own) way	they (now) delight in abomination;
I too will choose ways to mock them	to bring upon them the very things they fear.[51]

He then compares this with the following Hittite text.

When the army is defeated by an enemy, then the following sacrifice is prepared "behind" the river: "behind" the river, a man, a kid, a puppy

---

[48]Translation by A. Goetze, *ANET*, 351.
[49]Englehard, *Hittite Magical Practices*, 169-70.
[50]Jack Sasson, "Isaiah LXVI 3-4a," *VT* 26 (1976) 199-207.
[51]Translation by Sasson, "Isaiah," 200. Although there is some disagreement over the exact translation of these verses, there is essential agreement that unorthodox cultic practices are in view here.

dog, and a suckling pig are cut in half. One half is placed on one side, the
(other) half on the other. Before it, one makes a door out of *ḫatalkenaš*
wood and pulls over it a cord(?). Then one lights a fire before the door on
one side, and also on the other side one lights a fire. The troops go
through the middle. But as soon as it [the troops] reaches the bank of the
river, one sprinkles water on them. Afterwards one goes through the field-
ritual as is the custom of doing the field-ritual.[52]

This Hittite text and Isa 66:3-4a show the following points of similarity.

1. Both include the sacrifice of an adult male.[53]

2. Both include the sacrifice of a dog. (Hebrew has no word for
puppy, though it might have been something like *gūr kĕlābîm*.)

3. Both include the sacrifice of a pig.

4. Both arrange these three sacrifices in the same order.

5. Though individual texts outside the OT (especially in the Greco-
Roman world) mention each of these sacrifices separately, only the
Hittite text has all three in a single ritual. These similarities are
impressive, and the sacrifice of dog and pig in light of other Hittite texts
is significant for the Israelite treatment of both animals here in Isaiah
and elsewhere in the OT.[54] There is at least a strong likelihood that
Israel considered the pig and dog unclean because of negative rituals
associated with the Hittites or others.

VI. THE SCAPEGOAT RITUAL

Of all the peoples of the ancient Near East, the Hittites seemed to be
the most concerned about ritual purity though the Israelites come a close
second on this point.[55] There were both similarities and differences in
the things the two peoples defined as impure. We have already seen some
differences in the procedures for removing impurities. One important
similarity is the scapegoat ritual described in Leviticus 16. Here we learn

[52]Translation by Sasson, "Isaiah," 205.

[53]Human sacrifice is generally considered to be an archaic Hittite practice.
Since we only know of one other Hittite text (KUB XVII 17) that *may* indicate
human sacrifice we refrain from drawing any additional conclusions. For
additional discussion see Moyer, *Hittite Ritual Purity*, 95-99. For human sacrifice
in the ancient Near East see A. R. W. Green, *The Role of Human Sacrifice in the
Ancient Near East* (ASOR Dissertation Series 1; Missoula: Scholars Press, 1975).

[54]A tantalizing bit of evidence is that the mouse (*ᶜaḫbār*) is unclean
according to Lev 11:29 and is listed in Isa 66:17 where its flesh along with that of
pigs and other detestable things is being eaten. In KUB XXVII 67 ii 3 (Goetze,
ANET, 348 and see substitution rituals later in the text) the mouse is used as a
substitute to carry away evil. However, in the Hittite text the mouse is neither
eaten nor sacrificed so that no contrast should be drawn at present.

[55]Moyer, *Hittite Ritual Purity*.

that on the Day of Atonement Aaron is instructed to take two goats and, after casting lots, one goat is designated for Yahweh and one for Azazel (la ʿăzā ʾzēl) (16:8). The crux of the problem is the meaning of Azazel, which occurs four times in vv 8, 10 (twice), and 26. Although the etymology and meaning of the term are uncertain,[56] the meaning of the ritual as a whole is not really in doubt. Basically the sins of the Israelites are transferred from the people to the goat through the agency of Aaron. The goat then carries the sins to the desert (16:22).[57]

A. H. Sayce first drew attention to similar Hittite "scapegoat" rituals,[58] and several of these rituals have been discussed over the years. A selection of these follows.

1. Purification Ritual Engaging the Help of Protective Demons, KUB XXVII 67 ii 34-40.

> She wraps up a small piece of tin in the bowstring and attaches it to the sacrificers' right hands (and) feet.
> She takes it off them (again) and attaches it to a mouse (with the words): "I have taken the evil off you and attached it to this mouse. Let this mouse carry it on a long journey to the high mountains, hills and dales!"[59]

2. Ritual of Dandanku, KUB II 7 iii 11-18.

> They drive in a donkey—if it is a poor man, they make one of clay— and they turn its face to the enemy country and say: 'Thou, Yarri, hast inflicted evil on this country and its army. Let this donkey lift it and carry it into the enemy country.'[60]

3. Ritual against Pestilence, KUB IX 31 ii 45-60.

> If people are dying in the country, and if some enemy god has caused it, I act as follows. They drive up one ram. They twine together blue wool, red wool, green wool, black wool, and white wool, make it into a wreath and crown the ram with it. This ram they drive on to the road leading to the enemy and speak as follows: 'Whatever god of the enemy land has caused this pestilence—see! We have now driven up this crowned ram to pacify thee, O god. Just as the herd is strong and keeps peace with the ram, do thou, O god, who has caused this pestilence, keep peace with the Hatti Land.' And they drive that crowned ram towards the enemy.[61]

[56]See Wenham, *Leviticus*, 234ff., and Noth, *Leviticus*, 125 for discussion.
[57]Wenham, *Leviticus*, 233.
[58]A. H. Sayce, "The Scapegoat Among the Hittites," *ExpTim* 31 (1919) 283-84.
[59]Translation by A. Goetze, *ANET*, 348.
[60]Translation by O. R. Gurney, *Some Aspects*, 49.
[61]Ibid., 48.

4. Ritual of Pulisa, KBo XV 1.

If the king has been fighting the enemy and returns from the enemy country and out of the enemy country a pestilence comes and afflicts the people—they drive in a bull and a ewe—these are both from the enemy country—they decorate the bull's ears with ear-rings and (fasten on it) red wool, green wool, black wool, and white wool, and they say: 'Whatever has made the king red, green, black, or white shall go back to the enemy country.' . . . He also says: 'Whatever god of the enemy country has caused this pestilence if it be a male god, I have given thee a lusty, decorated bull with ear-rings. Be thou content with it. This bull shall take back the pestilence to the enemy country.' And he does the same with a decorated ewe if it be a female deity.[62]

In all of these texts one animal or another carries away the evil, infection, or whatever by analogy. Numerous other texts describe various kinds of substitute (*nakušši*) rituals. Animals, birds, and even human beings can carry away some type of defilement.

The Hittite rituals and the Israelite scapegoat ritual appear to be similar. Both seem to share the basic concept that evil can be transferred to an animal (or person) which can carry it away to a distant place where it will prove to be harmless. There are differences of carriers and differences of operation within the Hittite texts, but the basic substitutionary nature of the rituals is clearly indicated. Apparently in Israel the scapegoat ritual is a survival from an earlier period which is not conceived to be opposed to the worship of Yahweh and therefore is not condemned or prohibited.[63]

VII. THE CUSTODY AND POLICING OF RELIGIOUS SANCTUARIES

Another similarity between the Hittites and the Israelites has been drawn by Jacob Milgrom with regard to the custody and policing of religious sanctuaries.[64] He makes his comparisons in five points which we summarize below. The relevant Hittite text is Instructions for Temple Officials, KUB XIII 4. All translations are from Milgrom, and are essentially those of Goetze with some reversions to Sturtevant.[65]

---

[62]Ibid.

[63]Substitute rituals were widespread throughout the ancient Near East; Israel's ritual does not have to be dependent on Hittite ritual practices.

[64]J. Milgrom, "The Shared Custody of the Tabernacle and a Hittite Analogy," *JAOS* 90 (1970) 204-9; reprinted in J. Milgrom, *Studies in Levitical Terminology* (Berkeley: University of California Press, 1970) 50-59.

[65]See A. Goetze, *ANET*, 207-10, and E. H. Sturtevant and G. Bechtel, *A Hittite Chrestomathy* (Philadelphia: Linguistic Society of America, 1935) 149-67.

1. Two classes of guards.

On the outside beat keepers shall watch; inside the temples shall the
temple officials patrol all night through and they shall not sleep (III, 9; see
26-30).

The guards within the Hittite temple are priests, while outside the
temple the "keepers" are non-priests. Likewise in Israel the priests have
the guard duty inside the temple, and the Levites are on the outside
(Num 3:7; 18:3).

2. The guards at the gate.

Furthermore, someone of those who are priests shall be in charge of the
gate of the temple and guard the temple (III, 13f.).

The Hittite temple entrance is guarded by a priest and not a keeper. So
in Israel the Tabernacle entrance is guarded by the priests (Num 3:38;
18:26) not Levites.

3. The head of all the guards.

Night by night one of the high priests shall be in charge of the patrols
(III, 12).

As the Hittite high priests control the patrols so the high priest designate
in Israel is chief of all the Levite guards (Num 20:26-28; 3:32).[66]

4. The keepers assist the temple officials inside.

If a keeper is assigned to anyone he may also enter the enclosure. He must
not speak thus: "I am guarding the house of my god but I will not go in
there." If there is some talk of enmity, (namely), that someone will
undertake to defile Hattusa and (the keepers) at the outer wall do not
recognize him, but the temple officials recognize him inside, the keeper
shall definitely go after him. (In) such (situation the) keeper must not fail
to spend the night with his god (III, 24-30).

The Hittite "keeper" must leave his post outside to perform guard duty
on the inside or to search for the unauthorized who do not belong inside.
Similarly the Levite assists the lay worshipper (Num 16:9), and helps the
priest in the sacred places against any intrusion (Num 3:6b, 7a; 18:2-4).

---

[66]Milgrom does not adequately support this comparison since the Hittite
text does not explicitly say the patrols are made up of "keepers."

5. The responsibility of the guards.

But if it is [a foreigner], if it is not a Hittite man, and he ap[proach]es the gods, he shall be killed. And he who conducts him (into the temple), it makes him liable of the death penalty too (II, 9-11). . . . Furthermore, let the watch be divided among you; then the one in whose watch sin occurs shall die; let him not be pardoned (III, 18-20).

Approaching the gods is a capital crime for the offender, his escort (if he has one) and for the temple official on guard duty. In Israel the outsider and presumably all others who approached the sanctuary were killed.[67]

Though we have raised some problems in the notes on points 3 and 5 above, the other similarities are interesting and illuminating. There are differences that could be cited, but it is clear that some aspects of the functions of religious personnel in Israel can be similar to those of the Hittites and still be consistent with the worship of Yahweh.

VIII. CONCLUSION

In drawing our conclusions it is necessary to highlight the limitations of our study.

1. It has concentrated only on Hittite comparative evidence. Practices similar to Hittite practices can be cited from Ugarit which is certainly closer to Israel geographically. This is true for divination by consulting the dead, bestiality, and rites of transformation, though Ugaritic evidence is usually less explicit.[68] There is also evidence from archaeology that the pig was used cultically in Palestine.[69]

---

[67]To support his contention that the guards were killed, Milgrom has to resort to 2 Kgs 10:24b where Jehu places the guards around the Baal temple and threatens to kill them if any escape from inside the temple. Milgrom may be correct, but more caution should be exercised here.

[68]For consulting the dead or divination by the pit see Hoffner, "Second Millennium," 387. For rites of transformation see the Tale of Aqhat translated by H. L. Ginsberg in *ANET*, 149-55, esp. iv 200ff. p. 155. For bestiality see n. 18.

[69]See R. de Vaux, "The Sacrifice of Pigs in Palestine and in the Ancient East," *The Bible and the Ancient Near East* (London: Darton, Longman, Todd, 1972) 252-69 and A. von Rohr Sauer, "The Cultic Role of the Pig in Ancient Times," *In Memoriam Paul Kahle* (ed. M. Black and G. Fohrer; Berlin: Töpelmann, 1968) 201-7. G. E. Wright ("Judean Lachish," *BAR* 2 [ed. E. F. Campbell and D. N. Freedman; Garden City, N. Y.: Doubleday, 1964] 304-6) cites evidence for pigs at Lachish. However, his notion that they were brought there by Assyrian troops is unlikely in light of the Mesopotamian distaste for pigs. On this last point see B. Meissner, *Babylonien und Assyrien* 1 (Heidelberg: Carl Winter, 1920) 416.

2. A direct link between the Hittites of Anatolia and Canaan before 1200 B.C.E. is still very tentative. However, the archaeological evidence is growing. It can also be argued that cultic practices change slowly and at least some could have been transmitted to Neo-Hittites with whom Israel had contact.

3. We have not attempted to give a thorough point by point comparison of all Hittite and Israelite cultic practices.

4. In the nature of the case evidence for direct borrowing or reaction is not available.

Despite these limitations we have been able to refine and add to specialized comparisons between the Hittite and OT texts. In each of the six practices cited our comparison has resulted in a better understanding of the Israelite practice. We have seen more by way of difference than similarity. The contrasts certainly prove extremely valuable in understanding the OT prohibitions. The similarities may have been less striking, but still illuminating. They have shown that at least some Hittite cultic practices were not perceived to have been opposed to the worship of Yahweh. Yet overall Israel's religious practice is significantly different from that of her neighbors.

ANCIENT AMPHICTYONIES, SIC ET NON

HENRY E. CHAMBERS

California State University, Sacramento

I. INTRODUCTION: SURVEY AND CRITICISM

Confronted with a mass of unfamiliar or unorganized material we often analyze it according to familiar patterns. This new corpus of material must be comprehensible and reflect an already known precursor. When there is firm evidence for these analogies, paradigms, or models, this approach can be productive. In the study of history, however, analogies or paradigms can be misleading, for they often become fixed models that after a time demand the historical evidence fit the original analogy. The models then exist of themselves, separate from the very components of history—time and space. Instead of guides they become abstracts separate from their own historical context and act as Platonic forms for another period and subject. The Israelite amphictyony developed by Martin Noth in his 1930 monograph, *Das System der Zwölf Stämme Israels,* and used ever since as the structure for premonarchical Israel has undergone this very canonization.[1] It must now be withdrawn and a new formulation for Israelite unity sought.

Noth argued that the classical Italian-Hellenic amphictyonies provided a workable model to explain the unity enjoyed by the Israelite tribes between the Exodus and before Saul's monarchy. The classical sacred leagues' characteristic central shrines, common cult festivals, representatives, common shrine maintenance, and characteristic twelve members determined a religious league for a number of tribal or urban units without effecting a structured political unity. A further political unification could develop later, as indeed the Israelite monarchy would bring to the tribes. Though he cited many examples from classical Greek and Italian history, his strongest and most extensively known example was the Pylaeo-Delphic amphictyony of central Greece. This religious league, centered about the Apolline oracle at Delphi, became his paradigm.

Noth's classic analysis, detailed in the *Das System der Zwölf Stämme Israels* and set within his text, *The History of Israel,* has set the basic

---

[1] Martin Noth, *Das System der Zwölf Stämme Israels* (Stuttgart: W. Kohlhammer, 1930).

outline for premonarchic Israelite history up to recent years.[2] Besides
Noth's own successful work the model still organizes major histories,
most notably John Bright's *A History of Israel*, first published in 1959
and revised in 1972.[3] With much of the biblical work during Noth's own
time concentrating on textual and archaeological questions, his amphictyony provided the unity most scholars understood as a necessary precursor for Saul's monarchic union.

In the early 1960s several scholars began to examine the Old
Testament evidence for the Israelite amphictyony. H. M. Orlinsky (1962),
H. I. Irwin (1965), and G. Fohrer (1966) raised serious doubts about the
model's propriety.[4] Their negative conclusions gained telling support
with the careful critiques offered by R. de Vaux in a 1971 *Harvard
Theological Review* article which he expanded in his 1973 work, *Early
History of Israel*.[5] A. D. H. Mayes in a 1974 monograph, *Israel in the
Period of the Judges*, joined de Vaux's position and continued the
critique in his chapter in Hayes and Miller's *Israelite and Judaean
History* (1977). Like others he also concluded that the "attractive
analogy" of Greek and Italian amphictyonies must be given up.[6] Bright's

[2]Martin Noth, *The History of Israel* (2d ed.; New York: Harper and Row,
1960). Noth's 1930 monograph was based upon earlier suggestions by H. Ewald,
Geschichte des Volkes Israel I (Göttingen: Dieterich, 1864), M. Weber, *Gesam-
melte Aufsätze zur Religionssoziologie, III, Das Antike Judentum* (Tübingen:
J. Mohr, 1923), and A. Alt, *Die Staatenbildung der Israeliten in Palestina*
(Leipzig: Reformationsprogram der Universität Leipzig, 1930); reprinted in
A. Alt, *Essays On Old Testament History And Religion* (Oxford: Basil Blackwell,
1966) 173-237.

[3]John Bright, *A History of Israel* (Philadelphia/London: Westminster,
1959). Bright in his 1972 revision had already begun to reflect the critical
literature on the Israelite amphictyony. See also W. Albright, *The Biblical
Period From Abraham to Ezra* (New York: Harper and Row, 1963).

[4]H. M. Orlinsky, "The Tribal System of Israel and Related Groups in the
Period of the Judges," *OrAnt* 1 (1962) 11-20; reprinted in *Studies and Essays in
Honor of A. Neumann* (ed. M. Ben-Horin, B. D. Weinrub, and S. Zeitlin
[Leiden: E. J. Brill, 1962]) 375-87; and in H. M. Orlinsky, *Essays in Biblical
Culture and Bible Translation* (New York: Ktav, 1974) 66-77. G. Fohrer, "Altes
Testament—Amphiktyonie und Bund?" *TLZ* 140 (1966) I, 801-6, II, 893-904.
G. Fohrer, *History of Israelite Religion* (New York: Abingdon, 1972) 87-96. H. I.
Irwin, "Le sanctuaire central Israelite avant l'établissement de la monarchie,"
RB 73 (1965) 161-84.

[5]R. de Vaux, "La thèse de l'amphictyonie Israélite," *HTR* 64 (1971) 415-36.
A shorter English version of the same article appeared as "Was There an Israelite
Amphictyony?" *BARev* 3 (1977) 40-47. See also R. de Vaux, *The Early History of
Israel* (Philadelphia: Westminster, 1978) 695-749. The original French edition of
de Vaux's *Early History* first appeared in 1971-73.

[6]A. D. H. Mayes, *Israel in the Period of the Judges* (SBT 2/29; Naperville,
Illinois: A. R. Allenson, 1974). Mayes, "The Period of the Judges and the Rise of

1972 edition of his *History* reflected these criticisms, but at that time he was still reluctant to reject the amphictyonic parallel until a more satisfactory solution appeared.[7] No doubt his expected third edition will reflect the growing scholarly rejection of the parallel. The historiographic upheaval was complete with C. H. J. de Geus' 1976 publication *The Tribes of Israel*.[8] De Geus not only dismantled Noth's thesis, but he also reviewed its genesis, growth, and dissolution. Then with the theory thoroughly critiqued he suggested new grounds for the Israelite unity so sought after for the premonarchic period, an ethnic unity based on the recent work on Amorite semi-nomadism. Jacob Weingreen in a 1973 article did likewise as he argued for a unity based upon two groups of tribes clustered around the tribes of Joseph in the north and Judah in the south.[9] Otto Bächli in a 1977 in-depth analysis preferred to remain with some sort of league analogy if the materials warranted one, although he saw no need to remain close to the classical variation.[10] Applying recent sociological and anthropological studies of tribalism to premonarchic Israel, Norman Gottwald found a clearly decentralized agricultural tribalism united by common religious ties, which bore none of the traditional amphictyonic traits.[11] Thus the 1970s saw both the overturning of the Noth theory, the first stages in suggesting some form of replacement, and a full-fledged alternative model.

Interestingly, as recent research has dismantled Noth's theory for an Israelite amphictyony, a stronger case has emerged for a Sumerian cultic league. A Sumerian league would obviate objections by critics that there was no parallel amphictyony in the ancient world other than the considerably later Greek and Italian leagues, the original models. When D. Rahtjen in a 1965 article argued for a Philistine amphictyony, it was dismissed as not close enough to the Greek model for relevance.[12] Rahtjen's Philistine variant would have greater impact if another variant

---

the Monarchy," *Israelite and Judaean History* (ed. John H. Hayes and J. Maxwell Miller; Philadelphia: Westminster, 1977) 285-331.

[7]Bright, *History of Israel*, 2d ed., 158-62.

[8]C. H. J. de Geus, *The Tribes of Israel* (Assen/Amsterdam: Van Gorcum, 1976).

[9]Jacob Weingreen, "The Theory of the Amphictyony in Premonarchical Israel," *JANESCU* 5 (1973) 427-33. See also B. Lindars, "The Israelite Tribes in Judges," *VTSup* 30 (1979) 95-112.

[10]Otto Bächli, *Amphiktyonie im Alten Testament: Forschungsgeschichtliche Studie zur Hypothese von Martin Noth* (Basel: Friedrich Reinhardt, 1977) 181-82.

[11]Norman K. Gottwald, *The Tribes of Yahweh* (Maryknoll, N. Y.: Orbis, 1979) 347-48.

[12]B. D. Rahtjen, "Philistine and Hebrew Amphictyonies," *JNES* 24 (1965) 100-104.

league, the Sumerian Kengir League, could be established. With three possible models the need for an exact Israelite equivalent to the classical model is smaller and indeed unnecessary. An Israelite league, whether Noth's model or now a more likely revamped new tribal unity, could then be constructed as simply another form of religious league, one befitting an earlier and recently sedentary twelve tribes.

Three questions will be examined in this paper. First, how firm is the evidence for an Israelite amphictyony as such? If the Old Testament cannot support a reasonably strong foundation for an Israelite league and only suggests a weak circumstantial case, then the weight of comparative materials in the argument is lessened.

Second, were there other amphictyonies in the Ancient Near East prior to or simultaneous with a presumed Israelite version? Specifically for this discussion, was there a Sumerian Kengir League? How close a parallel might it offer to the amphictyonic model? Would any significant alterations in its structure disallow it for comparative purposes? If the Israelite strict amphictyonic model is rejected, as it seems it must be, then might not the Sumerian League prove even more pertinent in reconstructing an early Israelite unity? The Sumerian League's existence, regardless of its differences from other leagues, opens the way for accepting a variety of historical possibilities for cultic league unity in early Israel. The Old Testament materials might be finally freed from the need to be bound by amphictyonic league strictures to qualify as a cultic league.

Third, are these other sacred leagues a proper subject for comparison? How should they be used?

II. GREEK AMPHICTYONIES

The Greek amphictyonic model chosen by Martin Noth to explain the structural form of tribal unity for the period of the Judges offers little problem for this analysis. A number of Classical Greek sacred leagues are known to have existed. Among them were a Boeotian cult league at Onchestos for Poseidon, the Calaurian amphictyony on Aegina for Poseidon, the Ionian League centered at Panion on the Asia Minor central coast, and the Aeolic League of Apollo at Grynion on the southwest coast of Asia Minor.[13] Very little is known about these leagues

[13]F. Cauer, "Amphiktyonie," Pauly-Wissowa Real-Encyclopedie 1 (1894) 1904-35. De Vaux offers a good recent survey on the variety of Greek leagues, broader than Noth himself would suggest, in Early History, 697-700. For the Asia Minor leagues see J. M. Cook, The Greeks in Ionia and the East (London: Thames and Hudson, 1962). On the Calaurian League see J. Penrose-Harland, "The Calaurian Amphictyony," AJA 29 (1925) 160-71. The sacred leagues must be distinguished from the Greek federal leagues; see J. A. O. Larsen, The Greek Federal Leagues (Oxford: Clarendon Press, 1968).

except for the basic names, members, and cult sites. Yet it is interesting to note that the last three all preserved a tribal dialectical unity long after they had moved across the Aegean. The most famous league, and our source for details of amphictyonic structure, is the sanctuary at Delphi.[14]

Outside of Greece several sacred leagues are known. But again little else is clear except their names. We can list the *duodecim populi Etruscae*, the important northern neighbors and opponents of early Rome, a southern Etruscan league centered about Campagnia, leagues in Italian Bruttium, Iapygi, Messaepia, Poediculi, and the famous Latin League that played such a crucial role in Rome's early rise to power in the Fifth Century B.C.E.[15] These leagues were important in retaining the ethnic and religious unity of the Italian and Hellenic peoples during the First Millennium B.C.E.

Generally these leagues did not serve as vehicles for political unity. As de Vaux put it, "no wider political unity ever came from them."[16] Perhaps Rome's own emergence from the Latin League can be argued as an exception, but no other example exists from the classical world. The Greek city-states attempted to transform their early federal leagues into larger political structures in the third and second centuries B.C.E., but we must be careful to distinguish the early federal leagues, such as the Boeotian, Achaean, Phocian, and others from the sacred amphictyonies, our subject and Noth's model.

The oracular shrine at Delphi served as Noth's prototype. The league shrine, originally to Demeter, had first been at Anthela near Thermopylae, but by 600 B.C.E. the Delphic shrine had surpassed it and would remain the central cult center. The league encompassed twelve central Greek *poleis*. Its chief duties involved the operation, protection, and support of the Delphic oracle and its lands. Besides caring for the actual shrine complex with its temples to Apollo and later Athena Pronaia, they also staged the Pythian athletic games. Aeschines, the Fourth Century B.C.E. Greek orator, recalled the original oaths of the amphictyons to refrain from razing a member city or stopping any member's water supply in peace or war. Should a polis violate this injunction the league would go to war and raze the offending city.[17] Noth himself stressed the "twelve" member states, the central cult shrine and festival, the responsibilities for upkeep, the twelve representatives

---

[14]Aeschines, *On the Embassy*, 115.

[15]Again see De Vaux, *Early History*, 697, for a good survey. On the Etruscans there are a number of good treatments; among the best is M. Pallotino, *The Etruscans* (2d ed.; Bloomington/London: Indiana University, 1975).

[16]De Vaux, *Early History*, 698; and "La thèse de l'amphictyonie israélite," 419.

[17]Aeschines, *On the Embassy*, 115.

charged with guiding the god's activities, and the national historical
consciousness that accompanied the shrine.[18]

Others such as de Vaux and de Geus have argued that this model
was not as purely religious as Noth presumed. De Vaux noted the
political role of Delphi as it protected member cities from destruction
during any inter-league war and safeguarded water supplies.[19] Since the
members were neighbors in a context where almost all early wars
involved either territorial rights or water rights, this protection against
total destruction by a neighboring polis or elimination of water supplies
was terribly important. Such safeguards assured that any territorial
struggle would remain limited and thus survivable, a not unimportant
measure in Ancient Greece. Such a struggle between Croton and Sybaris,
neighbors on the instep of Italy during the sixth century B.C.E., led to
Sybaris' total destruction. Much later Athens regularly followed this
policy during the Peloponnesian War.

III. THE ISRAELITE "AMPHICTYONY"

Noth's case for an Israelite equivalent of the Greek amphictyony can
be summarized as follows. The Twelve Tribes of Israel under Joshua's
leadership assembled at Shechem to form a covenant and accept Yahweh.
They took oaths and agreed to send representatives, $n^e si^{\gamma} im$ according to
Noth, to yearly rites at the central cult shrine, now the home of the ark.
Thus Joshua and the tribes transformed Shechem from a local Canaanite
holy place to a central cult shrine of the new amphictyony. Since the
Old Testament offers a succession of additional shrines for Israel's tribes,
Noth assumed the ark must have been moved successively from Shechem
to Bethel, Gilgal, and Shiloh, until the Israelite monarchy established
Jerusalem as the permanent cult center for the twelve tribes.[20] Noth
placed great importance on the number "twelve" both for Israel and his
Delphic model. The *duodecim populi Etruscae* increased its significance
in establishing the parallel. This caused Noth problems in reconciling
the two tribal lists he selected from the Old Testament when membership
of the "twelve" changes.[21] Since then, others have lessened the burden of

---

[18]Noth, *Das System*, 47-60.

[19]De Vaux, *Early History*, 698.

[20]Noth, *History of Israel*, 85-109.

[21]See Genesis 49 for the tribal list including Levi and Numbers 26 for the list
without Levi. Mayes, *Israelite and Judaean History*, 304-6, discusses the intricacies
of the Levi tribal list. For a careful analysis of the Joseph tribal questions see de
Geus, *The Tribes of Israel*, 69-118. For a survey of the numerous possible tribal
lists see H. Weippert, "Das geographische System der Stämme Israels," *VT* 23
(1973) 76-89; and Koichi Namiki, "Reconsideration of the Twelve-Tribe System
of Israel," *Annual of the Japanese Biblical Institute* 2 (Tokyo: Yamamoto
Shoten, 1976) 29-59.

establishing the requisite "twelve" for Israel by pointing out that several
of the Greek examples also varied in membership—twelve to ten, six, or
even five at times. Yet as the critics aided Noth's theory by removing the
imperative for precisely twelve tribes and the same twelve, whatever the
status of Levi or Joseph, they simultaneously weakened his argument.
Noth's original parallel was based on a series of hypotheses, as Fohrer
pointed out in his 1966 article; and if one of the strongest parallels, i.e.
twelve members, is a variable, then the Israelite amphictyonic structure
rests even more precariously on the single, central cult shrine.[22]

Noth himself weakened the status of a single central shrine by
suggesting that the ark was the key element in the shrine. Since the ark
was formerly a traveling or portable religious symbol, the tribes would
see it as proper that the ark continue its journeys rather than become the
fixed shrine after the Canaanite manner.[23] And he agreed that the tribes
still used local shrines for local cults and individual tribal meetings.[24]

The major thrust of Noth's 1960s and 1970s critics has been directed
at the central shrine. Was there ever a single shrine serving as the central
shrine for all the tribes? Some cannot find evidence in Joshua or Judges
to accept Shechem, Bethel, or Gilgal as having the ark, much less
serving as a central shrine for all twelve tribes.[25] The ark, however, did
certainly reside at Shiloh prior to its capture by the Philistines in
battle.[26] De Vaux will accept the ark at Bethel, but not that Bethel
thereby became the sole sanctuary; only that there were then two
sanctuaries.[27] Nor can he agree that the ark's presence at Shiloh even
demonstrates the central sanctuary, for the tribes before doing battle with
the Benjaminites in Judges 20 and presumably meeting as a league met
at Mizpah, not Shiloh. What de Vaux finds is a series of shrines, not a
single cult shrine for an amphictyony.[28]

A. D. H. Mayes mirrors de Vaux's difficulties in finding amphictyonic and ark evidence at the shrines.[29] After some hesitation he can
accept a possible ark presence at Gilgal, but little more. Were all the
tribes visiting it as a central sanctuary and worshipping there at a
covenant festival? No. The twelve stones at Gilgal in Joshua 4:8-9
suggest a central tribal role; but, like much of Noth's other evidence,

[22]Fohrer, "Altes Testament," 801-6; and Mayes, Israelite and Judaean History,
304-5.

[23]Noth, Das System, 54; and History of Israel, 94.

[24]Noth, History of Israel, 96-97.

[25]See for example de Vaux, Early History, 704-6; and Orlinsky, "Tribal
System," 11-20.

[26]1 Sam 3:3; 4:1-7:1.

[27]De Vaux, Early History, 705.

[28]Ibid., 708-10; and "La thèse de l'amphictyonie," 430-31.

[29]Mayes, Israel in the Period of the Judges, 49-52.

that of the stones is circumstantial. With firm support from elsewhere they might help, but by themselves the mute stones are dubious witnesses. As H. I. Irwin comments, the twelve stones site may have been *a* shrine, but was it *the* shrine?[30] Bethel may have been a repository (Judg 20:24), but it is at Mizpah that the tribes assemble for the Lord. And it is at Mizpah (1 Sam 10:17) where the tribes proclaim their first king and Gilgal where they establish Saul as monarch (1 Sam 11:15), and Hebron where David is anointed king "before the Lord" (2 Sam 5:3). Orlinsky in his early 1962 article indicated the dilemma. There simply is no record in Judges that all the tribes met as an amphictyony at any of the shrine candidates. Likewise none of the judges was more than an individual war leader; they were not affiliated with any of the shrines nor did they serve as a Nothian amphictyon.[31]

What do we have then? Only Shiloh is a possible candidate for a central shrine attended by all the tribes and a site of a cult rite. The ark definitely resided there. The critics agree that this site could fulfill the requirements. And even there the tribes failed to assemble for their monarchy. As for the rest of the shrines, Irwin sums up very well the post-Noth quandary. "Evidence of a central sanctuary is fragmentary and difficult to prove. It is as difficult to prove the non-existence of something. But the evidence does not favor a central sanctuary."[32]

E. F. Campbell and G. E. Wright attempted to resuscitate the central shrine for the amphictyony in 1969. Like others they realized the increasing tenuousness of a single shrine, even if it was one that moved eventually from Shechem to Shiloh as Noth had originally proposed. They suggested a whole series of similar shrines as more suitable to a nomadic people, shrines identical in floor plan and proportions to the Shechem original. They reported on a small square temple excavated at Amman, Jordan, with a square holy of holies set within a larger square and bordered by outer walls. A stone pedestal sat in the middle square.[33] They likened this small temple to a proportionately identical one on Mt. Gerizim excavated in 1931.

Both shrines duplicate two courtyards with a similar pedestal found in the earliest phase of the Shechem tell dated as early as the 17th century.

[30]Irwin, "Le sanctuaire," 173.

[31]Orlinsky, "Tribal System," 15-17.

[32]Irwin, "Le sanctuaire," 182-83. See also G. W. Anderson ("Israel: Amphictyony: ꜤAM; ḴĀHĀL; ᶜĒḌĀH," *Translating and Understanding the Old Testament* [ed. H. T. Frank and W. L. Reed; New York: Abingdon, 1970] 145-46) who agrees that the period of Judges does not support a single central shrine. Gottwald (*Tribes of Yahweh*, 348-50) comes to the same conclusion.

[33]E. F. Campbell and G. E. Wright, "Tribal League Shrines in Amman and Shechem," *BA* 32 (1969) 104-16.

Revising Wright's earlier interpretation, Wright and Campbell now argued for a class of similar shrines used by semi-nomads returning to a shrine in the spring in an area where they had planted the previous fall. They propose then a number of shrines with identical cult shapes and functions serving as the physical manifestations of a single cult. They can then avoid the single cult shrine and replace it by one major cult center and several lesser ones. There would be no need presumably to demonstrate that eleven of the tribes assembled regularly at the central Shechem site. Wright and Campbell thereby save the league—pointing out how universally acceptable Noth's thesis is—while at the same time gutting the central shrine so essential to the classic amphictyony. Interestingly in their concluding remarks they refer to leagues among the desert fringe tribes.[34] Well might they, for Noth's "dwellers around" have been dispersed to multiple shrines. A more fruitful solution would have been to reconsider the entire thesis as others were already doing. Faced with multiple shrines and no specific central one, Irwin felt compelled to reinterpret Joshua's unity at Shechem as based upon Yahweh's service, not on an amphictyonic shrine cult.[35] Wright and Campbell may well have been on the right path from a single shrine to multiple shrines, and their material could prove helpful in any future reconstruction of the tribal unity. But they did not go far enough in their article.

Noth's representatives to the central shrine, the *neśi'im* have a similar tenuousness to them. As de Vaux made clear, they do not appear at the founding meeting at Shechem nor anywhere else in Judges. And Judges covers the entire amphictyonic era.[36] Hebrew uses the term broadly, generally referring to some level of chiefs.[37] The only dispute rests on their function within the tribes and not on whether they served as amphictyons.[38]

Most of the analyses of the late 1960s and 1970s focused on the web of specifics that constituted the amphictyony parallel; and, as we have shown, the web is quite weak. The conclusion is the same when one

[34]Ibid., 116.

[35]Irwin, "Le sanctuaire," 166.

[36]De Vaux, *Early History*, 711-12; and "La thèse de l'amphictyonie," 431-32. For Noth see *Das System*, 151-62 or *History*, 98. He suggests the usage of "speaker" and emphasizes that there were twelve, one for each tribe. Orlinsky ("Tribal System," 14) and Anderson ("Israel: Amphictyony," 147) attach similar value to the term as de Vaux.

[37]Irwin, "Le sanctuaire," 169.

[38]Mayes, *Israelite and Judaean History*, 307; E. A. Speiser, "Background and Function of the Biblical *nāśi*," *Oriental and Biblical Studies* (ed. J. J. Finkelstein and M. Greenberg [Philadelphia: University of Pennsylvania Press, 1967]) 113-22; J. van der Ploeg, "Les chefs du peuple d'Israel et leurs titres," *RB* 57 (1950) 40-61; and Gottwald, *Tribes of Israel*, 350-52.

considers the supposed overall parallels between the Greek amphictyony
and an Israelite confederacy. Gottwald in his massive 1979 study aptly
stresses the "fundamental structural discontinuity between the Israelite
confederacy and the Greek amphictyony."[39] He succinctly analyzes the
differing functions, scope, and role that the Greek amphictyony and the
Israelite tribal unity played for their respective societies.[40] Only on two
points can he find any comparability, the formal likeness of associate
autonomous political units and the primary definition of the league in
terms of a common religious cult.[41] On all else, their respective legal
status, cult shrine, conditions of membership, number of gods, military
obligations, the two are not compatible.

IV. SOLOMONIC ADMINISTRATIVE DISTRICTS AND AN EGYPTIAN PROTOTYPE

The Solomonic tax system might conceivably reflect an earlier tribal
unity. 1 Kgs 4:7-19 lists for Israel only twelve officials by name and their
respective geographic areas. Each was responsible monthly for providing
the food and provisions for Solomon's household. Judah had its own
unnamed official. Since the text specifies twelve officials and lists Judah
as a separate thirteenth district, apparently Judah was exempt from the
tax system. The twelve Israelite areas do not correspond to the tribal
areas and seemingly represent a real administrative district structure and
one tied to a twelve month support schedule.[42] G. E. Wright in a 1967
article interpreted the districts as a radical departure from the tribal areas
intended to create areas of similar economic wealth.[43] Wright like others
sees the districts as a move to emasculate the traditional tribal ties and
replace them by central administrative controls.[44] In fact he would trace
the origins of the district system back to the census list in 2 Samuel 24.
Only a strong public reaction attributed at the time to a plague sent by
Yahweh kept David from implementing the changes, leaving it to
Solomon to complete the centralization process. T. N. D. Mettinger's
recent analysis, however, suggests that Wright probably overemphasized
the alterations.[45] Whatever the degree of alteration, the new districts are

[39]Gottwald, *Tribes of Israel*, 383.

[40]Ibid., 376-86.

[41]Ibid., 377.

[42]A. Alt first began the discussion of the list in a 1913 article reprinted as
"Israels Gaue unter Salomo," *Kleine Schriften* 2 (Munich: C. H. Beck, 1953) 76-
89.

[43]G. E. Wright, "The Provinces of Solomon," *Eretz Israel* 8 (Jerusalem:
Israel Exploration Society, 1967) 58-68.

[44]Ibid., 67-68; Y. Aharoni, *The Land of the Bible* (Philadelphia: Westminster, 1967) 277-80.

[45]T. N. D. Mettinger, *Solomonic State Officials* (Coniectanea Biblica, Old
Testament Series 5; Lund: C. W. K. Gleerup, 1973) 111-27.

clearly not equivalent to the tribal lands that preceded them. If nothing else they incorporated within their boundaries some of the former Canaanite territory. As Y. Aharoni carefully pointed out, the six districts defined by towns are from the Canaanite regions on the plains. And they joined Israel only during David's reign. The remaining six encompassed traditional tribal districts.[46] If then the districts are not equivalent to tribal boundaries, then what structure or model was Solomon employing for his new system?

One solution has been that Solomon modeled his system on an Egyptian tax structure employed by a 22nd Dynasty pharaoh, perhaps Sheshonq I, a contemporary of Solomon. An Egyptian decree involved the restoration of an Herakleopolitan temple, part of a general Libyan revival of traditional Egyptian institutions.[47] The decree specified twelve groups of officials who for a month supplied the daily offerings needed by the restored temple. The groups of officials listed reflected particular geographic areas of the Herakleopolitan nome. It is this district system and the twelve month distribution that has suggested parallels to Solomon's system.

Both T. N. D. Mettinger and D. Redford agree that it is quite conceivable that Solomon might have borrowed the Egyptian temple support system. Mettinger finds Egyptian prototypes for some though not all of the higher government offices for Solomon.[48] Neither agrees on how knowledge of the system might have travelled to Israel. Redford suggests the former Egyptian presence in Canaan would be a possibility.[49] In this case simple Egyptian presence does not seem sufficient to explain knowledge of a particular temple decree, especially since it is likely that the pharaoh and the decree would overlap the end of Solomon's reign and not an earlier period. Certainly there was considerable contact, for the pharaoh contributed a royal daughter to Solomon's harem, a rare honor (1 Kgs 7:8). Mettinger distinguished a pattern of Egyptian prototypes, royal secretary, herald, and administrator of the royal estates, which might lay the groundwork for a borrowing of a tax system. If Solomon was borrowing this closely, then he may very well have been

[46]Aharoni, *Land of the Bible*, 278-80.
[47]D. B. Redford, "Studies in Relations between Palestine and Egypt during the First Millennium B.C. I. The taxation system of Solomon" *Studies on the Ancient Palestinian World* (ed. J. B. Wevers and D. B. Redford; Toronto: University of Toronto, 1972) 141-56. "II. The Twenty-Second Dynasty," *JAOS* 93 (1973) 3-17. For a good discussion of the Egyptian background see also K. A. Kitchen, *The Third Intermediate Period In Egypt, 1100-650 B.C.* (Philadelphia: Westminster, 1973) 85-88, 287-304.
[48]Mettinger, *State Officials*, 140.
[49]Redford, "Studies in Relations," 153-57.

aware of the innovative Egyptian system. Even so the analogy remains circumstantial.

Recently Alberto Green has challenged the direction of correspondence in a critique of Redford's article.[50] Green would reverse their roles, arguing that the pharaoh modeled his system upon Solomon's. Unable to discover an earlier calendric system of taxes like the decree prior to Sheshonq, Green maintains an Israelite origin. And Jeroboam's flight to Egypt in 1 Kgs 11:40 supplies a conduit for its transmission. Jeroboam had been a corvée official for Ephraim and Manasseh and would be knowledgeable in the workings of Solomon's system.

Green's proposal if correct has an intriguing effect, for it would shift the origin of the twelve month administrative division back to Israel where it could be a relic of an earlier league contribution system. One problem quickly emerges, the limited number of Egyptian tax records we have. In addition Green's reversal necessitates the derivation of the calendric divisional system subsequent to Sheshonq from a single source, the Herakleopolitan temple, a heavy but not impossible burden.

Green implies that the pharaoh would have no impetus to deviate from the traditional forms without the Solomonic model. The support needed by this temple was not the kind an annual tax could readily furnish. It required daily offerings and supplies. Normally a temple might expect its own nearby lands to supply it. In this instance the pharaoh was restoring a temple which had fallen into disrepair and was implicitly without its own lands. The restoration decree set an obligation on the Herakleopolitan nome for its various regions to send supplies. In a time of pharaonic regrouping there would be a natural disinclination to weaken the monarchy by diminishing its own lands. This relatively slight burden set upon geographically distributed officials representing other estates as well might seem a more tolerable solution. Participation by already functioning temples and estates in restoring an older complex would be difficult to reject. Alternatives would be detaching lands from present temples or lessening the bourse of the pharaoh. Pharaonic financial and political needs can supply the motivation. Nevertheless a definite origin for the district system remains arguable. The motivation would be present in Egypt, but the model could yet have originated with Solomon.

V. A PHILISTINE LEAGUE

In 1965 B. D. Rahtjen developed another candidate for a Near Eastern parallel, the five member Philistine league centered at the cult shrine at Ashdod.[51] The Philistine league met with not much more

[50]Alberto Green, "Israelite Influence at Shishak's Court?" *BASOR* 233 (1979) 59-62.

[51]Rahtjen, "Philistine and Hebrew Amphictyonies."

acceptance than the Sumerian League proposed years earlier. The Ashdod group did have a central fixed shrine and the members were city-states as were the Greek prototypes. De Vaux would reject it as having no religious character and an overly political and ethnic nature. He added that Dagon was not even a Philistine god.[52] Fohrer admitted it to be closer to the Greek model, but he could still not accept it as an amphictyony.[53] De Vaux illustrates the collective ambivalence of the critics. Careful demands are rightfully placed upon the Israelite material, but then he can dismiss the Philistine model as too ethnic and overly political. Were not the Greek versions ethnic and political for their times as well? And military at times? Yet others would give Israel more credence it if could be shown to have fought holy wars as a unit. Then they might see a stronger case.[54] Gottwald ironically adds that he doubts whether Rahtjen demonstrated a Philistine amphictyony, but he has shown the Philistine amphictyony argument is more "cogent" than the Israelite amphictyony.[55] What one must admit for the Philistine arrangement and especially in this present context is that the leagues no doubt did change, as Noth himself maintained for the original Israelite league.

VI. THE SUMERIAN LEAGUE

Solomon's monthly district system can provide another clue to its origins, one at least as intriguing as the Egyptian parallel. Solomon retained the twelvefold division and monthly format for the North despite its restructured base. This system parallels the BALA system for the Sumerian League of Ur III times. Fohrer in his brief note on the Sumerian amphictyony dismissed W. W. Hallo's article on the BALA contribution system as demonstrating nothing more than this very contribution parallel.[56] When the Israelite amphictyony still dominated the scholarly consensus, Aharoni believed the twelve unit monthly structure reflected an earlier system "fixed in tradition" long after its practical significance had departed.[57] The heavy financial burdens of the national kingship required new contributions far beyond any traditional tribal support. Thus the new districts incorporated Canaanite cities and rearranged Israel's internal boundaries to support the manpower and

---

[52]De Vaux, *Early History*, 701.

[53]Fohrer, *History*, 90.

[54]See Rudolf Smend (*Yahweh War and Tribal Confederation* [New York: Abingdon, 1970]) for a discussion of the holy war's role in the amphictyony theory. For an extensive review of the Philistine League see also Bächli, *Amphiktyonie im Alten Testament*, 35-41.

[55]Gottwald, *Tribes of Israel*, 356.

[56]Fohrer, *History of Religion*, 91, n. 10.

[57]Aharoni, *Land of the Bible*, 280.

construction projects, but Solomon retained the traditional twelve-unit month form. Or so Aharoni suggests.

As the Greek amphictyony is rejected as a model for Israel and a firm Sumerian League emerges, this very BALA parallel could prove quite suggestive in future attempts to reconstruct whatever form of unity the twelve tribes did have either during the period of the Judges or the early monarchy. Solomon's district model could reflect this earlier unity, just as undoubtedly the BALA system does for a Sumerian League—as we shall argue shortly. Some caution, however, is needed. As we have seen, the Biblical evidence does not support the single central shrine for a future reconstruction of the tribal unity. And a single central shrine would be the most likely though not an absolutely necessary focus for a support system.

Over the last twenty years as critics have overthrown the Israelite amphictyony, attempts to establish parallel leagues have had mixed success. In 1960 W. W. Hallo published his analysis of a contribution system by Sumerian Ur III *ensi*s or governors to the chief Sumerian sanctuary of Enlil at Nippur, starting a search that has not yet ended.[58] Among the numerous receipts from Drehem, a supply depot near Ur, Hallo distinguished a category called BALA. Drehem's function was to gather the livestock and other supplies needed by the temples and distribute them. His BALA survey found receipts from only the central Sumerian and Akkadian cities with none of the outlying Ur III dependencies represented except a certain Zariq of Susa. Hallo attributed his role to a personal obligation to the specific Sumerian Ur III ruler. Among the 19 Sumerian and Akkadian cities only Nippur itself was unrepresented in the BALA receipts. Since Hallo's 1960 article M. Tanret published another BALA text revealing that the Nippur *ensi* also contributed to Enlil's support.[59] The new tablet does not significantly alter the BALA argument. In a sense it would be strange perhaps if Enlil's own *ensi* did not participate. Hallo's analysis from the BALA to a Sumerian amphictyony still stands strongly in the wake of a larger and broader case for the religious, social and political role that can now be made for a Sumerian Kengir League centered around Enlil and his sanctuary at Nippur.

The BALA reveals a system of contributions rotating calendrically among league members. BALA's root meaning is "rotate" or "turn," and its noun form survived into Ur III as a generic word for "turn of

---

[58]W. W. Hallo, "A Sumerian Amphictyony," *JCS* 14 (1960) 88-114. See also W. W. Hallo, *The Ensis of the Ur III Dynasty* (University of Chicago M.A. thesis, 1953), where he first distinguished the two definite groups of *ensi*s.

[59]M. Tanret, "Nouvelles données à propos de l'amphictyonie neo-sumérienne," *Akkadica* 13 (1979) 28-45.

office"—for *ensis* as well as lesser officials.[60] The new tablet published by Hallo details clearly this calendric nature for the BALA, for it designates twelve 30 day units with one or more cities constituting a BALA depending upon their relative wealth. What we have here is a formal contribution system, just what Noth might have wished for his Shechem shrine. Hallo's tablet makes explicit this relationship as it assigns monthly BALA duties to specific *ensis* for the fourth year of Amar-Suen's reign. And the BALA are for a central cult shrine. Such a BALA system had been suggested in earlier publications by H. Radau (1900) and B. Landsberger (1917).[61]

In a 1976 dissertation R. Sigrist analyzed another Nippur cult contribution system, one for the Ešumeša temple of Ninurta, Enlil's son.[62] Sigrist examined the contributions called *sattukku* for the later Isin-Larsa period. Though he concentrated on the late period he noted that *sattukku* tablets first appear at Lagash during the pre-Sargonic era and were very abundant for Ur III.[63] Originally they designated a measure of capacity and then by extension rations and gifts; but their principal use was for gifts to the gods. He suggested that the connotation "regular" is not intrinsic to its Sumerian $sa\text{-}du_{11}$ form but is "shown by the nature of things."[64] With the specific term of Ninurta's temple contribution dating back to Early Dynastic times and despite slender other evidence for Ninurta's cult at Nippur itself that early, it is not unreasonable to assume that the BALA may also date back to pre-Sargonic times, especially in light of other supporting materials for an early Nippur League shrine to Enlil.

Hallo had added that the BALA system might accord well with Noth's position that an amphictyony characteristically precedes organization of a full-fledged national state. And he offered the Sumerian League as a clear case of an early league leading to such a state.[65] Unfortunately Noth's position is groundless. The Delphic League never served such a purpose for its members unless one counts Philip of Macedon's manipulations and military drives, and even that was only a temporary phenomenon. The Ionian, Aeolic, and Dorian Leagues never matured into a state or a reasonable facsimile. And the Etruscan cities might have survived Rome had they any political unity worthy of the

[60]Hallo, "Sumerian Amphictyony," 89.

[61]H. Radau, *Early Babylonian History* (Oxford: University Press, 1900) 299; B. Landsberger, *Der Kultische Kalender* (Leipzig dissertation, 1917) 65.

[62]R. Sigrist, *Ninurta à Nippur. L'économie du culte pendant la période d'Isin et Larsa* (Yale dissertation, 1976).

[63]Ibid., 1. 357-61.

[64]Ibid., 361.

[65]Hallo, "Sumerian Amphictyony," 96.

name. The Sumerian Kengir League could have provided such a political role model for Noth, one far better than his own Greek choice.

The Sumerian League provides an excellent parallel as one form of league. It was not directly equivalent to the Greek model, nor should we expect any league to be a direct parallel to the much later Greek case. Indeed, by virtue of its historical context the Sumerian League at Nippur has far more grounds for claiming the prototypical role. The Kengir League predated even the Israelite period by 1000 years and the Greek leagues by c. 1500 years.

The Sumerian amphictyony thesis has not met with anything like universal acceptance. Soon after its initial publication G. Fohrer set the critical tone when he could find no evidence for any amphictyonic league in the Ancient Near East.[66] Like others to follow he argued only for an obligation placed on several cities for the Nippur cult, paralleling Solomon's division of Northern Israel into administrative districts.[67] R. de Vaux (1968), G. Buccellati (1967), and C. H. J. de Geus (1976) would all echo Fohrer's stance that a possible Sumerian parallel should be abandoned and could at best apply to Solomon's system.[68] Even O. Bächli who agrees that the classical amphictyony cannot be forced upon the Israelite tribes judges the Sumerian parallel too distant to be instructive. Rather he finds the tribal and urban forms in the two different areas too much to overcome to make an instructive parallel.[69]

Gottwald's position on the Sumerian parallel is paradoxical. On the one hand he finds troublesome the fact that the BALA system was statist, imposed by Ur III imperial policy, and involved more than twelve member cities. This he judges "does not make an amphictyony."[70] Yet he himself is willing to suggest that the entire twelve tribe system was originated by David, perhaps using Saul's militia system as an administrative reform. This administrative application he holds solidified David's control on the "foundation of the tribal entities of the old Yahwistic association of Israelite peoples."[71] Additionally the soundness of "twelve" has already been undermined as a criterion for such a league. The parallel between the Sumerian League and the Israelite confederation still holds, especially if the Sumerian League exhibits a pre-BALA ethnic/religious origin as the unifying force for Sumer. This reluctance

[66]Fohrer, *History of Religion*, 90-91.

[67]Ibid., 91, no. 10.

[68]De Vaux, *Early History*, 700-701; G. Buccellati, *Cities and Nations of Ancient Syria* (Rome: Istituto di Studi del Vicino Oriente, 1967) 114-16; de Geus, *The Tribes of Israel*, 60-61.

[69]Bächli, *Amphiktyonie im Alten Testament*, 34-35, 178.

[70]Gottwald, *Tribes of Yahweh*, 751, n. 265.

[71]Ibid., 363-67.

among biblical scholars to accept such a role is not necessarily shared by Sumerologists or by other Sumerian materials.[72]

Biblical commentators such as de Geus and Fohrer consider the BALA system as a timeless unity with no past. Since Hallo has identified the contributing members as a limited number of specific Sumerian cities within the Sumer/Akkad region, then conceivably the BALA reflects a late remnant of the much earlier Kengir League, postulated by Thorkild Jacobsen in 1957.[73] Otherwise there would be little reason not to include the numerous Ur III dependent rulers outside the central Sumer/Akkad region. In an earlier article in 1939 Jacobsen suggested that the term *Kengir* began as a designation for Nippur itself.[74] Jacobsen also noted a puzzling collection of jar sealings inscribed with the names of major Sumerian cities which he thought implied evidence of official deliveries to Ur, an earlier parallel of the BALA deliveries.[75]

For the Sargonic, Ur III, and Isin-Larsa periods there is no doubt that the Enlil-Nippur cult supplied the social, cultural, and political underpinnings for Sumer and Akkad.[76] Nippur was not just a cult shrine due deliveries, rather it was the central fixed cult shrine for Sumer and Akkad which supplied the cosmic and intellectual credence for a political unity imposed by force, whether by the Sargonic dynasty, Ur III rulers, or the later Isin-Larsa kings. Each Sumerian city had its respective tutelary divinity associated normally with other divinities as well, but Enlil at this single shrine supplied the necessary royal legitimacy and cosmic order.

[72]H. Cazelles, "Mari et l'ancien Testament," *La civilisation de Mari* (Rencontre Assyriologique Internationale 15, 1967) 87-88; P. Michalowski, "Foreign Tribute to Sumer During Ur III," *ZA* 68 (1978) 34-49; J. J. Van Dijk, "Les contacts ethniques dans la Mésopotamie et les syncrétismes de la religion sumérienne," *Syncretism* (Stockholm: Almquist and Wiksell, 1969) 171-206, esp. 183-85; M. Tanret, "Nouvelles données"; R. Sigrist, *Ninurta à Nippur*, 23.

[73]T. Jacobsen, "Early Political Development in Mesopotamia," *ZA* 52 (1957) 91-140, esp. 99-109; reprinted in W. Moran (ed.), *Toward the Image of Tammuz* (Cambridge: Harvard University, 1970) 132-56. For a general discussion see N. Bailkey, "Early Mesopotamian Constitutional Development," *AHR* 72 (1967) 1211-36. Also H. Vanstiphout, "Political Ideology in Early Sumer," *Orientalia Lovaniensia Periodica* 1 (1970) 7-38; W. W. Hallo and W. K. Simpson, *The Ancient Near East: A History* (New York: Harcourt Brace, 1971) 42-46.

[74]T. Jacobsen, "The Supposed Conflict Between Sumer and Akkad," *JAOS* 59 (1939) 487, n. 11. Hallo also gives a brief account of the Kengir concept in his *Early Mesopotamian Royal Titles* (New Haven, Conn.: American Oriental Society, 1957) 77-89.

[75]Jacobsen, "Early Political Development," 109.

[76]Sigrist (*Ninurta à Nippur*, 7-84) gives a good discussion of the evidence before the Isin-Larsa period.

The numerous royal hymns of Sumer and Akkad analyzed by Hallo in a 1963 study describe a continuous political ideal of unity.[77] According to the cosmic-political theory the gods assemble at Nippur under Enlil's leadership and bestow the *illilutu* (executive authority) on one of its divine members. This deity then confers the earthly rule upon his king or *ensi*. Ur-Nammu left us a fine record of just this as he claimed his kingship from Enlil at Nippur.[78] The very term for this grant of authority betrays Nippur's central role: *illilutu* = ^{d}*en-lil-utu* or Enlil-ship.[79] Subsequent publications on the royal hymn genre by D. Reisman and J. Klein confirm and deepen Hallo's analysis. The three hymns founded the kings' right to rule on a grant of authority by Enlil.[80] All reflect a close and even proportional relationship between Enlil and the specific king, a relationship anticipating the divine right theory of kingship in Hellenistic and later periods.

Royal titularies substantiate the central role of Nippur. Hallo's 1957 examination of Ur III titles shows that the royal title *lugal ki-en-gi ki-uri* used for the period of Ur-Nammu to Hammurabi reflects a compound title, King of Sumer and Akkad.[81] And for a ruler to claim the title he had to possess Nippur, located between the two areas. Ur-Nammu first used it when he became a national figure, and the Isin-Larsa dynasties passed it back and forth as they alternated control of Nippur.[82]

Nippur's importance for the unitary cult of Sumer and Akkad originated in the Early Dynastic Period. The Sumerian King List reflects three major cities vying for predominance in the Early Dynastic Period, Kish in the north (Akkad) and Ur and Uruk in the south (Sumer). The Semitic names of many Early Dynastic kings of Kish strongly suggest an early Semitic presence. Other materials testify to these early Semites down at least to the Nippur vicinity.[83] A. Goetze argued that it was the Semites at Kish who elevated Kish to its early prominence and some

---

[77]W. W. Hallo, "Royal Hymns and Mesopotamian Unity," *JCS* 17 (1963) 112-18.

[78]W. W. Hallo, "The Coronation of Ur-Nammu," *JCS* 20 (1966) 133-41.

[79]T. Jacobsen, *Before Philosophy* (Baltimore: Penguin, 1949) 207-8. The usage is common. A recent text is D. Reisman, *Two Neo-Sumerian Royal Hymns* (University of Pennsylvania dissertation, 1968). Hallo's *Royal Hymns* treats the subject well.

[80]J. Klein, *Shulgi D: A Neo-Sumerian Royal Hymn* (University of Pennsylvania dissertation, 1968); D. Reisman, *Two Neo-Sumerian Royal Hymns*.

[81]Hallo, *Royal Titles*, 87-88.

[82]Ibid., 126-27; R. Sigrist, "Nippur entre Isin et Larsa de Sin-iddinam à Rim-Sin," *Or* 46 (1977) 363-74.

[83]M. Gibson, *The City and Area of Kish* (Florida: Field Research Projects, 1972) 11.

controlled Nippur itself.[84] According to the Tummal Inscription recording Nippur sanctuary constructions, Enmebaragesi, King of Kish, built the Enlil temple at Nippur during ED II and his son Agga continued the construction.[85] Agga of Kish was the famous antagonist of Gilgamesh in a short Sumerian text which surely retained memories of a struggle between Kish and Uruk or Sumer and Akkad. Once the southern cities had been successful in establishing their dominance over the North they too called themselves Kings of Kish.[86] When in turn Sargon of Agade sought acknowledgement of his supremacy over both areas he brought Lugalzagesi of Umma before Enlil at Nippur. His empire would then centralize the loose earlier unity.[87]

Simple administrative documents from Nippur itself also support such a central league role. A. Westenholz examined account records of Nippur scribes to compare the date system and the Sumerian King List.[88] The scribes dated these local peaceful records after the exploits of the kings of Uruk, Umma, and Akkad. Only a single king at a time was ever cited to date a document. This practice suggests that the scribes recognized a single king as primary ruler among the three at any one time. Three of these kings also appear on the Sumerian King List, suggesting both further historicity in the King List as well as implying that the other List names were also used singly for dating. Westenholz notes that Nippur remained simply a religious and administrative center with its god Enlil as the bestower of legitimacy. He too agrees that military victory would bring agreement by Enlil that the victor was king of all the land or lord of Sumer and Akkad.

J. J. van Dijk discussed the cult sanctuary's role in the Sargonic rise and fall.[89] First the Nippur priests accepted Sargon's victory as they would for any other military conqueror. And with good reason for Sargon remained careful in his relations with the Nippur priesthood. Later successors', especially Naram-Sin's, inscriptions much less frequently mention Enlil, and according to the Curse of Agade Enlil's temple itself may have been ravaged.[90] Nippur did not join any of the

---

[84]A. Goetze, "Early Kings of Kish," *JCS* 15 (1961) 105-11.

[85]E. Sollberger, "The Tummal Inscription," *JCS* 16 (1962) 40-47.

[86]Goetze, "Early Kings," 105-11.

[87]W. W. Hallo and J. J. Van Dijk, *The Exaltation of Inanna* (New Haven: Yale University, 1968) ch. 1; Vanstiphout, "Political Ideology," 30-37. Sigrist (*Ninurta à Nippur*, 17-18) has gathered the Sargonic materials neatly in his discussion of early Nippur.

[88]A. Westenholz, "Early Nippur Dates and the Sumerian King List," *JCS* 26 (1974) 154-56.

[89]Van Dijk, "Contacts ethniques," 206.

[90]Sigrist, *Ninurta à Nippur*, 17-18.

military coalitions against them, but the importance placed upon the Ishtar/Inanna cult and the possible Nippur ravaging led it eventually to support the resurgence of Sumerian Ur. N. Bailkey in his discussion of the same incident concludes that they set up an anti-king at Nippur and then were joined by eight other gods and their cities in their opposition.[91] As van Dijk phrased it, "the dynasty became the victim of an unalterable decree of the Nippur assembly," or more mundanely, the Nippur priesthood.[92] Enlil retained his supremacy as did his cult center as the source of religious, political, and cultural unity for the land of Sumer and Akkad.

Unlike the Israelite amphictyony the Nippur League has firm grounds for its important role in its members' lives. It fulfills most if not all the requirements for a sacred league. Possessing a fixed shrine, an early limited number of members, a calendric contribution system, a religious claim to supremacy in the Sumerian pantheon, a formal priestly structure, Nippur was a well developed religious league. If the Sumerian King List and the Tummal Inscription have been interpreted correctly, the Nippur pre-eminence dated from its early role, begun by the Kings of Kish, as the central shrine to bring together the portions of southern Mesopotamia, Sumer and Akkad, into a single loose confederation at a central sanctuary. Here truly member cities, probably 19 in all, "dwelt around." With its claim to grant Enlil-ship or *illilutu* the Nippur sanctuary preserved the fiction of an ordered universe under Enlil's rule despite the regular struggles for predominance among the cult's member cities. The Ur III period retained the memory of the Nippur League's origins in its BALA contribution members. Were these political functions? Certainly. Yet Nippur itself was not a political power; it remained a religious, cultural, cosmic, and occasional political arbitrator. And its scribal schools were continuously working to uphold Enlil's and thus their own central role as the earthly manifestation of the cosmic assembly. Eventually Nippur had to relinquish its preeminence to Marduk and Babylon. The Mesopotamian river valley would become a single political unity governed by an increasingly secular monarchy.

What do the Biblical critics wish for the Twelve Tribes? They seek a cultic league with some type of formal structure, one that might lead to a later monarchy. Bright says as much when he cautions against rejecting completely any sacral league for early Israel just because of the tenuous amphictyony parallel. He suggests "a sacred league of some sort" may yet be our most suitable approach.[93] And if the Greek leagues which

---

[91] Bailkey, "Early Mesopotamian Constitutional Development," 1226.

[92] Van Dijk, "Contacts ethniques," 206.

[93] J. Bright, Review of O. Bächli, *Amphiktyonie im Alten Testament, JSS* 24 (1979) 275-76.

served a temporary political function during their early days were judged proper amphictyonic prototypes until retreating before other more overtly political forms, then why not the Nippur League?[94]

VI. CONCLUSION

The Israelite amphictyonic model as formulated by Noth lies in disarray. It was a model which demanded that biblical texts fit it. Under the close examination of the 1960s and 1970s the texts failed to supply more than a web of circumstantial citations without a firm center. Without Noth's original thesis to support Joshua and Judges they cannot stand. The Greek leagues provided a fixed model which Israel cannot be forced to duplicate. Bächli in his exhaustive review concluded also that a true amphictyony can only be found in Greece.[95] The same problem originally faced other attempts to find Near Eastern parallels. They too could not be established as "amphictyonic" in the Greek mode. Now with the scholarly demolition of the Israelite amphictyony there is no longer any reason to deny valid attention to Near Eastern parallels, especially the Sumerian Nippur League. Fohrer's and others' dismissal of the Sumerian League can no longer stand.

The scholarly community must now reexamine and reconstruct the forms of tribal unity that preceded Saul's monarchy. Freed from the amphictyonic restraints they might find the early history of the Nippur League and its union of Sumer and Akkad into one nation a suggestive variant. The League stands on its own as one of a number of political forms that lead to a larger monarchic unity. Once again it is clear that the historian must move carefully from an era's own sources before seeking foreign models and imposing them. Once the texts suggest directions, the parallelism can be a productive tool. Comparative materials must remain precisely that—comparative, not imperative.

[94]A. Malamat in two articles has already offered some intriguing parallels. A. Malamat, "Organs of Statecraft," *BA* 27 (1965) 34-65; and Malamat, "Kingship and Council in Israel and Sumer; A Parallel," *JNES* 22 (1963) 247-53. D. G. Evans ("Rehoboam's Advisers at Shechem and Political Institutions in Israel and Sumer," *JNES* 25 [1966] 273-79) cannot find more than that the two groups of advisers are representatives of the same literary tradition.

[95]Bächli, *Amphiktyonie im Alten Testament,* 178.

AN HISTORICAL RECONSTRUCTION OF THE EMERGENCE OF ISRAELITE KINGSHIP AND THE REIGN OF SAUL

WILLIAM E. EVANS

Kansas State University

I. INTRODUCTION

The career of Saul, as the first Israelite monarch, is important for at least two reasons. First, it marks a revolution in Israel's political structure. Second, it is by general agreement the threshold of actual historical events in the Bible.[1] The material in 1 Samuel devoted to Saul's rise and fall and the rise of David tantalizes the reader: even though confronting him with doublets, the telescoping of events, the lack of a clear chronological order, and the differing attitudes toward Saul and the monarchy more generally, it creates a strong impression that he is seeing some reflection of what actually transpired. While there is no lack of critical examination of the book, much of the work has necessarily focused on textual difficulties. In a recent article, J. Blenkinsopp concludes his examination of Saul and his reign saying, "perhaps more than with any other major biblical figure. . . the modern historian finds himself working, so to speak, against the grain of his sources. This is always a hazardous task, but the importance of the period in question, not to say the reputation of Saul himself, demands that it be undertaken."[2] This paper will survey some of the pertinent criticism on 1 Samuel, emphasizing chapters 8-31, in an attempt to further elucidate

---

[1]Even for J. A. Soggin, "The History of Ancient Israel: A Study in Some Questions of Method," *H. L. Ginsberg Volume* (*Eretz-Israel* 14, Jerusalem: Israel Exploration Society, 1978) 51*, who proposes a new "datum point" for biblical history in the united monarchy under David but suggests that "some of the events preceding the united monarchy can be tentatively reconstructed: such events as those surrounding Saul's kingship." For a critique of Soggin's proposal, see W. W. Hallo, "Biblical History in its Near Eastern Setting," *Scripture in Context* (Pittsburgh: Pickwick Press, 1980) 1-18, esp. pp. 9-11.

[2]"The Quest of the Historical Saul," *No Famine in the Land* (Festschrift John L. McKenzie; ed. J. W. Flanagan and A. W. Robinson; Missoula: Scholars Press, 1975) 93.

the problems confronting the reader wishing to reconstruct the history of Saul's reign and to offer some tentative suggestions toward such a reconstruction.

Among the initial difficulties is the fact that one must rely primarily on the Masoretic text[3] because there is little corroborating evidence available from other sources. The only other significant biblical treatment of Saul appears in genealogical tables in 1 Chronicles and in chapter 10 of that book, which deals exclusively with his last battle and his death. Ironically, just at the point in history at which one would like to see related epigraphic and archaeological material to shed more light on this brief period, neither that nor much in comparative material from the Near East is available. Since the historical reconstruction must be drawn primarily from the biblical text, it is worthwhile to review the current state of literary analysis of 1 Samuel.

II. I SAMUEL: TEXTUAL CONSIDERATIONS

Most recent critics, with the notable exception of O. Eissfeldt,[5] have abandoned the Pentateuchal or Hexateuchal source extensions in their analyses.[6] P. K. McCarter's literary analysis, representative of the current trend, will be followed here, though his order of presentation will be reversed so as to move from the early sources to the later redactions.[7] The "oldest narrative sources" consist of "the ark narrative" (4:1b-7:1);[8] "the Saul cycle" including: (1) a "lost" account of Saul's birth (chap. 1), (2) the lost asses (9:1-10:16), (3) Saul's victory over the Ammonites (10:27b-11:15);

---

[3]For a discussion of the current state of scholarship on the text, including the Septuagint and Qumran materials, see P. K. McCarter, *I Samuel* (AB 8; Garden City, N. Y.: Doubleday, 1980) 5-11.

[4]For indications of the paucity of references to Saul in Jesus ben-Sirach and the scattered Talmudic references to Saul see Blenkinsopp, "The Quest of the Historical Saul," 75-76.

[5]He argues for the L, J and E strands continuing from the Heptateuch. See *The Old Testament: An Introduction* (New York: Harper and Row, 1965) 271-81.

[6]For general histories of literary analysis, see T. Ishida, *The Royal Dynasties in Ancient Israel* (BZAW 142; New York: de Gruyter, 1977) 27-28; P. K. McCarter, *I Samuel*, 12-14. See also B. C. Birch, *The Rise of the Israelite Monarchy: The Growth and Development of I Samuel 7-15* (SBLDS 27; Missoula: Scholars Press, 1976) 1-7; A. D. Ritterspach, *The Samuel Traditions: An Analysis of the Anti-Monarchical Source in I Samuel 1-15* (unpublished dissertation, Graduate Theological Union, 1967) 7-53.

[7]*I Samuel*, 12-30.

[8]References to chapters and verses in 1 Samuel from this point on will not be preceded by the book's title unless its omission would cause confusion.

and the history of David's rise (1 Sam 16:14-2 Sam 5). The middle stage of the book's growth is "prophetic history" in which the prophetic writer incorporated the older sources into his history, "amplified them and reworked parts of them, sometimes with considerable license, to reflect his *Tendenz.*"[9] The result was a systematic, three-section narrative: (1) the story of Samuel (chaps. 1-7), (2) the story of Saul (chaps. 8-15), and (3) the story of David's rise (chaps. 16ff.). The final stage is "the Deuteronomistic history." In Samuel, the hand of the Deuteronomist is sparse, presumably because the prophetic history was already long and basically in accord with his viewpoint; McCarter identifies nine brief additions by this source (e.g., 13:1-2; 14:47-51 and 23:14-24:23) which were meant to "impose a structure on them whereby they could be incorporated into a larger history."[10] While general agreement exists on the early sources, there is still debate over the later reworking. This analysis sees some older early sources (some favorable to Saul, some not), a prophetic stratum probably written in the northern kingdom in the late eighth century B.C.E., and a Deuteronomistic overlay dating from the Exile (or according to F. M. Cross, in two editions—one from Josiah's time, Dtr_1, the other from the Exile, Dtr_2).[11] It should be noted that some scholars have strongly disagreed with this approach and have put forth quite different alternatives.[12]

If this analysis is close to correct, it reveals a problem faced in an attempted historical reconstruction. The strands that pervade the entire 1 Samuel narrative, prophetic and Deuteronomistic, can clearly be seen as anti-Saul but not necessarily anti-monarchy. Their reasons for disliking Saul's monarchy were quite different. R. P. Knierim[13] has argued persuasively for a pre-Deuteronomistic stratum which dominates especially chaps. 9-31. Basically he sees both Saul and David as messiahs in this source. Recognizing that interpretation, the reader can then better understand why the two figures are judged as they are from this strand's perspective. As messiah, the Lord's anointed is required to obey Yahweh completely. The reader can then better understand why Saul is said to lose Yahweh's support completely in chapter 15, even in the face of Samuel's pleading and attempted intercession on Saul's behalf. As the

---

[9] *I Samuel*, 18.

[10] Ibid., 16-17.

[11] *Canaanite Myth and Hebrew Epic* (Cambridge: Harvard University, 1973) 178, n. 17; 287.

[12] See M. Tsevat, "Samuel, I and II," *IDBSup* (1976) 780-81, and H. H. Segal, "The Composition of the Books of Samuel, *JQR* 55 (1964) 818-339, *JQR* (1965) 32-50 and 137-57.

[13] "The Messianic Concept in the First Book of Samuel," *Jesus and the Historians* (ed. F. Thomas Trotter; Philadelphia: Westminster, 1968) 20-51.

Lord's anointed, Saul incurs special responsibilities as well as special
favor. He is to follow Yahweh's divine will to the letter. When Saul fails
to do so, he is condemned as harshly as Moses had been condemned
earlier for *one* failure to obey. Where Moses would not be allowed to
enter the promised land, Saul would not be allowed to succeed in his
role as king. "Although Saul fails in the testing and is therefore rejected,
David does not fail in the testing and is therefore finally confirmed
(2 Sam, chap. 7)."[14] The value of Knierim's study derives from its
identification of the systematic theology governing the stratum and
demonstrating it to be consistently anti-Saul and pro-David. The inference to be drawn from this is that the selection, ordering, and interpretation of events in this source serve the interests of a clear religious slant
rather than the interests of historicity.

The anti-Saul/pro-David position is reinforced by the Deuteronomistic layer. The Deuteronomist's interpolation, 8:8, and his additions
to Samuel's farewell address (12:6-15, 9b(?), 20b-22, 24-25)[15] both appear
to concern dire warnings to the people about the potential evils of
kingship. As J. A. Soggin has suggested, the Deuteronomist saw kingship
"as an institution which had the potential for either good or evil, and
was concerned to show how it could be compatible with the notion of
Israel as the people of Yahweh."[16] R. E. Clements[17] has further demonstrated this source's difficulty by asking how the accession, rule, and
failure of Saul, of whom the Deuteronomist disapproves, can be reconciled with Yahweh's choice of David, of whom he approves. Objecting to
I. Mendelsohn's suggestion that what was being rejected was the despotic
rule of Canaanite kings,[18] Clements feels that "although the Deuteronomists show at many points that kingship is neither a blameless, nor a
sacrosanct institution, nevertheless in their eyes it did have, in its
Davidic form, a special role to play."[19] This source is torn between the
idea that no king is necessary (that Yahweh can rule directly) and the
fact that the Davidic covenant is a Yahweh-ordained, eternal covenant.
Therefore, Saul can be condemned, but David cannot.

If the content of these two strata can be agreed upon, even in broad
outline, it seems obvious that there are two tendentious lines having as

---

[14]Ibid., p. 38. B. C. Birch comes to a similar conclusion, *The Rise of the
Israelite Monarchy*, 148.

[15]*I Samuel*, 16.

[16]In *Israelite and Judean History* (ed. J. H. Hayes and J. M. Miller;
Philadelphia: Westminster, 1977) 297.

[17]"The Deuteronomistic Interpretation of the Founding of the Monarchy in
I Sam. VIII," *VT* 24 (1974) 398-410.

[18]"Samuel's Denunciation of Kingship in the Light of the Akkadian Documents from Ugarit," *BASOR* 143 (1956) 17-22.

[19]R. E. Clements, "The Deuteronomistic Interpretation," 406.

their common focal point the disapproval of Saul's monarchy. The prophetic strand places special emphasis upon Samuel at the book's beginning and, with the Deuteronomist's later collaboration, upon David's rise from the book's midpoint to its end. Where, then, does Saul figure prominently on his own in the book? The instances are few: (1) 9:1-10:16, (2) 10:27b-11:15, (3) 13:2-7a, 15b-23; 14:1-46.[20] Of these instances, the folkloristic nature of the tale of the lost asses must be questioned in a historical reconstruction.[21] If this is ruled out, one is left with precious little "unbiased" material on Saul to work with. Historical reconstruction of Saul's reign cannot depend only upon these brief passages. However, one may use them as touchstones in sifting through the remaining parts of 1 Samuel. The following section of the paper will be devoted to questions about Saul's reign and will attempt to suggest what historical data may be reasonably ascertained from the book as a whole.

III. ISRAEL'S FIRST KING

One might begin with a consideration of what circumstances brought about the institution of kingship in Israel. Chap. 9 suggests that Yahweh had chosen a new leader, a nāgîd, to "save my people from the hand of the Philistines" (v 16), but chap. 8 says that the people had demanded a king "to govern us like all the nations" (v 5)—a king who will " 'go out before us and fight our battles' " (v 20). While the context of chapter 8 suggests that the people's major impetus for demanding a king, a wrongheaded demand, was merely the desire to emulate other nations, it seems far more likely that the demand actually centered on the recognized need for a stable, central leader who could defend Israel from its most serious external threat. The leaders of the previous period are said to have saved Israel from apparently isolated incursions into parts of their territory by fairly small enemy groups. The old system had not been successful in stopping the incursions of the technologically superior, professional Philistine armies that clearly wanted to control Palestine.[22] G. E. Wright says, "moving rapidly from their coastal base, the Philistines had Israel virtually surrounded. Theirs was a planned drive for the conquest of the whole land. The next move would obviously be a thrust directly into the center of Israelite power itself." Pointing to the biblical record, he cites the battle of Aphek, the Israelite defeat, the destruction of Shiloh and the removal of the ark, and the Philistine garrisoning of the hill country. "Only the installation of a monarchy

---

[20]*I Samuel*, 26-27.

[21]We cannot agree with H. W. Hertzberg, *I and II Samuel* (Philadelphia: Westminster, 1976) 78, who says, "true history is surely reflected here."

[22]O. Eissfeldt, *Cambridge Ancient History* (III, Part 2; 3rd ed.; London: Cambridge University, 1975) 570-71.

and the reigns of Saul and David frustrated the permanent success of the Philistine achievement."[23] It seems clear that the Philistine threat set the stage for a new kind of political organization in Israel.

While the military considerations were probably paramount for some Israelites who demanded the monarchy, it appears that they were not for others. We are told near the end of chapter 7 that under Samuel as judge the Lord routed the Philistines at Ebenezer and that "the Philistines were subdued and did not again enter the territory of Israel" (vv 10-12a). That statement is patently contradicted by later chapters and must surely be seen as an attempt to elevate Samuel's status at the expense of Saul and the monarchy. Another clue to a more personal anti-Saul reaction may be seen at the Mizpah episode where, after Saul has been chosen by lot, announced by Samuel, and acclaimed by the people, "some worthless fellows said, 'How can this man save us?' And they despised him and brought him no present" (10:27). After Saul's victory over the Ammonites (chap. 11) those same men were threatened with death but were spared by Saul (11:12-13). M. A. Cohen, reflecting on the tensions between the vested interests of tribal leadership and the new institution of kingship, says "the decision to create the monarchy could not have come without reluctance and regret. The pages of the Book of Samuel reflect the vacillation which must inevitably accompany so radical a departure from custom."[24] The temptation in reconstructing biblical history is to choose one path or one option over, or to the exclusion of, others. We suggest that even though the military threat showed a clear need for a new kind of leadership, in this case a king, the existence of various reactions to that political change are likely to be historically rooted.

What was Samuel's position in Israel and his role in initiating the monarchy? In view of the disparate conclusions reached by various scholars, it seems clear that there is no consensus of opinion in answer to the first part of the question. A range of opinion about Samuel's position is set forth briefly in T. Ishida's section, "The Samuel-Saul Complex."[25] The speculations as to whether Samuel is priest, prophet, seer, judge, or indeed something else have been far-ranging. W. A. Irwin, in an amusing but long since superseded article, concludes, "in the end we are, then, in the disturbing position of possessing not a single

[23]"Fresh Evidence for the Philistine Story," *BA* 29 (1966), 78-79. See also Y. Aharoni, *The Land of the Bible* (rev. and enl. ed.; Philadelphia: Westminster, 1979) 274-75.

[24]"The Role of the Shilonite Priesthood in the United Monarchy of Ancient Israel," *HUCA* 36 (1964) 67.

[25]In *The Royal Dynasties*, 28-29.

narrative of Samuel's activity that merits respect as good source material."[26] M. A. Cohen argues that he is a "seer-priest";[27] T. Ishida
sees him as a šōpēṭ;[28] J. L. McKenzie has suggested that the "real Samuel
is the leader of the sons of the prophets," characterizing them as
combining "a paradox of conservative and radical tendencies; they were
conservative in the sense that they were jealous of tradition, radical in
their violent opposition to any person or institution which they judged
dangerous to tradition. Their political activity is manifest in most of the
passages in which they appear."[29] There remain questions about Samuel's
role and title that may never reach general agreement. Part of the reason
for that results from an apparent reworking of the early chapters, which
may in fact have contained originally the story of Saul in some ways
comparable to that of Samson, to make him appear to be a more
important figure than he may have been historically.[30] Even without
being able to ascertain his exact status, it still seems reasonable to
assume that Samuel had some recognition as a religious figure and had
some part to play in Saul's inauguration—that part may have served two
interests, the preservation of some personal power[31] and the preservation
of some controls over the king.[32]

The question of what Samuel, Saul, and the people of Israel were
agreeing to in the initiation of the first monarchy is greatly complicated
by the passages on "the manner of the king" (8:11-17) and "the manner
of the kingdom" (10:25) which seem to establish the king's rights and
limitations and to bring them into the realm of the Israelite covenant
tradition.[33] Very briefly, I. Mendelsohn argues that the passage in chap.
8 could be patterned on the model of Canaanite city-states prior to and
contemporary with Samuel's time.[34] Z. Ben-Barak also argues for a

[26]"Samuel and the Rise of Monarchy," *AJSL* 58 (1941) 132.
[27]"The Role of the Shilonite Priesthood," 66ff.
[28]*The Royal Dynasties*, 33ff. See also A. D. Ritterspach, *The Samuel
Traditions*, 311 ff.
[29]"The Four Samuels," *BR* 7 (1962) 16.
[30]See Adolphe Lods, *Israel from its Beginnings to the Middle of the Eighth
Century* (New York: Knopf, 1932) 354-55; McCarter, *I Samuel* 62; and
J. Blenkinsopp, "The Quest of the Historical Saul," 92, who argues not only
this point but suggests further, from 4QSam[a], that Saul was also probably a
nazirite.
[31]See A. D. Ritterspach, *The Samuel Traditions*, 312-14, and M. A. Cohen,
"The Role of the Shilonite Priesthood," 69.
[32]See F. M. Cross, *Canaanite Myth and Hebrew Epic*, 221-22, and J. L.
McKenzie, "The Four Samuels," 17.
[33]For a brief history of the criticism on these passages, see T. Ishida, *The
Royal Dynasties*, 40-41.
[34]"Samuel's Denunciation of Kingship," *BASOR* 143 (1956) 17-22.

contemporary model, but she also establishes connections to past Israelite covenant traditions.[35] R. E. Clements feels that the passage is a retrojection from Solomonic times by the Deuteronomistic historian.[36] A satisfactory answer to the question of whether "the manner of the king" and "the manner of the kingdom" is modeled on contemporary monarchies or introduced later has not yet been provided. Nevertheless, the presence of these two passages may suggest that there were attempts to define the new institution's scope by indicating what the king could and could not do. Given the suddenness of the monarchy's emergence in Israel's history, the rather clear ties with the charismatic past in Saul's election as first king, and the political, military, and cultic tensions of the difficult time, it seems quite likely that an important part of Saul's problems stemmed from the lack of clearly defined and accepted rules of governance.[37] Yet, it does seem that there was a covenant agreement of some kind concerning the monarchy.[38]

In turning from the background material concerned with the emergence of kingship and Samuel's role in introducing the first king to comment on Saul's reign, we might keep in mind an historical cliché. J. Blenkinsopp[39] and T. C. G. Thornton[40] have pointed out that it is generally the winning side that writes the history, and we know that David won. Just as Samuel plays an important part in the early part of 1 Samuel, David begins to dominate the second half of the book. In the relations between Saul and David, Saul soon becomes the villain of the piece. There seems to be no question, as Thornton consistently argues, that the later chapters are largely Davidic propaganda.

We have already suggested that among Saul's difficulties as king is the misunderstanding of the king's role. We have also suggested that he came to Israel's attention in the manner of the older charismatic judges, possibly because of his success against the Ammonites (11:1-11). If this is

[35]*"The Manner of the King" and "The Manner of the Kingdom": Basic Factors in the Establishment of the Israelite Monarchy in the Light of Canaanite Kingship* (unpublished dissertation, Hebrew University, 1972), summary in English, dissertation in Hebrew.

[36]"The Deuteronomistic Interpretation of the Founding of the Monarchy in I Sam. VIII," 408-9.

[37]A. D. Ritterspach, 300.

[38]F. M. Cross, *Canaanite Myth and Hebrew Epic,* 221 says that the first monarchy was basically a covenant "conceived by the tribesmen as a conditional appointment or covenant, so long as the 'Spirit of God was upon him,' and so long as he did not violate the legal traditions or constitution of the league." We can agree with the concept of covenant, but not with the inference that Israelite monarchy was initially non-dynastic.

[39]"The Quest of the Historical Saul," 75.

[40]"Studies in Samuel," *CQR* 168 (1967) 413.

so, Saul provides an obvious transitional link between the older-style leader and the new concept of a covenanted dynastic leadership seen even more clearly in David. Yet, when Saul acts on his best judgment, as in 13:8-15 at Gilgal before a Philistine battle, Samuel condemns him for sacrificing. However, when Saul later builds an altar and presumably sacrifices in 14:35, there is no adverse reaction. Could he or could he not perform priestly functions? Granted that he seems to act with impetuosity on occasion, as in ordering his troops to fast during battle (14:24), Saul may have been acting from the religious zeal demonstrated elsewhere in chapters 9-15.

Saul also had to find a way to unite the Israelite tribes. While the Philistine menace seems to have been reason enough for such unification, it is difficult to assess the extent to which "all Israel" joined him. The text indicates (11:8) that Saul led three hundred thousand men of Israel and thirty thousand men of Judah. It is reasonable to suspect the numbers and even the presence of Judeans at this point. If one accepts this episode as the one bringing Saul to the foreground as a military leader, it is more likely that his troops came from the area of Benjamin; Judah would not seem to be threatened by this Transjordanian action. It might then follow that after this victory, Saul's leadership gradually extended to other tribes.[41] It can also be suggested that, as will be seen below, he eventually had ties with Judah.

Legitimation of his rule and the issue of dynastic succession are further problems for Saul. In opposition to Alt's thesis that Saul's reign and those of later northern kings during the divided monarchy are charismatic,[42] G. Buccellati asserts "that Saul's monarchy was dynastic, both *de jure* and *de facto*."[43] F. M. Cross agrees to an extent with him but still prefers Alt's view.[44] T. Ishida argues strongly in support of dynastic kingship in Saul's reign. He observes that when Gideon and Saul were offered the office of king, the people intended to change the inadequate institution of the judge; then, he asks, "if the new regime was, indeed, non-dynastic, what could have been the innovation? . . . Did an institution such as non-dynastic monarchy exist?"[45] These are, of course, rhetorical questions for him. The biblical text shows some

<hr>

[41]See C. E. Hauer, "Does I Samuel 9:1-11:15 Reflect the Extension of Saul's Dominions?" *JBL* 86 (1967) 307-10.

[42]A. Alt, "The Formation of the Israelite State in Palestine," *Essays on Old Testament History and Religion* (Garden City, N. Y.: Doubleday, 1968) 225-309, esp. pp. 255-57.

[43]*Cities and Nations of Ancient Syria* (Studi Semitici 26; Rome: University of Rome, 1967) 195-200.

[44]*Canaanite Myth and Hebrew Epic*, 222, n. 10, and cf. above, n. 38.

[45]*The Royal Dynasties*, 2, 51-54.

support for dynastic kingship in Saul's reign (cf. 13:13, 20:30-31). One might also consider that after Saul's death, his son Ishbaal ruled over the northern tribes[46] and that David, in his pursuit of legitimation over the north, insisted on Michal's return to him[47] and later renounced any complicity in Ishbaal's death. The northern suspicion of David's usurpation through the blood of Saul's family is clear (2 Sam 16:7-8). While Saul is supposedly stripped of dynastic succession in 13:13 and of his right to rule in 16:28, he continued as king until his death, one of his sons succeeded him, and David was very careful to avoid the appearance of being a mere usurper of the Saulide monarchy. This suggests that Saul was recognized, at least by many Israelites, as the legitimate ruler and that the dynastic principle operated during his time.

By no means did Saul deal successfully with all his problems. Although the anti-Saul bias must be considered, it appears that he may have failed to convert the priests (and possibly prophets) to his cause. This may reflect the historical situation. After Samuel's death, the prophet (if that is what Samuel was) is gone and not replaced. After the execution of the priests at Nob and Abiathar's escape to David, Saul is said to have no source for ascertaining Yahweh's will because it is a rare occasion, even in the early monarchy, when Yahweh appears directly to the king—even in dreams. If Saul was indeed without these religious functionaries, or at least those officially recognized by the people, his reputation among Israelites oriented to the older order may have declined, but that cannot be answered either way by the text.

Saul was apparently afflicted with an emotional disorder though it seems to have affected him only intermittently. Such a problem would not have been ameliorated by the purported relations of Michal, Jonathan, and David. We should observe that those passages dealing with Saul's family and David are clearly pro-David. One may have reservations about Jonathan's supposed recognition that David was destined to be Saul's successor and yet acknowledge that there could have been love and strong friendship for David from Michal and Jonathan. This speculation might be further advanced by entertaining the idea of a vicious circle in operation. As Saul became more suspicious of David, Michal and Jonathan became more protective of David. Whether this is the case is unprovable, but it is reasonable to suggest that Saul was bothered especially by Jonathan's behavior toward his friend.

[46]See J. A. Soggin, "The Rule of ʾEshbaᶜal, Son of Saul," *Old Testament and Oriental Studies* (Rome: Biblical Institute, 1975) 31-49, for an interpretation of the discrepancy between David's seven year reign in Hebron and Ishbaal's two year reign in the north.
    [47]See Z. Ben-Barak, "The Legal Background to the Restoration of Michal to David," in *VTSup* 30 (1979) 15-29, for why David could reclaim Michal and why Ishbaal had to surrender her.

On a more positive side, Saul appears to have had substantial military success prior to the battle of Gilboa. In his analysis of Saul's strategic military pattern, one that he recognizes might have emerged from short range plans and actions, C. E. Hauer shows three stages: "(1) the securing of the Israelite center as the aftermath of the battle of Michmash, (2) the securing of the (Judean) south, and (3) an abortive attempt to secure the far north."[48] Hauer argues that this was a rational plan and one that was quite successful before the end. That Saul might have been more successful than the text suggests is indicated by Hauer's observation that "prior to the [Michmash] battle the Philistines seemed able to work their will at the heart of the Israelite hill country. Not so afterward. Indeed, the Deuteronomic historians do not record a Saulide defeat at the Philistine hands from Michmash to Gilboa."[49] Y. Aharoni speculates on the area under Saul's control; it is surprisingly large and includes at least a tenuous relationship with Judah.[50] It seems that Saul was engaged primarily in defending the lands of Israelite occupation, not in territorial expansion. If the expanse of this territory is so large, it must raise another question about the historiographic intent of chaps. 16-25. How could a man deprived of Yahweh's spirit continue to succeed in Israel's behalf? The question is not easily answered, but we might consider a correlative question: "How much loyalty did Saul command from his people, even after his repudiation by Samuel?"

There may be a greater degree of loyalty to Saul than the text stresses. In connection with his military exploits, his victories may have been successful not only in that arena but also in Israel's response to him. When David flees Saul's court and goes to Adullam, he does not keep his parents with him; he leaves them instead with Mizpah of Moab. While the text does not state why David does this, it may be that he fears harm for them from Saul and that he cannot trust the Judeans to protect them. That conjecture may be supported by observing that when David goes to Judah and is told to save Keilah from the Philistines, his men respond, " 'Behold, we are afraid here in Judah; how much more then if we go to Keilah against the armies of the Philistines?' " (23:3). The first part of the verse suggests fear of Saul, even in David's homeland. Further, after delivering Keilah, David asks whether the men of that city will turn him over to Saul. Yahweh says that they will (23:5-12). Soon after, the Ziphites report David's whereabouts to Saul, again putting David in danger (23:19-20). Perhaps even in David's home territory the allegiance may have been far stronger to Saul than to David. It may not be too extreme to entertain the possibility that David was seen by the

---

[48]"The Shape of Saulide Strategy," *CBQ* 31 (1969) 153.
[49]Ibid., 153-54.
[50]*The Land of the Bible*, 288-90.

people of both north and south as pretender to the throne. In the aftermath of the battle of Gilboa, the men of Jabesh-gilead, hearing of the desecration of the bodies of Saul and his sons, marched all night and retrieved the bodies for proper burial, no doubt at the risk of their lives (31:11-13). Jabesh-gilead's indebtedness to Saul for their rescue in chap. 11 may be a strong motivation for their act, but it is still a remarkable demonstration of loyalty.

Loyalty to Saul might also be shown more indirectly through some of David's activities in 1 and 2 Samuel. David's position after leaving Saul's court became so precarious that he had to join the Philistines for protection. Before he takes that action, we are told that David has twice spared Saul's life (chaps. 24, 26). It might be argued that David's motive was respect for the Lord's anointed or that David would have set a precedent that might later make him victim, but it might also be argued that Israel's loyalty to Saul was too strong for David to risk such an action. At Saul's death and after, David shows outward respect for Saul's memory (his lament in 2 Sam 1:19-27), he kills the Amalekite who says he slew Saul, he remains in Hebron for seven years before assuming kingship over the north, he disclaims responsibility for Abner's death, and he kills the murderers of Ishbaal. These events may be reflections of David's genuineness, but they may also show that, at least in the north, loyalty to Saul's family continued and that David had to recognize it. Again, when David flees Jerusalem during Absalom's revolt, Shimei ("a man of the house of Saul") curses David saying, " 'The Lord has avenged upon you all the blood of the house of Saul, in whose place you have reigned' " (2 Sam 16:5-8).

IV. THE EMERGENCE OF KINGSHIP IN OTHER NEAR EASTERN CULTURES

Some notes on the kind and extent of comparative materials, especially that from Palestine and Mesopotamia, may be in order here. There is none that we are aware of dealing with the emergence of kingship. The silence on this point may not be difficult to understand. H. Frankfort says, "The Mesopotamians asserted that in the earliest time, and again after the Flood, 'kingship has descended from heaven.' This remarkable formula combines the awareness that kingship had not always existed with the fact that it represented the only known form of government in historical times."[51]

[51]*Kingship and the Gods* (Chicago: University of Chicago, 1958) 237. In his epilogue on the Hebrews, Frankfort says, "If kingship counted in Egypt as a function of the gods, and in Mesopotamia as a divinely ordained political order, the Hebrews knew that they had introduced it on their own initiative, in imitation of others and under the strain of an emergency. . . . If the Hebrews, like the Mesopotamians, remembered a kingless period, they never thought that 'kingship descended from heaven' " (p. 449).

Evidence of the Philistine presence in Palestine during Saul's time, based on archaeological data, is presented by G. E. Wright and T. Dothan. While in the latter part of his article, Wright is primarily interested in establishing that Philistine Gath is probably located at Tell Shariʾah, he argues in the earlier part that archaeological evidence from Egypt and Palestine along with Egyptian writings and the biblical tradition support the "Sea Peoples" presence in Egypt toward the end of the 13th century and during the 12th century B.C.E. and their presence as settlers along Palestine's southern coastal plain during the 12th and 11th centuries B.C.E. The records of Rameses III mention several different groups. The Egyptian Tale of Wenamon places another group at Dor. The biblical tradition remembers them by the name of one group, the Palishtu or Philistines. Arguing that the Sea Peoples may have invaded the Syro-Palestinian coast prior to Rameses III's time, based on letters from Ugarit, and that their power reached into the Jordan Valley as far as the Jabbok River, based on Philistine pottery found at Tell Deir ʿAlla and the bench-tombs found at Tell el-Farʾah, Wright then provides evidence for substantial 12th century expansion of Philistine power in Palestine and concludes that their permanent success was thwarted by the anti-Philistine achievements of Saul and David.[52]

In the conclusion to her recently published *Excavations at the Cemetery of Deir el-Balaḥ*, Trude Dothan summarizes, based upon comparative evidence with cemeteries at Tell el-Farʾah, Lachish, and Beth Shean:

> . . . the sequence of anthropoid burials in Canaan [is] as follows. The earliest appearance was at Deir el-Balaḥ in the late fourteenth century B.C. The thirteenth-century phase at Deir el-Balaḥ overlaps the early group of anthropoid burials at Beth Shean. Into this phase also falls Tomb 935 at Tell el Farʾah, while Tomb 570 at Lachish perhaps takes us a stage later to the turn of the thirteenth century B.C. Entering the twelfth and eleventh centuries, the Philistine tombs of el-Farʾah and the Beth Shean coffins with 'grotesque' lids showing the distinctive headgear of the Sea Peoples prove that the custom of anthropoid burial was adopted by the Philistines.[53]

She feels that the 13th century group of coffins is "most probably attributable to Egyptian officials or garrisons stationed in Egyptian strongholds in Canaan," and that the later group, dating from the 12th-11th centuries, is an adaptation by Philistines (who were first Egyptian mercenaries settled in Canaan) of the Egyptian burial custom.[54] Dothan's conclusions support Wright's conclusion that the Philistines were Egyptian mercenaries in the Beth Shean area in the twelfth century.[55]

[52]G. E. Wright, "Fresh Evidence," 70-86, esp. pp. 70-78.
[53](Jerusalem: Hebrew University, 1979) 103.
[54]Ibid., 98-104.
[55]G. E. Wright, "Fresh Evidence," 71-82.

As was mentioned earlier, there are also arguments that "the manner of the king" and "the manner of the kingdom" are based upon Canaanite models. I. Mendelsohn challenges the view that 1 Sam 8:4-17 is a late document denouncing kingship based on actual experience with Israelite and Judean kingship. Breaking down vv 11b-17 into four stages, Mendelsohn argues that Samuel's resentment of the elders' request for kingship "would result in abject slavery for the people." Using data from Alalakh and Ugarit, dating from the 18th to the 13th centuries, Mendelsohn says that the Samuel account authentically describes the semi-feudal Canaanite society prior to and during Samuel's day and that the prophet himself or a spokesman could have written the biblical passage to reflect contemporary anti-monarchical feelings. He concludes that the disputed passage "does not constitute 'a rewriting of history' by a late opponent of kingship but represents an eloquent appeal to the people by a contemporary of Saul not to impose upon themselves a Canaanite institution alien to their own way of life."[56]

To some extent, Zafrira Ben-Barak agrees with Mendelsohn's assessment. Based upon her investigation of epigraphic materials from the El-Amarna letters and the archives from Alalakh and Ugarit, she concludes that a qualitative-substantive (contents) and a quantitative (citing as many documents as possible) examination of these materials demonstrates that Samuel's concern over A) human resources in the service of the king, and B) royal control over the people's property expressed in 1 Sam 8:11-17 is based on a close relationship with contemporary Canaanite monarchy. She also argues that 1 Sam 10:25 ("the manner of the Kingdom") is of "exceptional importance in shaping the Israelite monarchy and in fixing its patterns for the remainder of its history." She concludes:

> It is from the event at Mizpah [1 Sam 10:25] that we come face to face with the true greatness of the leader of the age, Samuel. By virtue of his personality and his activity in connection with the Mizpah covenant he succeeds in warding off what was clearly a most serious danger to the ancient Israelite heritage. He was able to assimilate the *mišpaṭ hammelek* to the *mišpaṭ hammᵉlukā* in such a manner as to guarantee the integrity of both the Israelite monarchy and the Israelite tradition.

Ben-Barak argues that Samuel succeeds in placing a foreign conception within the framework of the Israelite covenant tradition.[57]

According to M. C. Astour, the anti-royalism manifested in Hosea, 1 Samuel, Deuteronomy, and Judges had precedents among non-Canaanites and among Canaanites of Syria and Palestine as well.

---

[56]"Samuel's Denunciation of Kingship," 17-22.
[57]"*The Manner of the King*" and "*The Manner of the Kingdom*," Summary (English) i-xix.

Quoting extensively from the Tell el-Amarna letters from Canaanite vassals to their Egyptian suzerains, Astour argues that pro-Habiru movements among Canaanite peasants encouraged those peasants to overthrow royal authority, to kill the king, and most important to introduce a republican regime. He suggests that the Canaanite anti-royalist ideology of the Amarna Age pre-dated and influenced the Israelite political organization after their conquest of Canaan and, further, that the ideology influenced the anti-royalist messages of Amos, Hosea, Isaiah and Micah during the social and political crisis of the eighth century.[58]

Comparative studies also treat the issue of monarchical legitimation during Saul's and David's time. Julian Morgenstern asks why Jonathan, the seemingly obvious choice as Saul's royal successor, seems to have regarded David as the natural and logical successor. His proposed solution rests upon an alternative principle of succession. As he examines the names and relationships of the eight Edomite kings recorded in Gen 36:31-39 (=1 Chr 1:43-51), Morgenstern conjectures that "each successive king was the son-in-law of his predecessor." Perhaps in Judah and in Israel "*beena* marriage or matriarchy may have obtained at this time." He concludes that the combination of David's military reputation and his "son-in-lawship" caused Jonathan to see David as "the natural and proper person to succeed his father as king."[59]

Drawing on biblical and Near Eastern materials, Zafrira Ben-Barak raises three important political, ethical, and moral questions associated with Eshbaal's return of Michal (who had remarried subsequent to David's flight from Saul) to David (2 Sam 2:12-3:1). In answer to why Eshbaal agreed to hand over Michal to David, she says that Eshbaal was anxious to create the image of a legitimate king who preserves law and order. She says that Mesopotamian law codes indicate that Michal's repeated remarriage can be explained by specific conditions. "After Michal has been living for years in the house of her husband David who is absent, and has been without sons, or father-in-law, she is married to Paltiel the son of Laish. Her remarriage to David is to be understood in the same way." Mesopotamian law codes also provide an answer to the question: how can David's remarriage to his former wife after her marriage to another be explained in the light of the express law in Deut 24:1-4? Ben-Barak suggests that the language of Deut 24:4b is a Deuteronomistic addition that apparently was not in force during David's time. David's justification for reclaiming Michal was based on the fact that he did not send his wife away of his own free will and at his own initiative;

[58]"The Amarna Age Forerunners of Biblical Anti-Royalism," *For Max Weinreich on His Seventieth Birthday: Studies in Jewish Language, Literature and Society* (The Hague: Mouton, 1964) 6-17.

[59]"David and Jonathan," *JBL* 78 (1959) 322-25.

therefore, David could take her back even though in the interim she had married another man. Only by understanding the Mesopotamian legal practice governing marriage obligations, also accepted in Israel, "can one adequately answer the questions posed at the beginning of this study."[60]

M. Tsevat examines the following document, found at the royal palace of Ugarit, authored by the Akkadian king, Ariḫalbu:

> To be effective immediately!
> Thus says Ariḫalbu, King
> of Ugarit:
> "Whoever, after my death, takes
> (in marriage) my wife Kubaba,
> daughter of
> Takan (?), from
> my brother—
> may Baal crush him,
> may he not make great (his) throne,
> may he not dwell in a (royal) house;
> may Baal of Mt. Casius
> crush him!"

Tsevat suggests that the legal concept underlying this document (a concept common to Israel, the Hittites, Assur, and Nuzi) is that of the levirate. He observes that curses are extremely rare in Akkadian legal documents and that this dying man's curse is meant to insure the continuation of Ariḫalbu's line through the levirate marriage involving his queen and his brother. The force of the curse is directed against any would-be violator of that marriage. Examining biblical material, Tsevat points out that "The early history of the Israelite kingdom affords several examples of the fact that the marriage of a former king's wife bestows legitimacy on an aspirant who otherwise has no sufficient claim to the throne." His examples derive from the period of David's and Solomon's reigns. This Akkadian document shows that the custom of securing the crown to the husband of the former king's widow can be set aside. Tsevat draws a parallel between the intended force of Ariḫalbu's curse and the Lord's judgment on David in 2 Sam 12:8.[61]

The comparative studies cited above shed some important light on a few issues involved in 1 Samuel, and the biblical scholar might well wish that more material of this kind were available. However, without additional non-biblical Near Eastern materials, one is left with the

[60]"The Legal Background . . . ," 28-29.
[61]"Marriage and Monarchical Legitimacy in Ugarit and Israel," *JSS* 3 (1958) 237-43.

impression that those available now do not yet provide enough historical data, directly concerned with the relevant biblical issues, to confirm or alter convincingly the biblical account of what actually transpired during the time of Samuel, Saul, and David in 1 Samuel.

V. CONCLUSION

In summary, the student who attempts a historical reconstruction of the emergence of kingship in Israel and the reign of Saul is confronted with great difficulties. He must rely almost exclusively on a biblical text that clearly demonstrates anti-Saul biases. The prophetic stratum might be seen as wishing to preserve the older order. In that stratum, Samuel is the dominant figure, making and breaking Saul. The Deuteronomistic stratum is suspicious of the institution of monarchy and has a vested interest in elevating David's career. Unfortunately, Saul is, in a sense, caught in the middle. In the absence of other significant biblical accounts of Saul's career and of comparative materials from that time, one can only sift and balance information from the tendentious narratives. That is what this paper has attempted to do.

From that sifting, a somewhat different picture emerges. The impetus for the origin of Israelite monarchy is the Philistine military threat. Saul comes to the foreground through the older charismatic kind of leadership, but now he is made a dynastic king and increases the territory over which he rules. The older religious leaders attempt to exert control over the monarchy, since they could not stop its coming, by creating a covenant kingship. Unfortunately for Saul, the leadership demands placed upon him bring him into conflict with the religious authorities, and they withdraw support from him. Still, faced with the external military threat and the internal political threat posed by a pretender, he is an effective military leader despite his emotional affliction. He is succeeded by his son, and the pretender to the northern throne is forced to play a careful political game before he is able to take over Saul's home territory. Even then, strong pro-Saul anti-David feelings are manifested by curse and later by open rebellion against David.

THE TESTAMENT OF DAVID AND EGYPTIAN ROYAL INSTRUCTIONS

Leo G. Perdue

The Graduate Seminary, Phillips University

I. INTRODUCTION

The Succession Narrative and Recent Research

Investigations of the Succession Narrative (2 Sam 9-20, 1 Kgs 1-2) in recent years have resulted in divergent assessments of the document's genre, purpose, authorship, redaction, and beginning point. The genre has been variously identified as court history,[1] royal novella,[2] or fiction,[3] while the purpose has been described as historiographical,[4] theological,[5] didactic,[6] political (pro- or anti-monarchy),[7] or entertainment.[8] The

---

[1]Leonhard Rost, "Die Überlieferung von der Thronnachfolge Davids," *Das Kleine Credo und Andere Studien zum Alten Testament* (Heidelberg: Quelle und Meyer, 1965) 119-253; Gerhard von Rad, "The Beginnings of Historical Writing in Ancient Israel," *The Problem of the Hexateuch and Other Essays* (London: Oliver and Boyd, 1966) 166-204; J. A. Montgomery, *A Critical and Exegetical Commentary on the Book of Kings* (ICC; New York: Charles Scribner's Sons, 1951) 67f.; Martin Noth, *Könige* (BKAT; Neukirchen-Vluyn: Neukirchener Verlag, 1968) 8f.; John Gray, *I & II Kings* (OTL; 2d rev. ed.; Philadelphia: Westminster, 1970) 14f.; and H.-J. Hermisson, "Weisheit und Geschichte," *Probleme biblischer Theologie* (ed. H. W. Wolff; Munich: Chr. Kaiser Verlag, 1971) 136-48.

[2]R. N. Whybray, *The Succession Narrative* (SBT 2/9; Naperville, IL: Alec R. Allenson, 1968) 47, 96.

[3]David Gunn, *The Story of King David* (JSOT SUP 6; Sheffield: Journal for the Study of the Old Testament, 1978) 13, 37f.

[4]See especially von Rad, "The Beginnings of Historical Writing," 176f.

[5]Von Rad ("The Beginnings of Historical Writing," 196) emphasizes that historical causality in the document is effectuated by providential control of events, though people and natural events are the avenue of divine activity. The ultimate result, of course, is Yahweh's bringing Solomon to the throne.

[6]Whybray, *The Succession Narrative*, 71.

[7]Scholars who believe the original document was written to justify Solomon's claims to the throne include Rost, "Die Überlieferung von der Thronnachfolge Davids," 227f.; Whybray, *The Succession Narrative*, 5f.; and T. N. D. Mettinger,

author has been described as an historian,[9] sage,[10] propagandist,[11] or literary aesthete.[12] In addition, the opinions of the extent to which the document was redacted vary from relatively little redaction by the Deuteronomistic school[13] to extensive editing by one or more redactors.[14] Finally, the pinpointing of the document's original beginning has continued to be a complex issue with options including chapters 2, 6, or 9 of 2 Samuel.[15] As a result of the lack of scholarly consensus on any of these issues, an obvious impasse has occurred. In my estimation, one conceivable way out of this maze of competing theories and positions may be a reconsideration of the relationship between the Succession Narrative and wisdom literature by using the contextual method advocated by W. W. Hallo.[16]

Wisdom and the Succession Narrative

Von Rad suggested the possibility of a relationship between the Succession Narrative and wisdom literature when he traced the origins

King and Messiah (Coniectanea Biblica, OT Series 8; Lund: CWK Gleerup, 1976) 21f. Others have argued that the original document was anti-Solomonic, but was later given a pro-Solomonic redaction (Ernst Würthwein, Die Erzählung von der Thronfolge Davids—theologische oder politische Geschichtsschreibung? (Theologische Studien; Zurich: Theologischer Verlag, 1974), 11f.; Timo Veijola, Die Ewige Dynastie (Helsinki: Suomalaisen Kirjallisuuden Kirjapaino, 1975), 130; and F. Langlamet, "Pour ou contre Salomon? La rédaction prosalomonienne de I Rois I-II," RB 83 (1976) 321-79, 481-528).

[8]Gunn, The Story of King David, 38.

[9]See n. 1.

[10]Whybray, The Succession Narrative, 56f.

[11]See n. 7.

[12]Gunn, The Story of King David, 37f.

[13]Rost, "Die Überlieferung von der Thronnachfolge Davids," 194f.; and Gunn, The Story of King David, 115-19.

[14]See especially Würthwein, Die Erzählung von der Thronfolge Davids; Veijola, Die Ewige Dynastie; and Langlamet, "Pour ou contre Salomon?"

[15]While many have regarded chapter 9 as the beginning point (see, for example, Whybray, The Succession Narrative), Gunn argues for chapter 2 through 4 as the original beginning (The Story of King David, 65f.). Both Rost ("Die Überlieferung von der Thronnachfolge Davids," 122f.) and von Rad ("The Beginnings of Historical Writing," 176f.) believed the beginning was interwoven with the ending of the "Ark Narrative."

[16]For a discussion and illustration of this method, see Hallo's article, "Biblical History in its Near Eastern Setting: the Contextual Approach," Scripture in Context (Pittsburgh: The Pickwick Press, 1980) 1-26. In this essay on historiography, Hallo emphasizes that both comparisons of and contrasts between biblical and other Near Eastern historiographies are important tasks, not only for establishing analogies, but also to determine if some impact may have been made on the biblical materials by Near Eastern Literature.

of the document to the Solomonic court during a socio-cultural enlightenment thought to cultivate international wisdom.[17] However, Whybray provided the first detailed discussion of von Rad's remark and concluded that the document was a didactic novel clothing wisdom themes in narrative dress.[18] Originating and continuing to be used within a wisdom circle, the narrative was written "to justify Solomon's claim to be the true king of Israel, and to strengthen the régime against its critics."[19] Significant wisdom themes embedded in the document, according to Whybray, included the importance of counsel, retribution, God as the controller of human destiny, and wisdom as an attribute of the king.[20] To buttress his conclusions, Whybray pointed to the royal novel and royal instructions in Egypt, particularly Amunemhet, as probable models influencing the Israelite author.[21]

In a study taking Whybray to task, James Crenshaw argued against a wisdom *provenance* of the text, believing instead that the narrative actually possessed an extremely negative view of wisdom, that the themes in Proverbs used by Whybray were far too general and could also be found in legal and prophetic literature, and that it is doubtful that Egyptian literature was known and used as early as the initial phase of Solomon's reign.[22] Even more important were the methodological issues raised by Crenshaw who stressed that a narrative could be convincingly identified as sapiential or shown to be influenced by wisdom only by pointing to stylistic and ideological elements unique to wisdom literature (Job, Proverbs, Qoheleth, Ben Sirah, and the Wisdom of Solomon). In addition, he argued that the changes in meaning of a wisdom phrase or motif, the negative attitude towards wisdom, and wisdom's own history must be carefully weighed.

As a result of Crenshaw's criticisms of Whybray's thesis, relatively few later studies have advanced a wisdom character for the narrative, and even these have not responded seriously to Crenshaw's critique.[23] Keeping Crenshaw's points in mind, what I propose to do in this article is to examine "The Testament of David" in 1 Kgs 2:1-12 in the light of royal instructions from Egypt in regard to three areas: genre, function, and themes. If indeed a wisdom *provenance* and character for this crucial part of the Succession Narrative can be effectively demonstrated by

---

[17]Von Rad, "The Beginnings of Historical Writing," 203-4.

[18]Whybray, *The Succession Narrative*, 56f.

[19]*The Succession Narrative*, 51-52.

[20]*The Succession Narrative*, 56f.

[21]*The Succession Narrative*, 96f.

[22]James L. Crenshaw, "Method in Determining Wisdom Influence upon 'Historical' Literature," *JBL* 88 (1969) 129-42.

[23]Hermisson, "Weisheit und Geschichte"; and Walter Brueggemann, *In Man We Trust* (Richmond: John Knox Press, 1972).

means of the contextual method, then a firm basis for further analyses of the relationship with wisdom will be established. In addition, the ramifications for the larger issues pertaining to the entire narrative outlined above would be significant. But first, a brief outline of the connections between Israelite and Egyptian wisdom is in order.

Egyptian and Israelite Wisdom[24]

The publication of "The Teaching of Amenemopet" by Budge in 1923 intitiated numerous studies over the past sixty years designed to demonstrate Israel's indebtedness to the Egyptian sages.[25] The dependence of the third collection of Proverbs (22:17-24:22) on Amenemopet has been proven to the satisfaction of many scholars, especially since the discoveries of a tenth century ostracon of Amenemopet in the Cairo Museum by Černy and of later papyrus fragments dating from the eighth to the sixth centuries, indicating both the popularity and the canonicity of this instruction in Egypt at an early date.[26] In addition to Amenemopet, an impressive number of studies have stressed important similarities between Egyptian and Israelite wisdom traditions with the strong probability of Egyptian influence in the areas of literary genres, social settings, themes, and motifs.

[24]For a survey of literary and linguistic parallels and possible mutual influence, see Ronald J. Williams, "Egypt and Israel," *The Legacy of Egypt* (ed. J. R. Harris; Oxford: Clarendon Press, 1971) 257-90. However, for a methodological essay concerned with establishing controls in comparative analyses, see Manfred Görg, "Komparatistische Untersuchungen an Ägyptischer und Israelitischer Literatur," *Fragen an die altägyptische Literatur* (Ed. Jan Assmann, Erika Feucht, and Reinhard Grieshammer; Wiesbaden: Ludwig Reichert, 1977) 197-215. For comparisons of Israelite and Egyptian wisdom, see S. Morenz, "Ägyptologische Beiträge zur Erforschung der Weiseitsliteratur Israels," *Les sagesses du proche-orient Ancien* (Paris: Presses Universitaires de France, 1963) 63-71; and Ernest Würthwein, "Egyptian Wisdom and the Old Testament," *Studies in Ancient Israelite Wisdom* (ed. James L. Crenshaw; New York: Ktav, 1976) 113-33. An important recent study of Egyptian wisdom is the collection of essays by Erik Hornung and Othmar Keel (eds.), *Studien zu altägyptischen Lebenslehren* (Orbis Biblicus et Orientalis 28; Göttingen: Vandenhoeck and Ruprecht, 1979).

[25]Sir E. A. Wallis Budge, *Facsimiles of Egyptian Hieratic Papyri in the British Museum with Descriptions, Summaries of Contents, Etc.* Second Series (London: Harrison and Sons, 1923). For additional surveys of the relationship between Israelite and Egyptian wisdom, see Paul Humbert, *Recherches sur les sources égyptiennes de la littérature sapientiale d'Israël* (Neuchâtel: Paul Attinger, 1929); and Glendon Bryce, *A Legacy of Wisdom* (Lewisburg: Bucknell University Press, 1979).

[26]Bryce, *A Legacy of Wisdom*, 54-56; and R. J. Williams, "The Alleged Semitic Original of the Wisdom of Amenemope," *JEA* 47 (1961) 100-6.

In regard to form criticism, Alt's conclusion that the *Naturweisheit* of 1 Kgs 5:13 was based on Egyptian onomastica was followed by a similar argument by von Rad in regard to Job 38.[27] Even more significant for our purpose have been studies by Whybray,[28] Bauer-Kayatz,[29] and McKane,[30] which have pointed to the likelihood that the Egyptian instruction was a major prototype for the same genre in Israelite wisdom circles. In addition, Bauer-Kayatz further suggested that the speeches of self-praise by Wisdom in Proverbs 1-9 are modeled on speeches of Egyptian goddesses, particularly Maat and Isis.[31] The social settings for Egyptian wisdom, the court and the school, have also been advanced for Israelite instructions. Hermisson thinks that the origins and continuation of this Israelite wisdom genre must have taken place within royal schools in the monarchial period and temple schools in the Post-Exile, following the demise of kingship.[32]

In addition, similar themes and motifs in both traditions have been advanced as evidence for significant Egyptian influence. For example, both Gese and Schmid have written monographs on the similar conceptions of "order" in Egypt and Israel, pointing in their estimation to Egyptian wisdom's impact on Israel's wisdom thought,[33] while Brunner

---

[27]Albrecht Alt, "Die Weisheit Salomos," *TLZ* 76 (1951) 139-44; and Gerhard von Rad, "Hiob 38 und die altägyptische Weisheit," *Gesammelte Studien* (München: Chr. Kaiser Verlag, 1958) 262-71.

[28]R. N. Whybray, *Wisdom in Proverbs* (SBT 45; Naperville, IL: Alec R. Allenson, 1965).

[29]Christa Bauer-Kayatz, *Studien zu Proverbien 1-9* (WMANT 22; Neukirchen-Vluyn: Neukirchener Verlag, 1966).

[30]William McKane, *Proverbs* (OTL; London: SCM Press, 1970) 51-150.

[31]*Studien zu Proverbien 1-9*, 76f. For a recent rejection of this thesis, however, see Bernhard Lang, *Frau Weisheit* (Düsseldorf: Patmos Verlag, 1975) 148f.

[32]H.-J. Hermisson, *Studien zur Israelitischen Spruchweisheit* (WMANT 28; Neukirchen-Vluyn: Neukirchener Verlag, 1968) 84f. Compare Williams, "Egypt and Israel," 273f. It should be noted, however, that Gerstenberger has argued that the roots of the prohibition which comes into both law-codes and instructions are located in a native clan wisdom (*Wesen und Herkunft des 'apodiktischen Rechts'* [WMANT 20; Neukirchen-Vluyn: Neukirchener Verlag, 1965]), while Richter has suggested that the admonition originated within native speech before coming into royal schools where admonitions were used for the instruction of young officials (*Recht und Ethos* [SANT 15; München: Kösel-Verlag, 1966]). Yet, it still remains probable that the entire instruction genre had its origins in Egyptian and Mesopotamian wisdom.

[33]Harmut Gese, *Lehre und Wirklichkeit in der alten Weisheit* (Tübingen: J. C. B. Mohr [Paul Siebeck], 1958) 5-50; and H. H. Schmid, *Gerechtigkeit als Weltordnung* (BHT 40; Tübingen: J. C. B. Mohr [Paul Siebeck], 1968).

has concluded that certain biblical expressions, "the hearing heart" (1 Kgs 3:9)[34] and "justice as the foundation of the throne" (Prov 16:12),[35] have their origins in Egyptian sapiential writings.

Furthermore, wisdom texts from Egypt have continued to be used in helping biblical scholars identify and define similar Israelite wisdom texts. Bryce, for one, has identified a loyalist collection in Proverbs 25 on the basis of the panegyric instruction of Sehetipibre.[36] The Israelite collection, in Bryce's estimation, aimed at teaching students the customs and mores of the court and the type of wise behavior necessary for advancement within the royal administration.

Finally, in spite of some doubts expressed,[37] the probable date for the beginning of Egyptian wisdom influence on Israel is the reign of Solomon, whose court would have provided a cultural and intellectual environment ripe for stimulation from Egypt.[38] Factors pointing to this period include the native tradition in 1 Kings 3-11, the continuing topos of Solomonic authorship or patronage of wisdom texts (Proverbs, Qoheleth, and the Wisdom of Solomon), and the political connection between the Solomonic and Egyptian courts, indicated by the marriage of Solomon to a pharaoh's daughter, the cabinet offices which may have been modeled on Egyptian proto-types,[39] the suggested Egyptian title of David's secretary, Seraiah, and name of his son (Elihoreph),[40] and the possible adoption by Solomon of an Egyptian tax system in the establishment of the twelve administrative districts.[41] Certainly the convergence of the streams of royal, judicial, and literary wisdom evidenced in the Solomonic narrative in 1 Kings 3-11 is paralleled by Egyptian

[34]Hellmut Brunner, "Das hörende Herz," *TLZ* 79 (1954) 697-700.

[35]Hellmut Brunner, "Gerechtigkeit als Fundament des Thrones," *VT* 8 (1958) 426-28.

[36]*A Legacy of Wisdom*, 135f. Also see the study by Udo Skladney who concluded that Prov 16:1-22:16 could be understood as an instruction to officials and diplomats while Proverbs 28-29 comprised an instruction to a prince (*Die ältesten Spruchsammlungen in Israel* [Göttingen: Vandenhoeck und Ruprecht], 1962).

[37]For example, see R. B. Y. Scott, "Solomon and the beginnings of wisdom in Israel," *VTSup* 3 (1955) 262-79.

[38]See, for example, Gerhard von Rad, *Old Testament Theology* I (New York: Harper and Row, 1962) 48f., 312f.; Martin Noth, "Die Bewährung von Salomos 'Göttlicher Weisheit'," *VTSup* 3 (1955) 225-37; Henri Cazelles, "Les débuts de la sagesse en Israël," *Les sagesses du proche-orient ancien*, 27-40; and Williams, "Egypt and Israel," 272f.

[39]See the detailed study by T. N. D. Mettinger, *Solomonic State Officials* (Coniectanea Biblica, Old Testament Series 5; Lund: CWK Gleerup, 1971).

[40]Mettinger, *Solomonic State Officials*, 25-30.

[41]D. B. Redford, "Studies in Relations between Palestine and Egypt during the First Millennium B.C.," *Studies in the Ancient Palestinian World* (Toronto: University of Toronto Press, 1972) 141-56. A recent article by Alberto Green,

wisdom from the Old Kingdom well into the New Kingdom. It is difficult to ignore these arguments by simply dismissing the native tradition as legendary, unhistorical, and dubious. In spite of the legendary character of the Solomonic history, Noth's conclusion that the material still reflects the atmosphere of the Solomonic court remains a cogent assessment.[42]

II. ROYAL INSTRUCTIONS IN EGYPTIAN LITERATURE

The Instruction for Merikare

During the First Intermediate period (2160-2040 B.C.E.), Herakleopolis and Thebes established rival dynasties competing for hegemony over Upper and Lower Egypt.[43] Around 2100 a royal instruction claiming to come from the predecessor of Merikare was written in Herakleopolis, and perhaps was first read when Merikare ascended to the throne.[44] That the text continued to have at least some literary import is indicated by the three extant copies dating some seven centuries after the original composition.[45]

The genre of Merikare, well represented in scribal literature for over two millennia, is the instruction ($sb3yt$),[46] as evidenced by the fragmentary

---

however, argues for Israelite influence on Egypt ("Israelite Influence at Shishak's Court?" *BASOR* 233 [1979] 59-62).

[42]Noth, "Die Bewährung von Salomons 'Göttlicher Weisheit'," 237.

[43]For a description of both the period and the conditions of the reign of Merikare, see William C. Hayes, "The Middle Kingdom in Egypt," *Cambridge Ancient History* (3rd ed.; Cambridge: At the University Press, 1971) 464-531.

[44]Though the text is mutilated at this point, the deceased predecessor is usually identified as Wahkare Akhtoy III (R. J. Williams, "Literature as a Medium of Political Propaganda in Ancient Egypt," *The Seed of Wisdom* [Toronto: University of Toronto Press, 1964] 16). Recently, however, Lopes has argued for Meryibre Akhtoy I, the founder of the dynasty who was known for his cruelty ("L'auteur d'Enseignement pour Mérikarê," *REg* 25 [1973] 178-91. Whoever the king, that he was presented as deceased when he gave the instruction is indicated by the statement, "while I was still alive," and by the fact that the name of Merikare is enclosed in a cartouche, demonstrating he is a reigning monarch (see Williams, "Literature as a Medium of Political Propaganda," 16).

[45]Wolfgang Helck, *Die Lehre für König Merikare* (Kleine ägyptische Texte; Wiesbaden: Otto Harrassowitz, 1977) 1. Helck's text provides the most current and detailed transcription, translation, and notes.

[46]See Hellmut Brunner, "Die Weisheitsliteratur," *Ägyptologie* (Handbuch der Orientalistik I; Leiden: Brill, 1952) 90f.; Jan Bergman, "Gedanken zum Thema 'Lehre-Testament-Grab-Name'," *Studien zu altägyptischen Lebenslehren*, 73-104; and K. A. Kitchen, "The Basic Literary Forms and Formulations of Ancient Instructional Writings in Egypt and Western Asia," *Studien zu altägyptischen Lebenslehren*, 235-82.

form of the typical title, reconstructed by Helck to read: "(The beginning of the instruction which King Achto)es (has made) for his son Merikare," and by the linking together of admonitions in contiguous sections in the instruction proper.[47] However, while the major generic structure of the text is the instruction, the composer has inserted other genres rather freely, including the autobiography and the hymn.[48] While several other instructions, notably Ptahhotep (*ANET*, 412-14), do have separate autobiographical narratives attached at the beginning, what is unique about Merikare and, as we shall see, Amunemhet is the interlacing of autobiographical material with the admonitions in the instruction proper.[49]

In deriving the original purpose and function of this instruction, many Egyptologists view the text as royal propaganda setting forth Merikare's own platform of rule at the time he ascended the throne.[50] Other political elements include the official legitimation of Merikare as the dead king's successor, the former king's admission of serious mistakes (most unusual in Egyptian literature), the emphasis on beneficial treatment of nobles, officials, the army, and the populace in order to quell internal discord, and the extending of the olive branch to Thebes in order to bring an end to the civil war. By placing his new policies on the lips of his dead predecessor in the form of an instruction, Merikare hoped to acquire greater authority and to achieve stability for his reign in ameliorating the oppressive rules of his predecessors in the dynasty.

The major theme pervading the entire instruction is that of royal responsibility for the establishment of order (justice, truth, $m^{3c}t$), a theme pervading the admonitions pertaining to meting out swift punishment to rebels, beneficent and just treatment to every rank of citizenry, reward of loyal supporters, and divine retribution on the day of judgment. For our purposes, most noteworthy are the fragmentary initial section and a later section in 11. 49-50 (*ANET*, 414f.) which deal with the punishment of revolutionaries. According to Poláček's interpretation, there are three types of rebels: the rebellious vassal, the disobedient rebel who has a significant number of supporters, and the rebel who instigates

[47]Helck, *Die Lehre für König Merikare.*

[48]For the autobiographical materials, see lines 70-110, 120f., while the hymn to god is inserted in lines 132f. (*ANET*, 414f.).

[49]For the synthesis of instruction and narrative, see Georges Posener, "Literature," *The Legacy of Egypt*, 253f.

[50]Aksel Volten, *Zwei altägyptische politische Schriften* (Analecta Aegyptiaca 4; Copenhagen: Einar Munksgaard, 1945) 85; Eberhard Otto, "Weltanschauliche und politische Tendenzschriften," *Ägyptologie*, 114f.; and Williams, "Literature as a Medium of Political Propaganda," 16-18. However, for a dissenting view, see Siegfried Herrmann, *Untersuchungen zur Überlieferungsgestalt mittelägyptischer Literaturwerke* (Deutsche Akademie der Wissenschaften zu Berlin Institut für Orientforschung 22; Berlin: Akademieverlag, 1957) 62.

social unrest and creates factions among the youth by means of rhetoric.[51] The punishment of the latter two, according to Poláček, is of significant interest. The rebel in active revolt who has a considerable following should be exterminated without hesitation, along with his children, and his name should be removed from memory. Likewise, the orator who incites rebellion should be liquidated. However, the political agitator who causes unrest by means of oratory but has not yet incited a revolution should be judged before a royal court and, following conviction, exiled. Only when delay is considered to be dangerous is the king justified in executing the rebel without trial. Otherwise, trial and exile are the proper procedure. The instruction warns the king never to punish unjustly and especially never to take a life, except in the case of the rebel.[52]

Immediately following the fragmentary section introducing the instruction proper is the emphasis that this treatment of revolutionaries will be justified in the eyes of the god and the population. This in turn is followed by a section that places emphasis on the royal cultivation of proper speech and the study of wisdom so that the king may become a model wise man who, by means of his wise speech, is able to circumvent discord and strife. Certainly the legal sphere is one arena in which royal wisdom is of considerable importance in handling the threats posed by rebels.

The Instruction of Amunemhet

The reunification of Egypt and the re-establishment of centralized rule by the 12th dynasty at the beginning of the Middle Kingdom was aided by the frequent use of literature as propaganda: the "Prophecy of Neferti" (commissioned by Amunemhet I), "The Tale of Sinuhe," "The Instruction of a Man for his Son," and "The Instruction of Amunemhet" (the last three commissioned by Sesostris I).[53]

---

[51]Adalbert Poláček, "Gesellschaftliche und juristische Aspekte in altägyptische Weisheitslehren," *Aegyptus* 49 (1969) 14-34.

[52]Ibid.

[53]Volten, *Zwei altägyptische politische Schriften*; A. de Buck, "La littérature et la politique sous la douzième dynastie égyptienne," *Symbolae ad jus et historiam antiquitatis peritinentes Julio Christiano van Oven dedicatae* (Leiden: Brill, 1946) 1-28; Otto, "Weltanschauliche und politische Tendenzschriften," 111-19; G. Posener, *Littérature et Politique dans L'Égypte de la XIIe Dynastie* (Paris: Librairie Ancienne Honoré Champion, 1956); Williams, "Literature as a Medium of Political Propaganda," 14f.; and Hellmut Brunner, *Grundzüge einer Geschichte der altägyptische Literatur* (Grundzüge 8; Darmstadt: Wissenschaftliche Buchgesellschaft, 1966) 46-76.

The origins of Amunemhet I, the founder of the 12th dynasty, are obscure, though he is considered to have been both a commoner and the vizier of the last king of the 11th dynasty.[54] The process by which he established a new dynasty remains unclear, though the legitimacy of his rule was seriously contested, a factor of significance in his presumed assassination. In "The Instruction of Amunemhet" the deceased king recounts the circumstances of his death, indicating that he was overcome at night while fighting alone, due to the betrayal of his bodyguard and the absence of his co-regent, Sesostris I, who was with the army in Libya. "The Tale of Sinuhe" suggests that the conspiracy and assassination were undertaken by a court faction supporting another royal son's claims to the throne, though neither the instruction nor Sinuhe specify the murderers and the rival party.[55]

The external framework of "The Instruction of Amunemhet," a popular literary text,[56] is the instruction, as indicated by both the title and the typical call to listen so that, in this case, the young king may rule successfully.[57] Following the title and introduction is the standard section of admonitions which in this text centers on the subject of disloyalty. Atypical, however, are the inclusions of stylized autobiographical statements common on tomb inscriptions of nobles, the autobiographical narrative account of the king's assassination, and the later autobiographical narrative depicting in grandiose terms the spectacular accomplishments of the deceased king.[58]

The function of the text also appears to be propagandistic as implied by the following: the emphasis on the important accomplishments of the dead king which validate the legitimacy of the dynasty, the theme of disloyalty which may have been used to support oppressive features of Sesostris' rule, and the specific designation of Sesostris as the chosen successor.[59] Thus, the instruction is placed on the lips of a dead

[54]See Rolf Tanner, "Bemerkungen zur Sukzession der Pharaonen in der 12., 17., u. 18. Dynastie," ZÄS 101 (1974) 126f.

[55]Volten speculates that the wife of Sesostris I was the main conspirator in the harem and that even Sesostris was implicated (Zwei altägyptische politische Schriften, 125f.).

[56]Helck, who provides a recent transcription, translation, and notes, lists five papyri, one leather roll, three wooden tablets, and fifty-nine ostraca discovered thus far, proving the canonical status and popularity of the text (Der Text der 'Lehre Amenemhets I. für seinen Sohn' [Kleine ägyptische Texte; Wiesbaden: Otto Harrassowitz, 1969] 1-5). Also see ANET, 414-18.

[57]See Brunner, "Die Weisheitsliteratur," 102.

[58]For a detailed discussion, see A. de Buck, "La composition littéraire des Enseignements d'Amenemhet," Muséon 59 (1946) 183-200.

[59]See the works cited in n. 53.

pharaoh who speaks in a divine revelation to his successor.[60] However, one problem emerges from this interpretation: Sesostris had already been the official co-regent with his father for some ten years before the assassination.[61] And yet, in the instruction, Amunemhet states that his assassination had occurred before the courtiers had heard that he was handing the rule over to Sesostris. Simpson has suggested that this remark indicates Amunemhet had already decided to abdicate in favor of his co-regent, but was murdered before he had made this decision public.[62]

III. THE SUCCESSION NARRATIVE: THE TESTAMENT OF DAVID

In turning to the Succession Narrative, embedded within the document is the "Testament of David" (1 Kgs 2:1-12) which appears to have all the earmarks of a royal instruction. But first, the question of whether or not the text is a later redactional insertion into the narrative needs to be addressed.

Redaction Criticism

Every critical investigation of 1 Kgs 2:1-12 has recognized the presence of a Deuteronomistic hand, responsible at least for vv 2-4 and

[60]Most Egyptologists have agreed that the king is presented in the text as deceased, thus giving a posthumous instruction (A. de Buck, "The Instruction of Amenemmes," *Mélanges Maspero* I [Orient Ancien; Cairo: Imprimerie de l'Institut Français d'Archéologie Orientale, 1935-38] 847-52; Battiscombe Gunn, "Notes on Ammenemes I," *JEA* 27 [1941] 2-6; Herman Grapow, "Die Einleitung der Lehre des Königs Amenemhet," *ZÄS* 79 [1954] 97-99; Volten, *Zwei politische Schriften*, 125; Posener, *Littérature et politique*, 75; Williams, "Literature as a Medium of Political Propaganda," 19f.; Hellmut Brunner, "Zitate aus Lebenslehren," *Studien zu Altägyptischen Lebenslehren*, 144; and Helck, *Der Text der 'Lehre Amenemhets I. für seinen Sohn'*, 12-13). The precedents for this are "letters to the dead" and grave inscriptions which instruct tomb visitors. For an opposing viewpoint which suggests the instruction was given at the time of the official designation of Sesostris as co-regent ten years before Amenemhet's death, see Rudolf Anthes, "The Legal Aspects of the Instruction of Amenemhet," *JNES* 16 (1957) 176-91; and "Zur Echtheit der Lehre des Amenemhet," *Fragen an die Altägyptische Literatur*, 41-54.

[61]For monumental evidence pertaining to the co-regency of these two kings, see William Kelly Simpson, "The Single-dated Monuments of Sesostris I; an Aspect of the Institution of Coregency in the Twelfth Dynasty," *JNES* 15 (1956) 214-19.

[62]William Kelly Simpson, *The Literature of Ancient Egypt* (New Haven: Yale University Press, 1972) 195, n. 7.

10-11.[63] The intent of this redaction is to emphasize that the king who rules according to the Mosaic law will prosper and the dynasty will continue. In addition, this redaction may have been undertaken in order to lessen the impact of David's counsel to execute his enemies. More problematic is the assessment of vv 5-9. While some scholars have argued that the verses are a part of the original narrative,[64] others believe that they are the result of a later redaction.[65] In summary the arguments for attributing these verses to a later redactor include:

1. The reason for executing Joab in the Testament, blood-guilt, differs from the one mentioned in v 28 (Joab's support of Adonijah).
2. The command to reward the sons of Barzillai in the Testament is not carried out by Solomon in the later narrative.
3. The Testament does not mention Abiathar's exile and Adonijah's execution which are described in the later narrative.
4. In the Testament, Shimei is to be executed for cursing David, but in the later narrative he is interned in Jerusalem and executed for having left the city.
5. The theme of wisdom in vv 6 and 9 is thought to presuppose the Solomonic history in chaps. 3-11.
6. The style of the verses is said to reflect a redactional style evidenced in other parts of the Succession Narrative.

In response to these arguments, first of all, it must be noted that the narrative in 1 Kings 1 emphasizes that Joab's complicity in the Adonijah conspiracy to seize the throne is revealed to David by Nathan and Bathsheba. While it is plausible to suggest that David may have wished Joab executed for a variety of reasons, including his murder of Absalom and his involvement in the Adonijah conspiracy, the emphasis in the Testament is placed on establishing a legal basis upon which to execute the military commander: blood-guilt. A similar rationale is at work in the counsel to execute Shimei. Shimei's execution could not be legally carried out on the basis of cursing the king, albeit a capital offense, since David had given him a royal pardon in the form of an oath (2 Sam 19:16-23). David is presented in the Testament then as counseling

---

[63]For a detailed examination, see Moshe Weinfeld, *Deuteronomy and the Deuteronomic School* (Oxford: Clarendon Press, 1972) 13f.

[64]For example Whybray, *The Succession Narrative*, 8-9.

[65]Noth, *Könige*, 9; Gray, *I and II Kings*, 15-16; Würthwein, *Die Erzählung von der Thronfolge Davids*, 20f.; Veijola, *Die Ewige Dynastie*, 19f.; and Langlamet, "Pour ou contre Salomon?," 378-79. Noth argues that this addition was made after an earlier redactor had added much of vv 13-46a, while Langlamet and Würthwein point to a pro-Solomonic redactor who wished to shift the blame for the executions from Solomon to David. Veijola is the only one, however, to identify this redactor as the Deuteronomistic Historian.

Solomon to discover a legal reason for executing this dangerous member of the house of Saul. Thus, Solomon interns Shimei in Jerusalem, has him swear upon pain of death to abide by the ruling (internment), and then legally executes him for breaking his oath by leaving the city. There is no compelling reason to suggest that David is fearful of the power of a curse that would harm the dynasty. The reason for wanting Shimei executed seems obvious: he is a former revolutionary who as a Saulide threatens the Davidic dynasty. It is important to note, in addition, that in the case of Adonijah's execution the same pattern of finding a legal basis for execution is present: the request for a member of David's former harem could be interpreted as a seditious request, a precedent thoroughly grounded in the case of Absalom earlier in the narrative (2 Sam 16:20).

Furthermore, the references to wisdom in the Testament certainly have precedents in other parts of the narrative, particularly in judicial and political contexts. These are the episodes involving the wise woman of Tekoa (2 Sam 14) and the wise woman of Abel of Beth-maacah (2 Sam 20). In addition, leaving aside the truncated state of the Testament, one still would hardly expect David to order the exile of his priest, Abiathar, and the execution of his own son, Adonijah. Similarly, the absence of a reference in the later narrative to the sons of Barzillai may simply be due to the insignificance of the matter in the eyes of the author.

Two literary arguments remain which suggest that the Testament was an integral part of the original narrative. First, throughout the Succession Narrative an important theme is the conflict between David and two sons of Zeruiah (Joab and Abishai) over the proper way to rule the kingdom: with compassion and forgiveness or merciless retribution (2 Sam 16:5-14, 19:16-23). The striking irony is that the first time David follows the policy of stern retribution advocated by the sons of Zeruiah is when he counsels Solomon to execute Joab.[66] Second, in unique fashion speeches are the major narrative technique used by the author in order to advance the action of the plot.[67] This is illustrated by the extensive speech placed in the mouth of the wise woman of Tekoa by Joab in chap. 14 which leads to the eventual restoration of Absalom to David's court and paves the way for the later revolutions. If the Testament were entirely eliminated there would be no characteristic speech between the death of David and the executions by Solomon.

Finally, the propagandistic utility of the text, that is, placing the responsibility for executing two dangerous rebels on the shoulders of David, is in keeping with the shaping of the entire narrative which is designed to legitimate Solomon's accession to the throne over his older

[66]Gunn, *The Story of King David*, 39f.
[67]Hermisson, "Weisheit und Geschichte," 137f.

brothers in spite of the importance of primogeniture.[68] While Amnon is characterized as a sadistic rapist and Absalom as an arrogant schemer whose foolishness in accepting the deceptive counsel of Hushai leads to his ultimate undoing, the description of Adonijah and his actions is most telling. This description almost exactly parallels Absalom's early moves to gain the throne, and it is preceded by the narrator's comment: "Adonijah, the son of Haggith, exalted himself, saying, 'I will be king'." The term מתנשא ("exalted himself") in this context refers to political hubris (Num 16:3 and Dan 11:14). Even the physical appearance of Adonijah recalls the description of Absalom. Clearly, the narrator wishes the point well understood: Adonijah's claim to the throne is as illegitimate as that of Absalom's. Finally, several other sons of David, if still alive, were older than Solomon, but the narrative's placing them at Adonijah's investiture suggests that they too were implicated in the conspiracy.[69]

In regard to Solomon, his unusual accession to the throne is presented with the best possible face by the narrator. Unlike David, Solomon had no royal covenant with the elders of Israel (2 Sam 5:3),[70] but their duplicity in supporting the Absalom rebellion, underlined clearly by the narrator, would suggest the elimination of their political power in selecting a king. A similar case for the elders of Judah is implicitly present in 2 Sam 19:11.[71] In addition, while there is no anointing of Solomon by the men of Judah and Israel, as was the case with David (2 Sam 2:4, 5:3), presumably an act originally indicating civil legitimation, Solomon's anointing is a sacral one, carried out by Zadok and perhaps Nathan. Hence, a sacral anointing replaces a civil one.[72] In addition, even though Solomon's investiture and coronation are presented as being undertaken with due haste, the narrative still describes the cry of acclamation by "all the people," even though "all the people" in this case seem only to be Zadok, Nathan, Benaiah, and the mercenaries.[73] Furthermore, while Solomon may not have been the people's

---

[68]For a discussion of primogeniture, see I. Mendelsohn, "On the Preferential Status of the Eldest Son," *BASOR* 156 (1959) 38-40. While primogeniture was a strong social force, it was not always followed in succession to the throne (see, e.g., Rehoboam's choice of Abijah who was not the eldest son; 1 Kgs 11:18-20).

[69]See the genealogies of David's sons in 2 Sam 3:2-5, 5:13-16, and 1 Chr 3:1-9.

[70]For the importance of the covenant between the people and the king, see Georg Fohrer, "Der Vertrag zwischen König und Volk in Israel," *ZAW* 71 (1959) 1-22.

[71]See Geoffrey Evans, "Rehoboam's Advisers at Shechem, and Political Institutions in Israel and Sumer," *JNES* 25 (1966) 273f. Also see A. Malamat, "Kingship and Council in Israel and Sumer: A Parallel," *JNES* 22 (1963) 247-53.

[72]A point argued by Mettinger, *King and Messiah*, 185f.

[73]Mettinger, *King and Messiah*, 119f.

choice, the narrator still explicitly affirms that he was God's and David's choice. Yahweh's choice is evidenced in the Solomonic birth narrative (2 Sam 12:24-25), where Yahweh's love for Solomon is stated and encapsulated in the name Yedidiah, a name apparently modeled on the same root as the throne name of David (דוד).[74] Moreover, typical for royal ideologies in Egypt and Mesopotamia is the affirmation that the king is "the beloved of the god(s)," a title indicating both personal religion and royal legitimacy.[75] Further, while Absalom's foolish rejection of Ahithophel's good counsel is described by the narrative as due to providence, Adonijah is presented as admitting that, while he and all Israel expected that he would succeed David, Solomon's obtaining the kingdom was "from the Lord" (1 Kgs 2:15).

Divine legitimation, while restrained, is paralleled by David's choosing of Solomon. The scene involving Nathan and Bathsheba, which precedes David's oath and proclamation of Solomon as nāgîd ("successor"),[76] could be interpreted as the deception of a senile old man, especially since they rehearse what they will say to the king.[77] However, the narrative presents David as oblivious to Adonijah's royal proceedings, so that when they inform him and remind him of his private oath to Bathsheba that Solomon would reign in his stead David acts immediately to proclaim Solomon as successor and co-regent. David is described as old and uninformed, but there is no evidence that he is senile. If Nathan were being deceptive, as believed by those arguing for an anti-monarchy viewpoint in the original narrative, one is at a loss to explain how this would conform to Nathan's earlier characterization as the righteous prophet condemning the sinful king. In addition, if Nathan wishes to deceive, why not have him simply lie and give a divine oracle proclaiming God's command to have Solomon succeed to the throne? If this section is anti-Solomonic, why is there no explicit remark that Nathan and Bathsheba were lying?

Unless one removes every conceivably favorable remark concerning David and Solomon by arguing that these belong to a pro-Solomonic redactor living in a later period, a questionable process undertaken by Langlamet, Würthwein, and Veijola, it would appear that the entire

---

[74]A. M. Honeyman, "The Evidence for Regnal Names among the Hebrews," *JBL* 67 (1958) 13-25.

[75]For Egyptian kings, see Siegfried Morenz, "Die Erwählung zwischen Gott und König in Ägypten," *Sino-Japonica* (FS André Wedemeyer; Leipzig: Otto Harrassowitz, 1956) 118-37. For Mesopotamian kings, see M.-J. Seux, *Épithetes royales akkadiennes et sumériennes* (Paris: Letouzey et Ané, 1967) 22.

[76]Mettinger, *King and Messiah*, 23-24.

[77]Langlamet, "Pour ou contre Salomon?," 330f.; and Würthwein, *Die Erzählung von der Thronfolge Davids*, 13f.

narrative has been subtly shaped to underline the legitimation of Solomon's accession. Thus, "The Testament of David" appears to be an integral part of the original narrative and serves the political purpose of demonstrating David's authority for the executions of Joab and Shimei and the legal basis for carrying out these executions. As seen above, the Egyptian royal instructions provide an important analogy.

The Genre of "The Testament of David"

In turning to the matter of genre, the Testament preserves at least part of a royal instruction comparable to the Egyptian royal instructions examined earlier.[78] While the original introduction of the Testament has presumably been obscured by the Deuteronomistic redaction in vv 2-4, it is important to notice that some features of the typical introduction of the instruction genre are present, especially the emphasis placed on the successful results for Solomon's rule if he obeys the Torah of Moses. In addition vv 5-9 contain two vetitives (לא תורד in v 6, and אל תנקהו in v 9), the second of which is followed by a circumstantial clause: כי איש חכם אתה. This, of course, parallels the main section of the classical instruction. More intriguing is the autobiographical form interlaced with the vetitives, a characteristic of the two royal instructions from Egypt. Poetic autobiographies coupled with proverbs and admonitions are found in several Hebrew wisdom texts (Prov 4:3-5, 7:6-23, 24:30-34, and Ps 37:35-36), while the substantial example in prose occurs in Qoh 1:12-2:17.[79] The prosaic autobiographical form in the Testament may be due to the prose cast given by the author of the narrative, but the same combining of autobiographical prose with admonitions in the Egyptian royal instructions at least suggests this feature was a characteristic of royal instructions in general.

Major Themes in "The Testament of David"

Three major themes appear in the Testament of David: execution of revolutionaries, reward of loyal servants, and wisdom as an important characteristic of the king. David's counsel to eliminate Joab and Shimei is paralleled in the Instruction for Merikare. Similar to this Egyptian analogue, two specific rebels are represented: Joab, the military commander who probably had a large number of supporters and who conspired with Abiathar to place Adonijah on the throne, and Shimei, the descendant of the house of Saul whose rhetoric against David involved the rebellious curse of the king. Also analogous to Merikare is

[78]For a recent form critical analysis of the instruction genre, see Bernhard Lang, *Die weisheitliche Lehrrede* (SBS 54; Stuttgart: KBW Verlag, 1972) 31f.

[79]For a discussion of the autobiographical form, see Whybray, *The Succession Narrative*, 73f.

the punishment: Joab, active in the Adonijah conspiracy, is executed without trial, while Shimei, not active in the conspiracy, apparently is tried by Solomon, interned in Jerusalem, and executed only when he breaks his oath and leaves the city temporarily. Finally, the same concern for acting justly, that is, on a legal basis acceptable to the people, is evidenced in both texts.

Reward of loyal servants, underlined in David's directions to provide a royal pension for the sons of Barzillai due to their father's hospitality to David during his flight from Jerusalem (2 Sam 17:27-29, 19:31-40), is also a significant theme in Merikare. In both texts the implication is that reward of loyalty brings stability to the throne. By contrast the treachery experienced by Amunemhet leads to his counsel that Sesostris should withdraw from close relationships.

Finally, David admonishes Solomon to utilize his wisdom to find a legal means by which to execute Joab and Shimei.[80] In the Testament and elsewhere in the narrative, political and judicial wisdom is understood as necessary in the establishment of order in a strife-ridden kingdom. This type of wisdom reflects the rational and empirical character of a royal wisdom nurtured by kings and statesmen in their efforts to establish and maintain stable rule, and is present in many places in the Succession Narrative, including the counsel and actions of Ahithophel, Hushai, the wise woman of Tekoa who was aided by Joab, and the wise woman of Abel of Beth-maacah. Such wisdom reflects a class ethos of statesmen, the chief of whom was the king himself, an ethos reflected in both the Testament and the royal instructions from Egypt.[81] In a court setting, furthermore, one wonders if the political executions by Solomon, as expedient as they were, would have been taken as anti-Solomonic? If the document was intended to be read by a sophisticated, courtly audience among whom wisdom would have

[80]Whybray notes that the root *ḥkm* occurs eight times in the Succession Narrative and nineteen times in the Solomonic History (1 Kings 3-11). Otherwise, it occurs only once in the rest of the entire Deuteronomistic History—Judg 5:29 (*The Intellectual Tradition in the Old Testament* [BZAW 135; New York: de Gruyter, 1974] 77, 89-91). This is important evidence in sifting the evidence for wisdom dimensions of the document. However, unlike Whybray who argues the wise are an educated class of aristocrats, and not counselors and statesmen, I am more persuaded that at least in the monarchial period sages were a class that included statesmen (Norman Porteous, "Royal Wisdom," *VTSup* 3 [1955] 247-61).

[81]See William McKane, *Prophets and Wise Men* (SBT 44; Naperville: Alec R. Allenson, 1965) 16f. In an essay dealing with Proverbs, Kovacs argues convincingly that this wisdom material does reflect a class ethic ("Is there a Class-Ethic in Proverbs?" *Essays in Old Testament Ethics* [ed. James L. Crenshaw and John Willis; New York: Ktav, 1974] 171-90).

flourished, would not the construction of a royal instruction around this ethos and the emphasis upon Solomon wisely finding a legal basis upon which to execute dangerous rebels have been admired and appreciated as evidence of a wise king sitting upon the throne? Indeed, modern readers whose ethical sensibilities are shocked by Solomon's executions may be basing their reactions on different ethical standards than those present in a *Gruppenethos* of the court.

<h2 style="text-align:center">IV. CONCLUSION</h2>

In conclusion, it has been suggested that "The Testament of David," an important part of the original Succession Narrative, is a royal instruction strongly resembling two possible Egyptian prototypes: the Instruction for Merikare and the Instruction of Amunemhet. Each one comes from a deceased or dying king and is intended to legitimate the policies and actions of new successors whose thrones were insecure. At least Sesostris I and Solomon both faced political parties in opposition to their rule. In addition, while none of the instructions mentions co-regency, monumental evidence for Sesostris and the earlier narrative in 1 Kings 1 demonstrate both kings were chosen as co-regents in order to establish dynastic stability.[82]

If the above conclusions are correct, several important ramifications are established. First, in terms of the comparisons with Egyptian wisdom, it is possible that these two royal instructions were known and used by the writer of the Succession Narrative. Obvious dependence is not evidenced, but what Bryce calls the "integrative" process may well be at work.[83] In regard to genre and themes, important parallels have been underlined. Even if the Egyptian texts were not used by the author of the Testament, they still shed important light on the genre and function of the biblical text. Second, in regard to the larger narrative, the discovery of a wisdom form should support efforts to assess further possible sapiential dimensions of the text. Obviously, the partial existence of a wisdom form does not prove the entire narrative is a product of the wise, but it at least adds viability to further examination of the thesis. An important place for further work would be an assessment of speeches, particularly the one by Joab and the wise woman of Tekoa. Third, the reference to the murder of Abner in the Testament lends credence to Gunn's argument that the beginning section of the document is chaps. 2-4 of 2 Samuel, since the description of the murder and David's reactions occur here. Finally, if the Testament is part of the original narrative, some restraint upon extensive redactional analyses recently undertaken would be in order.

[82]See E. Ball, "The Co-Regency of David and Solomon," *VT* 27 (1977) 268-79. He suggests that this may have been a process borrowed from the Egyptians.
[83]Bryce, *A Legacy of Wisdom*, 113f.

NARAM-SIN AND JEROBOAM:
THE ARCHETYPAL *UNHEILSHERRSCHER*
IN MESOPOTAMIAN AND BIBLICAL
HISTORIOGRAPHY*

CARL D. EVANS

University of South Carolina

I. INTRODUCTION

Even the most casual reader of the Book of Kings cannot avoid noticing a salient claim of deuteronomistic historiography, viz., that Jeroboam ben Nebat, the first monarch of the north Israelite kingdom, committed great "sins" and thereby set his kingdom on a fateful course which others after him followed to the ruin of the nation. The Deuteronomist first connects the calamitous end of Israel with Jeroboam's actions in his assessment of Jeroboam's reign in 1 Kings 14.[1] Then, having persistently reminded his readers of the perpetuation of Jeroboam's "sins" in his negative evaluation of virtually every north Israelite king,[2] the Deuteronomist returns to the same cause-effect correlation in his discourse on the fall of Israel in 2 Kings 17. He says:

*Work on this project was supported by a Research and Productive Scholarship grant from the University of South Carolina.

[1]Especially vv 15-16: "The Lord will strike Israel, till it trembles like a reed in the water; he will uproot its people from this good land which he gave to their forefathers and scatter them beyond the Euphrates, because they have made their sacred poles and provoked the Lord's anger. And he will abandon Israel for the sins that Jeroboam has committed and has led Israel to commit" (NEB). Even though the words are attributed to the prophet Ahijah, it is generally recognized that they are part of the Deuteronomist's expansion of the prophet's oracle of condemnation. Cf. J. Gray, *I & II Kings*, 2nd edition (London: SCM, 1970) 334 and M. Noth, *Könige* (BKAT 9; Neukirchen-Vluyn: Neukirchener Verlag, 1968) 310-11.

[2]On the basis of certain variations in the judgment formulas, H. Weippert has recently argued that a three-stage development in the redactional history of the Book of Kings must be posited—one pre-deuteronomistic and the other two deuteronomistic: *idem*, "Die 'deuteronomistischen' Beurteilungen der Könige von Israel und Juda und das Problem der Redaktion der Königsbücher," *Bib* 53 (1972) 301-39. A refinement of Weippert's three-redaction scheme has been offered by W. B. Barrick, "On the 'Removal of the "High-Places"'" in 1-2

The Israelites persisted in all the sins that Jeroboam had committed and did not give them up, until finally the Lord banished them from his presence, as he had threatened through his servants the prophets, and they were carried into exile from their own land to Assyria; and they are there to this day (vv 22-23, NEB).

This point of view, so prominently featured in the Deuteronomist's work, invites more careful examination, not only because it differs so sharply from more objective assessments of the collapse of Israel,[3] but also because it is unique among the native Israelite assessments preserved in the Hebrew canon. With regard to the latter, the following data is pertinent. The Chronicler, characteristic of his limited attention to the affairs of the north Israelite kingdom, passes over the collapse of Israel without notice.[4] He does offer at another point, however, a lengthy condemnation of Jeroboam, but in doing so he doesn't so much as offer a hint that the "sins" of Jeroboam contributed to the collapse of Israel (2 Chr 13:4-12). In the prophetic portion of the canon, we find that the great prophets, though never tiring in their efforts to connect great calamities with unfaithfulness to the national Deity, do not go so far as to connect the collapse of Israel with the "sins" of Jeroboam. Isaiah, for example, can give a vivid description of the moral decay that led to the ruin of the Northern Kingdom, and even attribute it to a failure in leadership, without offering the slightest suggestion that Jeroboam was the primary, or even a notable, culprit in the matter (Isa 9:8-21 [Heb 9:7-20]). Only in the Book of Kings is the collapse of Israel said to be the consequence of the "sins" of Jeroboam.

It is this state of affairs that prompts the present investigation. If we may anticipate for just a moment, we shall find that the Deuteronomist fashioned his portrait of Jeroboam out of traditions that portrayed Jeroboam's rise to power and reign from various perspectives, some favorable and some not. Conflicting assessments were more or less reconciled by subjecting them to a one-sided interpretation, and this

---

Kings," *Bib* 55 (1974) 257-59. One must observe, however, that judgment formulas alone constitute a very narrow base on which to construct such a general theory of redactional history. See also M. Weinfeld, *Deuteronomy and the Deuteronomic School* (Oxford: Clarendon, 1972), esp. pp. 332-41, whose analysis shows that the phraseology characteristic of the judgment formulas is deuteronom(ist)ic throughout.

[3]For a recent treatment which gives special attention to the sources available to the historian, see H. Donner, "The Syro-Ephraimite War and the End of Israel" in *Israelite and Judean History*, ed. J. H. Hayes and J. M. Miller (Philadelphia: Westminster, 1977) 421-34.

[4]There is a possible allusion to the calamity in 2 Chr 28:23, but it is unclear whether the downfall of "all Israel," which is attributed to Ahaz's sacrifice to "the gods of Damascus," is a reference to the collapse of Israel or Judah or both.

view of matters was reinforced by means of recurring literary patterns throughout the Book of Kings. Indeed, we find here a complex of motifs that calls to mind various Mesopotamian materials, especially the literary tradition that portrays Naram-Sin of Akkad as Mesopotamia's archetypal *Unheilsherrscher*.[5] We shall begin with the pertinent Naram-Sin materials to gain an understanding of the typology of the *Unheilsherrscher* and to provide a comparative literary context for considering the Deuteronomist's special treatment of Jeroboam.

II. NARAM-SIN AND THE MESOPOTAMIAN TRADITION

Ever since Güterbock's publication of several Naram-Sin texts in 1934,[6] it has become commonplace to recognize that this illustrious Sargonic ruler was remembered in later traditions as the epitome of what Güterbock called the *"Unheilsherrscher."*[7] To be sure, the later traditions do not render a unanimous verdict on Naram-Sin, but there is evidence of an enduring tendency over a period of a millennium and a half to portray him in this light. As noted by Finkelstein, it is difficult to find an idiomatic English equivalent of *Unheilsherrscher* which connotes, as the German term does, "the element of the king's own instrumentality in bringing about the misfortune (by real or alleged misdeeds)."[8] Inasmuch as this element is such an important topos in the typology itself, and in deference to Güterbock's place at the beginning of the discussion of the subject, we prefer to retain the German term. But, terminology aside, the full dimensions of the typology in question can be supplied only by an analysis of the pertinent texts, to which we now turn.

The earliest text for this discussion is the Sumerian composition known as "The Curse of Agade."[9] This literary work is known from

[5]Our preference for the German term will be explained presently.

[6]H.-G. Güterbock, "Die historische Tradition und ihre literarische Gestaltung bei Babyloniern und Hethitern bis 1200 (Erster Teil: Babylonier)," *ZA* 42 (1934) 1-91.

[7]Ibid., esp. pp. 75-76.

[8]J. J. Finkelstein, "Mesopotamian Historiography," *Proceedings of the American Philosophical Society* 107 (1963) 467, n. 23, who proposes the translation "calamitous ruler" as an improvement (which he himself admits is "hardly idiomatic") over "ill-fated ruler" as rendered by O. Gurney, "The Cuthaean Legend of Naram-Sin," *Anatolian Studies* 5 (1955) 96. Cf. Hallo's use of the term "hapless ruler" in his discussion of Naram-Sin in W. W. Hallo and W. K. Simpson, *The Ancient Near East: A History* (New York: Harcourt Brace Jovanovich, 1971), esp. p. 63.

[9]The most recent edition is by A. Falkenstein, "Fluch über Agade," *ZA* 57 (1965) 43-124. An English translation of the text is provided by S. N. Kramer in J. B. Pritchard, ed., *Ancient Near Eastern Texts Relating to the Old Testament*, 3rd edition (Princeton: Princeton University, 1969) 646-51.

numerous exemplars from the Old Babylonian period, but it was probably first composed during the Neo-Sumerian literary renaissance of the
Ur III period.[10] This would place it no more than a century or two after
the reign of Naram-Sin. Most of the exemplars come from Nippur which
is indicative of the interest that the composition held for the Old
Babylonian scribes of that city. That this should be the case is readily
explained by the fact that the desecration of Enlil's temple in Nippur by
Naram-Sin is a central theme of the text.

The Curse of Agade is a poetic narrative which, according to
Kramer, seems to allude to historical events "in a style and manner
consonant with the Sumerian world view."[11] The opening lines, which
claim that Enlil angrily destroyed Kish and Uruk and then gave the
kingship to Sargon of Akkad, probably refer to conquests of Sargon
known from other sources.[12] The text then describes how the goddess
Inanna devoted herself to making Akkad, the Sargonic capital, a prosperous and influential city with the result that it became, at the time of
Naram-Sin's reign, a magnificent trading center with goods brought by
merchants from near and far.[13] The fortunes of the city changed,
however, when Inanna, presumably at Enlil's command, abandoned her
shrine in Akkad and turned against the city. As other gods, too, withdrew
their favors from the city, it soon suffered from a loss of might and
prosperity. Because of a certain vision, presumably about the Ekur,
Naram-Sin seems at first to accept this fate and even displays signs of
genuine humility. But after seven years of forbearance, he turned to
defiance when a request for an oracle from the Ekur in Nippur was not

---

[10] According to A. Sjöberg and E. Bergmann (*The Collection of the Sumerian
Temple Hymns* [Texts from Cuneiform Sources III; Locust Valley, NY: J. J.
Augustin, 1969] 7) there is an unpublished Ur III text of the Curse of Agade.

[11] Kramer, *ANET*[3], 646, n. 1. On this view, however, see the reservations of
Falkenstein ("Fluch über Agade," 48-50) who stresses that the work reflects more
of an "anti-akkadische Tendenz" than a concern for historical truth. See now
also C. Wilcke, "Politische Opposition nach sumerischen Quellen: Der Konflikt
zwischen Königtum und Ratsversammlung. Literaturwerke als politische
Tendenzschriften," in *La Voix de l'Opposition en Mésopotamie*, ed. A. Finet
(Brussels, 1973) 37-65, esp. pp. 63-64.

[12] Cf. Kramer, *ANET*[3], 646, n. 5, who states: "The reference here is probably
to Sargon's victory over Ur-Zababa of Kish, and Lugalzaggesi, originally of
Sumer who made Erech [i.e., Uruk] his capital."

[13] Cf. T. Jacobsen, "Ipḫur-Kīshi and His Times," *AfO* 26 (1978/79) 13 who
observes that it is "likely that 'The Curse of Akkadê' retains essentially correct
memories when it depicts the Akkadê of those years [i.e., the early years of
Naram-Sin] as a prosperous trading center with goods brought from Elam in the
east, Subartu in the north, and Mardu and Meluḫḫa in the west, as well as by
traders from Sumer in the south."

granted. Thereupon he marched his troops to that city and destroyed the Ekur in what is portrayed as a defiant act of desecration. Angered by what Naram-Sin had done, Enlil avenged the sacrilege by calling the Gutians from the distant mountains to invade the land. They swarmed over the land like devastating locusts, and nothing escaped. They brought desolation, famine, and death. Although the people in their suffering pleaded to Enlil, he would not listen. Just when the whole land was certain to be destroyed, a group of Sumerian gods interceded to "soothe (and) comfort the heart of Enlil," saying:

> "Oh, valiant Enlil, the city that has destroyed your city may it become like
>   your city,
> (The city) that has demolished your *giguna*, may it become like Nippur."[14]

The gods then proceed to utter a lengthy curse against Akkad, dooming it to utter destruction, presumably so that the rest of the land could be spared. The composition concludes by claiming that this is precisely what happened; Akkad was destroyed.

To what extent the details of this composition reflect a Sumero-centric perception of events known from other sources is debatable. Jacobsen, however, has recently suggested that Naram-Sin's alleged desecration of the Ekur in Nippur can be interpreted as an attempt on Naram-Sin's part to "treat Enlil's city well."[15] This interpretation is based, in part, on an Old Babylonian copy of a Naram-Sin inscription[16] which reads:

> "(and) washed his weapons in the Lower Sea. Naram-Sin, the mighty, on
> Inanna's errand, when Enlil judged his case so as to give the reins of the
> people into his hand, and also gave him none who could turn him back,
> broke the shackles of the forces of Nippur. . . ."[17]

This inscription, reflecting the victor's point of view, indicates that Naram-Sin felt secure that Enlil had delivered Nippur into his hands, so the victorious ruler "freed the labor and soldier forces of Nippur from service. . . ."[18] Jacobsen also calls attention to a date formula and a brick

---

[14]Lines 211-12, Kramer's translation.

[15]Jacobsen, "Ipḫur-Kīshi," 14.

[16]Hand copy published by A. Poebel, *Historical and Grammatical Texts* (Publications of the Babylonian Section, Vol. V; Philadelphia: University Museum, 1914), no. 36. Poebel's transliteration and translation of this inscription appears in the same series, Vol. IV 209-15.

[17]This is the obverse (not reverse as per Poebel), col. iii, with Jacobsen's restorations ("Ipḫur-Kīshi," 12).

[18]Ibid., 14.

stamp which, he believes, indicate that Naram-Sin actually began the task of rebuilding Enlil's temple.[19] Jacobsen speculates that the old structure was torn down so the new one could rise in its place, but the task of rebuilding was left unfinished or interrupted for a considerable period of time while Naram-Sin attended to trouble spots elsewhere, now attested in several new sources.[20] Due to some such set of circumstances, Jacobsen contends, "the demolition could well have been reinterpreted in later memory as a hostile act."[21]

Although one must admit that this reconstruction of matters is rather hypothetical, the fact remains that the Curse of Agade identifies Naram-Sin as the culprit whose sacrilege was requited by the invasion of the Gutians. This, most certainly, is a distortion of history, for the earliest contemporary attestation for the Gutians is found in date formulas that come from the reign of Shar-kali-sharri, the son and successor of Naram-Sin,[22] and, contrary to the Curse of Agade, the fall of Akkad must be placed in the period of anarchy that set in following Shar-kali-sharri's twenty-five year reign—that is, much later than the time of Naram-Sin. Although the date formulas indicate that Shar-kali-sharri had a number of military encounters with the Gutians, we can assume from the length of his reign that the claims of victory are essentially correct. At his death, however, the situation changed. The Sumerian King List alludes to a period of anarchy with its rhetorical "Who was king? Who was not King?" and records that the next four kings ruled for a total of three years.[23] They are followed in some versions of the King List by two more kings who ruled for a total of thirty-six years, but the region they controlled was only a shadow of the empire at its height. Thus the collapse of Akkad must be seen in the context of the anarchy in the years following Shar-kali-sharri's reign. Although not the sole cause, the Gutians were certainly a factor in the

[19]Ibid., nn. 55 and 56. For the date formula, see F. Thureau-Dangin, *Recueil de Tablettes Chaldéennes* (Paris, 1903), no. 144. For the brick stamp, see F. Thureau-Dangin, *Die sumerischen und akkadischen Königsinschriften* (Leipzig, 1907) 166, 2a. The stamp reads: "The divine Narām-Suen, builder of the Temple of Enlil" (Jacobsen's translation). Jacobsen also observes (n. 56) that bricks bearing this stamp have been found in Ekur by various excavators, indicating that it was actually used.

[20]See especially A. K. Grayson and E. Sollberger, "L'insurrection générale contre Narām-Suen," *RA* 70 (1976) 103-28.

[21]Jacobsen, "Ipḫur-Kīshi," 14.

[22]W. W. Hallo, "Gutium," in *Reallexikon der Assyriologie und vorderasiatischen Archëologie* III/8 (Berlin: Walter de Gruyter, 1971) 708-20, esp. section 2 ("Gutian contacts in the reign of Šarkališarri").

[23]See T. Jacobsen's edition, *The Sumerian King List* (Assyriological Studies 11; Chicago: University of Chicago, 1939), col. vii, lines 1-7.

empire's demise.[24] In this light it can be seen that the Curse of Agade, by placing the calamity in the time of Naram-Sin and at the hands of the Gutians, distorts certain facts and thereby paints the first strokes of a portrait of Naram-Sin that, in later tradition, becomes more and more a depiction of the archetypal *Unheilsherrscher.*

Additional features of this portrait come into view in the so-called "Cuthean Legend of Naram-Sin"[25] and a related fragment published by J. J. Finkelstein.[26] Although parts of the Cuthean Legend have been known since the early days of Assyriology, the full scope of the composition has come to light only in the last twenty-five years with Gurney's publication of a well-preserved exemplar from the Sultantepe tablets.[27] In addition to the Gurney tablet, parts of the legend are preserved on four other Neo-Assyrian tablet fragments from Nineveh as well as a Hittite text which represents the same or a closely related story.[28] The existence of the Hittite counterpart to the Assyrian legend indicates that a forerunner of the composition must have existed as early as the Old Babylonian period. Earlier estimates of the related fragment published by Finkelstein had proposed that it represented the Old Babylonian forerunner, but a re-examination of the matter by Finkelstein has made clear that, while this text is related to the Cuthean Legend, especially in the similarity of a few lines, it "can no longer be regarded simply as an Old Babylonian version of the Assyrian story."[29] A major difference between the two is that the Morgan fragment is from a tablet which, on Finkelstein's estimate, would have contained a composition of 250 to 300 lines,[30] whereas Gurney's publication has now made clear that the

[24]C. J. Gadd in *The Cambridge Ancient History*, 3rd edition, I/2 (Cambridge: University, 1971) 454-61, esp. pp. 455-56; cf. Hallo, "Gutium," sect. 3 ("Gutium and the fall of Akkad").

[25]Latest edition and bibliography by O. R. Gurney, "The Cuthaean Legend," 93-113. For corrections, see Gurney, *Anatolian Studies* 6 (1956) 163-64.

[26]J. J. Finkelstein, "The So-called 'Old Babylonian Kutha Legend'," *JCS* 11 (1957) 83-88.

[27]Above, n. 25.

[28]For the Hittite text, see E. Forrer, *Die Boghazköitexte in Umschrift* II, nos. 4 and 5, and comments on p. 2*; H.-G. Güterbock, "Die historische Tradition und ihre literarische Gestaltung bei Babyloniern und Hethitern bis 1200 (Zweiter Teil: Hethiter)," *ZA* 44 (1938), esp. pp. 49-67; and more recently, H. A. Hoffner, Jr., "Remarks on the Hittite Version of the Naram-Sin Legend," *JCS* 23 (1970) 17-22.

[29]Finkelstein, " 'Old Babylonian Kutha Legend'," 87. The older assumption had gained currency after H. Zimmern ("'König Tukulti bēl niši' und die 'kuthäische Schöpfungslegende'," *ZA* 12 [1897] 317-30) had called attention to the close similarity between the fragment in question (based on the published portion by P. Scheil) and the earlier published fragments of the Assyrian story.

[30]Finkelstein, " 'Old Babylonian Kutha Legend'," 83.

Assyrian story consisted of only 175 lines. Although the Old Babylonian version of the Cuthean Legend has not yet come to light, we can cite the Morgan fragment as a related text which, as we shall see, adds chronological depth to the depiction of Naram-Sin that we find in the Assyrian story.

The Cuthean Legend belongs to a literary type formerly called *"narû*-literature."[31] This designation was used because texts in this category are cast in the form of a royal inscription, usually found on a *narû* or stele, and purport to narrate the king's first-person account of his experiences. However, since this designation leads to possible confusion between the genuine *narû*-inscriptions and those in the category to which the Cuthean Legend belongs, other labels for the latter have been proposed. "Poetic autobiographies,"[32] or, alternatively, "pseudo-autobiographies"[33] have been suggested because "what distinguishes these [texts] from royal inscriptions is the fact that the autobiographies are composed not at the king's command but by scribes, presumably some time after the king's death, on their own initiative."[34] From the Cuthean Legend and the other representatives of the genre,[35] it can be gathered that the main purpose of these texts was to exhort future rulers to heed the counsel of the gods lest great misfortune be encountered.

In the Cuthean Legend Naram-Sin's empire is invaded by a horde of warriors who are called "umman-manda," an enigmatic term which in this context may mean simply "barbarians."[36] They are described in fanciful terms: "Warriors with bodies of 'cave-birds', a race with ravens' faces" (Gurney, line 31). They are led by seven kings and joined in alliance by seventeen more. Their combined troop count is 450,000. They are known for devastating campaigns over virtually the entire map

[31]Güterbock first proposed this designation ("Die historische Tradition: Babylonier," 19-21) and it has been commonly used until recently.

[32]Proposed by the first author in A. K. Grayson and W. G. Lambert, "Akkadian Prophecies," *JCS* 18 (1964) 8.

[33]An alternative offered more recently by Grayson in his *Babylonian Historical-Literary Texts* (Toronto and Buffalo: University of Toronto Press, 1975) 7-8 and also in the work cited in the following note, pp. 2-3.

[34]Grayson, *Assyrian and Babylonian Chronicles* (Texts from Cuneiform Sources V; Locust Valley, NY: J. J. Augustin, 1975) 2.

[35]The other texts include the Sargon birth legend, another Sargon autobiography, an autobiography of a king in the Isin II dynasty, a Kassite autobiography, and possibly others. See bibliography for these texts in Grayson, *Babylonian Historical-Literary Texts*, 8, n. 11. On the first of these see now B. Lewis, *The Sargon Legend* (ASOR Dissertation Series 4; Cambridge: American Schools of Oriental Research, 1980) who also discusses briefly the others, esp. pp. 88-90 and nn. 4-21 on pp. 115-16.

[36]So Gurney, "The Cuthaean Legend," 97.

of the Near East. To Naram-Sin they seem supernatural, and he instructs an officer to prick them with his lance to see if they bleed like other human beings. They do, but this does not diminish their threat to Naram-Sin. He is ready to take up arms against them, but first he seeks the counsel of the gods. Their advice is not to go out against the invaders, but Naram-Sin chooses to ignore their warnings. The result was devastating as the following lines indicate:

> When the first year arrived,
> I sent out 120,000 troops, but none of them returned alive.
> When the second year arrived, I sent out 90,000 troops, but none of them
>   returned alive.
> When the third year arrived, I sent out 60,700 troops, but none of them
>   returned alive.
> I was bewildered, confused, *sunk in gloom*, sorrowful, exhausted.
> Thus I spoke in my heart—these were my words:
> "What have I to show for my reign?
> "I am a king who brings no prosperity to his country,
> "a shepherd who brings no prosperity to his people.
> "How am I to *proceed* and *keep myself out of trouble*?"[37]

These are the lines which bear a striking similarity to a section of the Morgan fragment,[38] but apart from this there is little likeness between the two compositions. Still, the similarity is revealing, for it suggests that both compositions draw upon a tradition of portraying Naram-Sin as an *Unheilsherrscher*. Although Naram-Sin in the Cuthean Legend seems to emerge from his difficulties with victory, presumably

[37]Lines 84-93, Gurney's translation. Italics indicate uncertain translations.

[38]Cf. column iii of the Morgan fragment (the end of column ii is not preserved):

> He inflicted a defeat, he left no [one alive].
> The second time 120,000 troops I sent forth;
> He inflicted a defeat, he filled the plain.
> The third time 60,000 troops I sent forth;
> He made that one (i.e., his victory) exceed even (that) of before.
> When he had slain 360,000 troops,
> He had inflicted a great defeat.
> I became confused, I was bewildered.
> I despaired (?), I groaned, I grieved, I grew faint.
> Thus I thought: 'What has God brought upon my reign.
> I am a king who has not kept his land prosperous.
> And a shepherd who has not kept his people prosperous.
> Upon myself and my reign what have I brought?
> How shall I proceed?' (lines 1-14, Finkelstein's translation).

after following the counsel of the seers whom he consulted again, the fact remains that a portion of the text portrays the king as a beleaguered, confused, and despairing figure. Finkelstein has aptly observed that despite the ultimate outcome "the king suffers many serious defeats before his final victory, and in his advice of passiveness and humbleness to future rulers he sounds like one chastised by a lifetime of misfortune and adversity rather than a buoyant victor."[39]

Although scholars have been reluctant to treat the Cuthean Legend as a historical source, and rightly so, it may be conceded that the story in its own fabulous way recalls wars that Naram-Sin is known to have fought against various coalitions of kings.[40] Since our purpose here is to concentrate on the portrait of Naram-Sin, we may spare ourselves the trouble of trying to reconstruct from other sources the events that conceivably lie at the basis of the legend. What we have found is a king who is remembered for great misfortunes, as well as times of happier fate. The misfortunes, in the form of invaders that overtake the land, are reminiscent of the misfortunes related in the Curse of Agade, although the name of the invaders has changed. We have found, too, that the cause of the invasion was the king's disregard of the divine counsel given by the seers. Moreover, the king's ultimate victory seems to result from his later decision to consult the seers again and follow their counsel, although the text is too poorly preserved at this point to be certain about the matter. And, finally, this understanding of the king's fateful experiences is offered as a lesson for future rulers. What stands out most clearly, however, is the king's bewilderment and self-abasement in the face of repeated misfortune.

The Weidner Chronicle offers still another example of a text wherein the tradition of the *Unheilsherrscher* is reflected, although in this case Naram-Sin is but one of a number of rulers whose reigns come under scrutiny.[41] This text, which exists in Neo-Assyrian and Neo-Babylonian copies, narrates events which cover the period from Early Dynastic times down to the reign of Shulgi where the tablet fragments either are broken off or become too illegible to read. The central concern of this chronicle is the city of Babylon and the cult of its patron deity Marduk. In particular, it attempts to show that those rulers who did not show proper regard for Babylon or provide fish offerings for Marduk's temple

---

[39]Finkelstein, "'Old Babylonian Kutha Legend'," 88.

[40]So Gurney, "The Cuthaean Legend," 96. For a discussion of several historical-literary texts that relate rebellions against Naram-Sin, see Grayson and Sollberger, "L'insurrection générale," 103-20. See also Jacobsen, "Ipḫur-Kīshi," 1-14.

[41]For the most recent edition see A. K. Grayson, *Assyrian and Babylonian Chronicles*, 145-51. See also pp. 43-45 for Grayson's discussion of the chronicle.

experienced great misfortunes, whereas those who did attend properly to such matters fared well. Like the Cuthean Legend, this chronicle has a didactic purpose. Grayson prefers to regard it as a "blatant piece of propaganda" which was designed to be an "admonition to future rulers to pay heed to Babylon and its cult."[42]

Consistent with its purpose the Weidner Chronicle does not attempt to provide a complete survey of the past. Only certain rulers are included, and they are brought into the account only to illustrate the importance of properly serving Babylon and its Marduk cult. The reigns of the kings mentioned are depicted as either "good" or "bad," a feature which is more characteristic of the so-called "prophecies"[43] than of chronicles. Of the Sargonic kings, only Sargon and Naram-Sin are mentioned. Sargon, we are told, refused an order from Ur-Zababa to alter the offerings at Marduk's temple for which Marduk "looked with joy upon him and gave him sovereignty over the Four Quarters."[44] Then Sargon did wrong by founding the city of Akkad as a counterpart to Babylon and for this an angry Marduk sent rebellions againt him and afflicted him with insomnia.[45] As for Naram-Sin, the text states:

[42]Ibid., 43-44. [Note also the additional duplicates newly published by I. L. Finkel, *JCS* 32 (1980) 65-80, which take matters down to the reign of Shu-Sin. Ed.]

[43]For a discussion of this genre and bibliography, see Grayson, *Babylonian Historical-Literary Texts*, 13-20, to which should now be added H. Hunger and S. A. Kaufman, "A New Akkadian Prophecy Text," *JAOS* 95 (1975) 371-75 and S. A. Kaufman, "Predictions, Prophecy, and Apocalypse in the Light of New Akkadian Texts," *Proceedings of the Sixth World Congress of Jewish Studies* 1 (1977) 221-28.

[44]Line 48, Grayson's translation.

[45]Lines 50-52b. This passage has a close parallel in the Chronicle of Early Kings (lines 81-23, also in Grayson, *Assyrian and Babylonian Chronicles*) and the portion of the passage pertaining to the founding of Akkad also occurs in the Neo-Assyrian omen collection, for which see L. W. King, *Chronicles Concerning Early Babylonian Kings* II (London: Luzac and Co., 1907) chronicle no. 3 (pp. 25-39). For a discussion of the relationship of the Weidner Chronicle and the Chronicle of Early Kings to the omen literature, see A. K. Grayson, "Divination and the Babylonian Chronicles," *XIVe Rencontre Assyriologique Internationale* (Paris: Presses Universitaires de France, 1966) 69-76. In this study, Grayson also brings the Religious Chronicle into the discussion, but he concludes that only the Chronicle of Early Kings used omen literature as a source and that the Religious Chronicle and the Weidner Chronicle have only a superficial relationship to omen literature (the last of these, e.g., has taken its omen-like material from the Chronicle of Early Kings). Thus ". . . divination plays no essential rôle in the origin or development of the chronographic literature of ancient Mesopotamia" (p. 76). Contrast Finkelstein, "Mesopotamian Historiography."

Naram-Sin destroyed the population of Babylon.
Twice he (Marduk) brought against him (Naram-Sin) an attack of the
    army of the Guti. His people as with a goad [. . .]
He (Marduk) gave his sovereignty to the army of the Guti.[46]

The text continues by describing the reign of the Gutians which turned
out to be "bad" and then states that sovereignty was taken away from
them and given to Utu-hegal, and so on and so forth.

What is most clearly evident in this chronicle is a highly schematic
presentation. While most reigns are depicted as "bad," occasionally there
is a "good" reign (that of Ku-Baba being a case in point, lines 42-45).
Some, like that of Sargon, begin "good" but turn out "bad." But in
every case the fate turns on the regard or disregard for Babylon or its
cult. Herein lies one of the most interesting features of the text, for the
city of Babylon and especially the cult of Marduk did not enjoy the
prominence assumed by the chronicle until much later than the third
millennium rulers named in the text. To make the fate of each turn on
what was done for Babylon or its cult is to present an account of matters
which employs striking anachronisms, a feature which has an interesting
parallel in the Deuteronomist's treatment of Jeroboam and the past in
general.[47]

Just when and why the Weidner Chronicle was originally composed
is a matter of conjecture, but Grayson has cogently argued for a date in
the latter Kassite or, more likely, early Isin II period.[48] If such a date
proves to be correct, this chronicle would be a product of the same
general period that spawned several of the so-called "prophetic" texts. It
may be no coincidence, then, that the Weidner Chronicle contains
features more common to these texts than to other Assyrian and

[46]Lines 53-55, Grayson's translation.

[47]Cf. E. Osswald, "Altorientalische Parallelen zur deuteronomistischen
Geschichtsbetrachtung," *Mitteilungen des Instituts für Orientforschung* 15 (1969)
286-96, esp. pp. 288-93.

[48]Grayson, *Assyrian and Babylonian Chronicles*, 278-79. He states: "At this
stage in history there is a surprising lack of references to fish and fishing (an
industry that had earlier been of major importance); the Kassites created a new
capital, Dur-Kurigalzu, about ninety kilometers from Babylon (the early Isin II
kings presumably had their capital at Isin rather than Babylon); the rise of
Marduk to the pinnacle of the pantheon took place during this period and
reached a climax with the reign of the fourth Isin II king, Nebuchadnezzar I. No
other period of time, it seems to me, is such a reasonable choice and therefore I
offer the suggestion that the Weidner Chronicle was composed about this time
(probably early Isin II) with the purpose of magnifying the position of Marduk
and castigating those who had built a rival capital to Babylon and were
responsible for piscine poverty" (p. 279).

Babylonian chronicles, viz., the phenomenon of direct divine speech[49] and the schematic depiction of "good" or "bad" reigns as discussed above. It is tempting, but this is mere speculation, to regard the Weidner Chronicle as an officially sanctioned effort to support the reform program of Nebuchadnezzar I who, as Lambert has shown, was responsible for elevating Marduk to the head of the Babylonian pantheon.[50] Surely such a change was accompanied by literary attempts at legitimation, such as occurred in another setting when the first edition of the Deuteronomistic History was produced to legitimate King Josiah's reform program.[51]

Fortunately, modern historiography is not limited by the materials reviewed above for its assessment of Naram-Sin. Diverse kinds of evidence have survived which not only allow but demand a much different accounting of Naram-Sin's place in history.[52] Inscriptions, date formulas, rock reliefs, etc. record Naram-Sin's impressive conquests near and far, as all of Mesopotamia and expansive regions beyond were brought under Sargonic control. Economic texts from the period indicate that active commerce existed throughout much of this far-flung empire, and a text preserving a treaty with Elam further attests to Naram-Sin's influence abroad. Thus the more or less contemporary documentation of the king's military, commercial, and diplomatic activity offers evidence of an enormously successful ruler, an empire builder whose achievements surpass even those of his illustrious grandfather, Sargon. Add to this the record of his institutionalization of various practices begun by Sargon,

---

[49]One might compare this to the Marduk and Shulgi prophetic speeches, although in these cases the address takes the form of an autobiography. The Marduk prophetic speech has been dated to the reign of Nebuchadnezzar I by Borger who also dates the Shulgi prophetic text to the first half of the twelfth century (R. Borger, "Gott Marduk und Gott-König Šulgi als Propheten," *BiOr* 28 [1971] 3-24, esp. pp. 22-23). Grayson, however, thinks it plausible that the Shulgi text could also be dated to the reign of Nebuchadnezzar I (*Babylonian Historical-Literary Texts*, 16 and n. 20).

[50]W. G. Lambert, "The Reign of Nebuchadnezzar I: A Turning Point in the History of Ancient Mesopotamian Religion," in *The Seed of Wisdom: Essays in Honour of T. J. Meek*, ed. W. S. McCullough (Toronto: University of Toronto, 1964) 3-13.

[51]On this view of the setting and purpose of the Deuteronomistic History in its original formulation, see esp. F. M. Cross, "The Themes of the Book of Kings and the Structure of the Deuteronomistic History," in *Canaanite Myth and Hebrew Epic* (Cambridge: Harvard University, 1973) 274-89.

[52]See, e.g., the treatment by Hallo in *The Ancient Near East: A History*, 60-63. The following sketch is drawn from Hallo's discussion whose notes should be consulted for this reconstruction. Cf. C. J. Gadd in *CAH*³, esp. pp. 440-45 ("The ·Reign of Naram-Sin").

such as the appointment of sons and daughters to high offices, cultic
and civil, in various key centers and the use of year names for calendrical
reckoning, and Naram-Sin's place as an unparalleled figure in Mesopotamian history begins to emerge. The innovations in the royal titulary
likewise give telling testimony to the stature of the king. Midway
through his reign the title "king of the four quarters" appears on his
inscriptions and becomes henceforth a title commonly claimed by "all
those kings who proudly aspired to universal dominion from a Mesopotamian base."[53] In addition, the title "god of Akkad" was thereafter
given to Naram-Sin, and whatever this may have signified initially it
soon developed into a full-fledged apotheosis of the king, including "a
cult of the living ruler and of deceased predecessors that was, for
practical purposes, indistinguishable from the cult of the 'real' gods and,
like theirs, centered around the king's statue."[54] And, finally, the title
"strong (male)" (dannum), which may have signified something like the
more common epithet "the great," is also attested from the latter part of
Naram-Sin's reign.[55] All of this adds up to an impressive amount of
evidence which conflicts sharply with the later traditions that portrayed
Naram-Sin so negatively.

Why the negative assessment developed and became so dominant in
later tradition surely has something to do with the distinctive way that
the Mesopotamians viewed and made use of the past.[56] Finkelstein has
stated the matter so well that I can do no better than quote his words:

> Contrasted with our sense of the uniqueness of past events which, of
> course, distinguishes the Western sense of history, it will be seen that the
> significance of past events for the Mesopotamians lay rather in their
> exemplificative value. The basic concerns and aspirations of a society or
> state, domestic prosperity, success in foreign affairs and in wars, remain
> constant throughout time. The experience of a single dynasty, if it was of
> sufficient duration, and spectacular in its rise, its glories as well as its
> reverses and final demise, constituted, as it were, the complete requisite
> paradigm for the fortunes that any ruler or dynasty would be likely to
> encounter in the future. For the Mesopotamians, the fortunes of the Akkad
> dynasty served precisely as that paradigm.[57]

[53]Hallo, The Ancient Near East: A History, 60-61.

[54]Ibid., 61.

[55]See now W. W. Hallo, "Royal Titles from the Mesopotamian Periphery,"
Anatolian Studies 30 (1980) 189-95.

[56]See J. Krecher's discussion of this general question in J. Krecher and H.-P.
Müller, "Vergangenheitsinteresse in Mesopotamien und Israel," Saeculum 26
(1976), esp. pp. 14-30.

[57]Finkelstein, "Mesopotamian Historiography," 466.

In the development of "the complete requisite paradigm" the two principal figures of the Akkad dynasty, Sargon and Naram-Sin, became the archetypes of good and bad fortune, respectively, so that together they represented the entire range of success and failure with which any ruler, dynasty, or nation could readily identify. It was Naram-Sin's misfortune that he chanced to be the one principal figure around whom the images of the *Unheilsherrscher* tended to crystallize. Thereby, the real image of the man became distorted, sometimes almost beyond recognition.

We would be remiss if we did not mention, before concluding this survey, that Naram-Sin is by no means the only figure who is portrayed after the pattern of the *Unheilsherrscher* in the Mesopotamian historical-literary tradition. It would take us too far afield, however, to provide a comprehensive survey of this literature in the present study. Only a few remarks can be offered here. Ur III kings in particular are cast in this role. An Old Babylonian text portrays Amar-Sin in this fashion,[58] but as one would expect it is Ibbi-Sin, the last member of the dynasty, who in tradition became "the typical figure of an ill-starred king, remembered only for his captivity and death in a strange land."[59] The Ibbi-Sin lamentation,[60] now recognized to be part of a longer composition known as the "Lamentation over the Destruction of Ur and Sumer,"[61] recalls Ibbi-Sin's capture and deportation as a part of the tragic fate decreed by the Sumerian gods for the land of Sumer, culminating in the collapse of the nation and the removal of kingship to a foreign land. The same fate of Ibbi-Sin is recalled in an omen text,[62] and the omen literature also records the disintegration of the empire and its final demise. In this connection one might also mention the Ibbi-Sin correspondence, as portions of it were favorite texts for exercises in the Old Babylonian scribal schools, especially at Nippur. One of the preserved letters, from Ibbi-Sin to Puzur-Numushda, the governor of Kazallu,[63] has the former chastising the latter for inaction in the face of Ishbi-Irra's usurpation of

[58]P. Michalowski, "Amar-Su²ena and the Historical Tradition," in *Essays on the Ancient Near East in Memory of Jacob Joel Finkelstein*, ed. M. de Jong Ellis (Hamden, Conn: Archon, 1977) 155-57.

[59]C. J. Gadd in *CAH³*, 617.

[60]A. Falkenstein, "Die Ibbīsîn-Klage," *WO* 1/5 (1950) 377-84.

[61]S. N. Kramer, "Literary Texts from Ur VI, Part II," *Iraq* 25 (1963) 171-76, esp. pp. 171-72. English translation by Kramer in *ANET³*, 611-19.

[62]E. Weidner, "Historisches Material in der babylonischen Omina-Literatur," *Mitteilungen der altorientalischen Gesellschaft* 4 (1928) 236.

[63]A. Falkenstein, "Ibbīsîn—Išbi²erra," *ZA* 49 (1950) 59-79. English translation by Kramer in *ANET³*, 480-81.

authority over various Sumerian provinces. Ishbi-Irra, a non-Sumerian general under Ibbi-Sin who deviously undermined the king's authority and assumed it himself, maneuvered into an advantageous position so that, when Ibbi-Sin was captured and Ur was overthrown by the invading Elamites, he dared to claim that Ur's kingship had passed legitimately to him. That this same sentiment, viz. that Enlil had given the kingship to Ishbi-Irra, appears in the same letter, despite the fact that the letter goes on to express Ibbi-Sin's confidence in eventual deliverance from his troubles, suggests that the scribes who copied the correspondence have perhaps embellished it with flourishes that reflect the ultimate outcome.[64] Beyond the Old Babylonian period, Ibbi-Sin's memory is kept alive in the omen tradition,[64a] as is true also for Amar-Sin.[64b] In the later historical-literary texts, however, Shulgi is often recalled when the other Ur III kings are not. Indeed, there is a notable tendency to telescope the entire Ur III dynasty into this one reign, and, interestingly, we find that the portrait of the *Unheilsherrscher* becomes attached to Shulgi himself. This characterization appears in both the Weidner Chronicle and the Chronicle of Early Kings, indicating again that later tradition tended to affix the typology to the most illustrious, if not the most deserving, member of a dynasty. The aforementioned Shulgi "prophetic" text[65] indicates, however, that this negative characterization was not the only way that this Ur III king was portrayed in later tradition.[65a]

Testimony to our typology's longevity within cuneiform literature is provided by various materials from the Persian and Hellenistic periods. As examples, the texts which attribute the fall of the Neo-Babylonian empire to the sacrilege of Nabonidus may be cited. In addition to the

[64]The authenticity of Ibbi-Sin's correspondence has been questioned, primarily because of the literate style and the theological interpretation of matters here and there, but the letters are generally regarded as historically trustworthy, though perhaps stylistically reworked by the later scribes. Cf. Falkenstein in the article cited in the previous note (p. 73) and T. Jacobsen, "The Reign of Ibbī-Suen," *JCS* 7 (1953) 40, n. 45 (= *Toward the Image of Tammuz and Other Essays on Mesopotamian History and Culture*, 412, n. 45).

[64a]See Weidner, *Mitteilungen der altorientalischen Gesellschaft* 4 (1928) 236. For the later omen literature referring to the crumbling of Ibbi-Sin's kingdom, see n. 18 of Jacobsen's "Reign of Ibbī-Suen" (cited in the previous note).

[64b]I. Starr, "Notes on Some Published and Unpublished Historical Omens," *JCS* 29 (1977) 160-62.

[65]Borger, "Gott Marduk und Gott-König Šulgi."

[65a]For additional Middle Assyrian and late Neo-Babylonian omens and chronicles about Shulgi, see W. W. Hallo, "Simurrum and the Hurrian Frontier," *Revue Hittite et Asianique* 36 (1978) 75-76.

Cyrus cylinder[66] and the Nabonidus Verse Account,[67] both of which provide elaborate characterizations of Nabonidus as an *Unheilsherrscher*, we now have the Dynastic "prophecy," recently published by Grayson,[68] which extends the use of the typology to Hellenistic times. Although names of rulers do not appear in this latter text, the reigns of various dynasts from (apparently) Nabopolassar to the early Seleucid kings are depicted as "good" or "bad" as the rise and fall of dynasties is "predicted." The section which pertains to Nabonidus (ii, 11-16) describes his reign in negative terms, and seems to allude (ii, 14), as do the Verse Account and the Nabonidus Chronicle,[69] to the interruption of the Akitu festival during his reign. This is followed by the "prophecy" of the rise of Cyrus who "will remove him [Nabonidus] from his throne," and so forth. The Dynastic "prophecy" now corroborates the close relationship that had been suggested for the Akkadian "prophecies" in general and biblical apocalyptic literature, especially the Book of Daniel which also "predicts" the rise and fall of empires.[70] For our purposes, however, this latest text indicates that the typology of the *Unheilsherrscher* was being used in the composition of cuneiform texts until the very end of the period during which the biblical literature was being composed.

When the entire scope of Mesopotamian historiography is considered, however, it was Naram-Sin who was cast in the role of the *Unheilsherrscher* more frequently and over a longer period of time than any other figure. However different his fortune may have been in history, he was fated to be remembered in tradition as the archetypal *Unheilsherrscher*.

---

[66]F. H. Weissbach, *Die Keilinschriften der Achämeniden* (Vorderasiatische Bibliothek 3; Leipzig, 1911), pp. 2ff. English translation by Oppenheim in *ANET*[3], 315-16. For the new fragment of the cylinder, see C. B. F. Walker, "A Recently Identified Fragment of the Cyrus Cylinder," *Iran* 10 (1972) 158-59 and P.-R. Berger, "Der Kyros-Zylinder mit dem Zusatzfragment BIN II Nr. 32 und die akkadischen Personennamen im Danielbuch," *ZA* 64 (1974) 192-234.

[67]For bibliography see Grayson, *Assyrian and Babylonian Chronicles*, 57, n. 62. English translation by Oppenheim in *ANET*[3], 312-15.

[68]A. K. Grayson, *Babylonian Historical-Literary Texts*, 13-37.

[69]This is a recurring motif in the Nabonidus Chronicle, for which see now Grayson, *Assyrian and Babylonian Chronicles*, 104-11.

[70]The relationship was proposed by Grayson, "Akkadian Prophecies," and developed more fully by W. W. Hallo, "Akkadian Apocalypses," *IEJ* 16 (1966) 231-42. Cf., most recently, W. W. Hallo, "The Expansion of Cuneiform Literature," *Jubilee Volume* (The American Academy of Jewish Research; Jerusalem, 1980) 307-22, esp. pp. 313-16 and notes 25-39.

III. JEROBOAM AND THE BIBLICAL TRADITION

When we turn to the biblical materials, we find that a similar contrast exists between the Jeroboam as depicted in certain older, more or less contemporaneous sources, and the Jeroboam portrayed in later, especially deuteronomistic, tradition. Although the Jeroboam of history bears little likeness to the Naram-Sin of history, we shall see that the Jeroboam of tradition is Israel's historiographical counterpart to the Naram-Sin of Mesopotamia's *Unheilsherrscher* traditions. Our task now is to examine this relationship more closely.

At the outset, one must acknowledge that any attempt at comparisons is confronted immediately by an obvious and important difference between the Mesopotamian and biblical historiographical materials. Whereas the former exist in more or less separate and discrete genres and texts—chronicles, pseudo-autobiographies, "prophecies," etc.—with only occasional indications of the influence of one genre on the development of another, on the biblical side we find that the "raw materials," so to speak, have been preserved only to the extent that they are now a part of extensive, chronologically arranged, historiographical works, such as the Deuteronomistic History. Fortunately, however, as is often the case in biblical historiographical works, certain unmistakable remnants from the raw materials concerning Jeroboam survive so that it is possible to reconstruct at least the general outlines of how he was viewed in history and tradition before the time of the Deuteronomist.

As stated in our introductory remarks, the Deuteronomist's connection of Jeroboam's "sins" with the fall of Israel is without parallel outside the Book of Kings. This is all the more remarkable in view of the fact that the tradition of the condemnation of Jeroboam began, as we shall see, during his own lifetime and was traded over several centuries in different forms, some of which took shape before and some after the Deuteronomist, and yet only he blamed Israel's national calamity on Jeroboam's "sins." Add to this the fact that historical traditions more or less contemporaneous with the king portrayed him as an Israelite hero, and a picture not unlike Naram-Sin's fate in history and tradition begins to emerge. After examining the materials which provide a positive assessment of Jeroboam, our procedure will be to trace the development of the negative portrait in the context of the biblical traditions, on the one hand, and to set this portrait in the larger context of the Mesopotamian typology of the *Unheilsherrscher*, on the other hand. This will enable us to highlight points of contrast as well as similarity both within the biblical traditions and between those traditions and the Mesopotamian materials cited earlier. This approach will avoid the pitfalls of superficial comparison, and will allow us to see the Deuteronomist's portrait of Jeroboam in its proper context.[71]

The Deuteronomist's account of Jeroboam's activities, from his aborted rebellion as an official in Solomon's administration to his actions as the first king of Israel, is related in a complex of materials (1 Kgs 11:26-14:20) which, fortunately, preserve a variety of traditional perspectives on the course of events. To be sure, the Deuteronomist by means of selection, arrangement, and commentary has cast the whole complex in a deuteronomistic mold, but it is still possible to identify the substance, if not the details, of the sources that were used. They include historical reports, extracts from archival texts, and prophetic oracles and legends.[72]

It is now generally recognized that 1 Kgs 12:1-19 preserves an historical report about the secession of northern Israel from the Davidic kingdom. The account's starkly realistic references to the oppressiveness of Solomon's rule and the unwillingness of Rehoboam to make concessions to the discontented north Israelites have frequently been noted. This realism has led some to compare the account with other examples of early Israelite historiography, notably the throne succession narrative (2 Samuel 9-20 and 1 Kings 1-2),[73] while others who do not press this comparison have acknowledged that the account "bears the clear stamp of reliability and a historical sense corresponding to the really important political situation described."[74] In any case, the account's attention to the political and economic factors that led to the secession contrasts sharply with the prophecy-fulfillment context in which it has been set by the Deuteronomist, who says "for the Lord had given this turn to the affair, in order that the word he had spoken by Ahijah of Shiloh to Jeroboam son of Nebat might be fulfilled" (1 Kgs 12:15; cf. 11:29-39).

[71]Cf. W. W. Hallo, "Biblical History in its Near Eastern Setting: The Contextual Approach," in *Scripture in Context: Essays on the Comparative Method*, ed. by C. D. Evans, W. W. Hallo, and J. B. White (Pittsburgh Theological Monograph Series 34; Pittsburgh: Pickwick, 1980) 1-26 for a recent discussion of methodology which has the same goal in view: "The intention is not to repudiate the comparative approach, but to define it, refine and broaden it, notably by wedding it to the 'contrastive approach.' The resulting blend can perhaps avoid both of these somewhat controversial labels and qualify instead as a 'contextual approach' " (p. 2).

[72]Justification for identifying these sources will be provided in the discussion that follows.

[73]I. Plein, "Erwägungen zur Überlieferung von I Reg. 11:26-14:20," *ZAW* 78 (1966) 8-24. Cf. Noth, *Könige*, 270-71 and E. Würthwein, *Das Erste Buch der Könige* (Das Alte Testament Deutsch 11/1; Göttingen: Vandenhoeck & Ruprecht, 1977) 150.

[74]Gray, *I & II Kings*, 299.

The preceding chapter in Kings seems to preserve portions of a related historical report about Jeroboam's rebellion under Solomon and subsequent refuge-taking in Egypt under the protection of Shishak (1 Kgs 11:26-28, 40).[75] From this report, incomplete as it is, we learn that Solomon had put Jeroboam in charge of the entire *sêbel* of the "house of Joseph," i.e., of the temporary levy-force drawn from the north Israelite tribes (as distinct from the permanent, institutionalized force of corvée-workers [*mas-ᶜobêd*] drawn from the Canaanite population).[76] While serving in this official capacity, Jeroboam rebelled against Solomon and fled to Egypt when Solomon attempted to kill him. A recent study, which sets Solomon's internal policies in the ambit of his relationships with Phoenicia and Egypt, has plausibly suggested that Shishak's (Sheshonq I's) accession in Egypt brought about a rapid deterioration in Solomonic-Egyptian relations and that Jeroboam hoped to gain Egyptian support in his move against Solomon.[77] But whatever Jeroboam's ultimate hopes may have been, this historical report, like the one previously discussed, preserves the memory of northern discontentment over Solomon's policies. It is possible that the continuation of this account is preserved in 1 Kgs 12:2-3a, 20 where Jeroboam's return from Egypt and subsequent elevation to the kingship over north Israel are reported.[78] If so, Jeroboam is presented as nothing less than an Israelite hero who champions the cause of his people, and when the time comes for selecting their own king he apparently has no rival.

These early historical reports, which may have originated within a generation of the events depicted, are supplemented by an account of prophetic designation in 1 Kgs 11:29ff. by which Jeroboam receives divine authorization to lead the secessionist cause. Although the account

[75]Cf. Würthwein, *Das Erste Buch der Könige*, 141.

[76]Cf. T. N. D. Mettinger, *Solomonic State Officials: A Study of the Civil Government Officials of the Israelite Monarchy* (Coniectanea Biblica—Old Testament Series 5; Lund: C. W. K. Gleerups, 1971) 128-39 for an analysis of the technical terms, and p. 138 for Jeroboam's position. Mettinger draws no conclusion as to whether Jeroboam was in charge of the Israelite levy from all of the northern tribes or only Ephraim and Manasseh (as "house of Joseph" might indicate).

[77]B. Halpern, "Sectionalism and the Schism," *JBL* 93 (1974) 519-32. For the possibility that Jeroboam could have introduced the Solomonic model of a twelve-fold division of the levy to Shishak, see Alberto R. Green, "Israelite Influence at Shishak's Court?" *BASOR* 233 (1979) 59-62.

[78]Reading *wayyāšob . . . mimmiṣrayim* ("and he returned from Egypt") instead of *wayyēšeb . . . bᵉmiṣrayim* ("and he dwelt in Egypt") in v 2b as attested in 2 Chr 10:2 and various versions. Cf. Gray, *I & II Kings*, 301 and note a. Vv 2-3a, as is often noted, intrude into the report in 1 Kgs 12:1-19 and appear to link backward with the account in 11:26-28, 40 and forward with 12:20.

as we have it has undergone considerable deuteronomistic expansion, it is possible that at least vv 29-31, relating the incident of the mantle-rending, preserves a portion of the original tradition.[79] The prophet who designates Jeroboam is Ahijah who hails from Shiloh. Being from Shiloh, which had once been an important Israelite tribal center when the ark of the covenant was located there, Ahijah may have entertained hopes that Jeroboam would select Shiloh for the religious center of his new kingdom.[80] Despite the fact that Ahijah later turned against Jeroboam, as reflected in his oracle of doom in 1 Kings 14, this does not remove the obvious confidence that underlies the designation scene in 1 Kgs 11:29-31(32). Thus, this prophetic account provides another glimpse of old traditions which portrayed Jeroboam as an Israelite hero devoted to the cause of his people. We may be confident that this assessment was shared by many north Israelites in the years leading up to and following the secession.

This mainly favorable, pre-deuteronomistic depiction of Jeroboam made a lasting impression on later tradition, as reflexes of it are still found in the Septuagint's alternative account of Jeroboam (Codex Vaticanus, 3 Kgdms 12:24a-z). Although scholars are sharply divided on the historical value of the alternative account, and its literary relationship to the Hebrew account in Kings,[81] more than a few have argued that despite its later literary form it preserves authentic echoes of early Jeroboam traditions.[82] We find in this account some additional information which can be said to enhance Jeroboam's reputation, such as the claim that he had three hundred chariots prior to his escape to Egypt (v 24b) and that the Egyptian king gave a daughter in marriage to Jeroboam (v 24e). While this latter detail may derive from a confusion of Jeroboam with Hadad, another rebel against Solomon (1 Kgs 11:14-25, esp. v 19),

---

[79]Cf. Plein, "Erwägungen," 18-20; J. Debus, *Die Sünde Jerobeams: Studien zur Darstellung Jerobeams und der Geschichte des Nordreichs in der deuteronomistischen Geschichtsschreibung* (FRLANT 93; Göttingen: Vandenhoeck & Ruprecht, 1967) 10; and Gray, *I & II Kings*, 288 (who includes vv 29-32 in the account which "may be drawn from the annals of the kings of Israel or . . . from a prophetic legend centring [*sic*] upon Ahijah and preserved in prophetic circles").

[80]Cf. A. Caquot, "Ahiyya de Silo et Jéroboam Ier," *Sem* 11 (1961) 17-27, esp. p. 25.

[81]For the most recent discussion and an assessment of the various views, see R. P. Gordon, "The Second Septuagint Account of Jeroboam: History or Midrash?" *VT* 25 (1975) 368-93.

[82]Cf. A. T. Olmstead, "Source Study and the Biblical Text," *AJSL* 30 (1913) 1-35; Debus, *Die Sünde Jerobeams*, 80-87; H. Seebass, "Zur Königserhebung Jerobeams I," *VT* 17 (1967) 323-33; M. Aberbach and L. Smolar, "Jeroboam's Rise to Power," *JBL* 88 (1969) 69-72; and Gray, *I & II Kings*, 310-11.

it has the effect, as pointed out by Aberbach and Smolar, of making Jeroboam a "worthy antagonist" of Solomon.[83] These and other details, it seems, are reflexes of a favorable portrait of Jeroboam, portions of which we have seen in the traditions discussed earlier. In this respect, then, what has been said about Naram-Sin must also be said about Jeroboam: the portrait of the *Unheilsherrscher* conflicts with other traditions, both early and late, about the fortunes of the king.

If we turn now to the origins of the tradition that portrayed Jeroboam as Israel's archetypal *Unheilsherrscher*, our attention is drawn to the narrative and oracle complex in 1 Kgs 14:1-18. As we now have it, this passage narrates an incident about Jeroboam's sending his wife, in disguise, to "seek a word" from the prophet Ahijah concerning their son, Abijah, who was ill. The answer given by the prophet, in the present form of the text, is a prediction of the child's imminent death and a prophecy of doom on the house of Jeroboam as well as the whole kingdom of Israel. All of this will transpire, we are told, because of the "sins" committed by Jeroboam which led Israel astray (v. 16). Here the main motifs of the typology appear together—the king's religious offenses bring condemnation on himself and ruin to his family and nation—but to determine whether these motifs appeared together from the beginning we must inquire about the tradition-history of this complex.

Although scholars are agreed that 1 Kgs 14:1-18 has received its present form from the Deuteronomist, there is equal assurance that the account preserves relics of an old tradition associated with Ahijah. Noth has suggested that the basic Ahijah tradition included not only the prediction that the sick child would die but also the oracle of doom on the house of Jeroboam.[84] This view, which is supported now by Gray,[85] gains much favor from the observation that the oracle of doom on Jeroboam's house (vv 10-11) is cast in "graphic language" quite unlike the stock phraseology of the Deuteronomist.[86] The oracle states:

> Therefore, I will bring evil to the house of Jeroboam and cut off from Jeroboam every male, whatever his status,[87] and I will consume the house

---

[83]Aberbach and Smolar, "Jeroboam's Rise to Power," 72.

[84]Noth, *Könige*, 311, 316-17.

[85]Gray, *I & II Kings*, 333.

[86]Ibid., 333, 337-38.

[87]The difficult phrase ʿāṣūr wᵉʿāzūb ("whatever his status") is rendered "bond and free" in RSV and JPS and "whether still under the protection of the family or not" in NEB. The phraseology chosen here follows Cross, "The Themes of the Book of Kings," 280. For a discussion of the various proposals, see Gray, *I & II Kings*, 337-38.

of Jeroboam as a man burns up dung, until it is all gone. As for him who belongs to Jeroboam who dies in the city, the dogs shall eat; as for him who dies in the field, the birds of the air shall eat.

In addition, we find that the same oracle is also adapted for Jehu ben Hanani's condemnation of Baasha (1 Kgs 16:4) and again for Elijah's censure of Ahab (1 Kgs 21:24). It is recalled once more by the prophet who anointed Jehu to supplant the house of Ahab. Significantly, the several occurrences of the oracle are used to announce divine judgment on the first three dynasties of the Northern Kingdom, though in each case the Deuteronomist has expounded the condemnation differently.[88] Whether this indicates that a cycle of dynastic doom oracles circulated among early northern prophets, or whether it was the Deuteronomist who adapted Ahijah's oracle to the other situations, is debatable. It seems likely, however, that this tradition was well-known in prophetic circles so that it could be recalled when later prophets had their turn at condemning royal dynasties, as they frequently did.[89] At the very least, it is virtually certain that this version of the oracle pre-dates the Deuteronomist, and most likely goes back to the Shilonite prophet himself. Ahijah had good reason to turn against Jeroboam, especially if he had hoped, as suggested above, that the new king would make Shiloh the religious center of his kingdom. Those hopes had been dashed by Jeroboam's selection of Dan and, especially, Bethel. The prophet's motivation for the doom oracle, assuming that it was stated in the original tradition, has been unfortunately lost to the stock phraseology substituted by the Deuteronomist at this point.

In this old Ahijah tradition, then, we see the emergence of the tendency in biblical tradition to portray Jeroboam as Israel's archetypal *Unheilsherrscher*. This tradition, as suggested above, became firmly embedded in the memory of later prophets and thus served as the chief vehicle for transmitting the unfavorable picture of Israel's first king until the time of the Deuteronomist. There remains a gap of more than two hundred years, however, between its reflexes in the doom oracles of the ninth century prophets and its revival by the Deuteronomist in the late seventh century. Surprisingly, the fall of later dynasties and the fall of Israel in the meantime did not spark others, not even the great prophets, to revive the tradition. But the tradition was not forgotten, as is indicated by the Deuteronomist's development and extension of its main features to connect the fall of Israel with Jeroboam's "sins." The

[88]Cf. P. R. Ackroyd, "The Vitality of the Word of God in the Old Testament," *ASTI* 1 (Leiden: E. J. Brill, 1962) 7-23.

[89]Cf. Gray, *I & II Kings*, 358: ("probably the relics of a prophetic source from North Israel on which the Deuteronomistic compiler drew").

tradition also survived in the Septuagint's alternative account (v. 24m), but here we find again the older form—the announcement of doom on the house of Jeroboam alone (and, interestingly, with no reasons given!). Thus, the Deuteronomist's special treatment appears all the more distinctive within its total biblical context. Only the Deuteronomist placed the blame for the demise of Israel on its first king! Although Jeroboam experienced a notable setback (Ahijah's turn-about) during his own lifetime which helps explain the early attachment of the *Unheils-herrscher* tradition to him, the typology in its fullest (deuteronomistic) form has little, if anything, to do with the historical realities that underlie the earliest stages of the tradition.

The Deuteronomist's negative assessment of Jeroboam, of course, rests on grounds much different from those of Ahijah's condemnation. This is especially evident in the Deuteronomist's objections to virtually every aspect of Jeroboam's religious program—the iconography, the cult places, the priests, the religious calendar, etc.—about which we are informed by the account in 1 Kgs 12:26-33. Although the account is overlaid with the Deuteronomist's polemical judgments, there is good reason to believe that the details pertaining to Jeroboam's cultic program are essentially reliable; some have suggested that they have been taken from an archival source.[90] The Deuteronomist's purpose in this account is to show the extent to which Jeroboam's religious establishment was "apostate," so he carefully singles out each of its main features and pronounces his judgment on it. The golden calves, their placement in Bethel and Dan, the appointment of priests "from the whole range of the people" (*miqṣôt hāᶜām*), the observance of the fall festival in the eighth month instead of the seventh, etc. are all mentioned only to be condemned. Thus, the account preserves valuable information despite (or because of!) the polemical purpose which it serves. The basis for the Deuteronomist's judgments, as generally acknowledged, was a commitment to the cultic order prescribed in the torah scroll (i.e., proto-Deuteronomy) "found" during Josiah's reign. Adopted in solemn ceremony, the scroll served the important function of sanctioning the king's religio-political program. The Deuteronomist used the scroll's religious requirements as the underlying principles of his historiographical work which served as propaganda, official or otherwise, for Josiah's program.[91] In this work Jeroboam becomes the symbol of "what is wrong in the eyes of the Lord," a paradigm of the ruler who, because of cultic offenses, brings doom and destruction to himself and

---

[90]Cf. H. Donner, "The Collapse of the Davidic-Solomonic Empire," in *Israelite and Judean History*, 383.

[91]For an excellent statement of this view, see Cross, "The Themes of the Book of Kings."

his family, and, more importantly, to the entire nation. No doubt this presentation of matters would have been regarded as strange and unwarranted by the majority of Jeroboam's subjects, and presumably even the likes of Ahijah would have thought it off-base and extreme.[92] Such is usually the case when standards that belong to another time and place are applied in the manner done by the Deuteronomist. From the late seventh-century perspective, however, and given the Deuteronomist's propagandistic objectives, Jeroboam's cultic measures become the "sins" that undermine a nation's integrity and lead to its ruin. It happened in the case of Israel, it could happen again in Judah's case—that is, unless everyone rallies around the program of Josiah. Thus Josiah, like his prototype David, serves as the paradigm of Jeroboam's opposite; they do "what is right in the eyes of the Lord."

The Deuteronomist thus brings all the motifs of our typology together and with them constructs his striking historiographic theme: the fall of Israel was due to the "sins" of Jeroboam. A similar claim, it will be recalled, is made in the Mesopotamian materials about Naram-Sin's alleged religious offenses and the end of Akkad. True, there are significant differences between the two: unlike Naram-Sin, Jeroboam is the first member of his "dynasty" and nothing like the telescoping of the Gutian invasion into the reign of Naram-Sin occurs in the Deuteronomist's scheme. However, the same result, viz., illustration of a cause-effect relationship, is achieved by the Deuteronomist in another way: he persistently maintains that none of the successors abandoned Jeroboam's sinful ways so that in the end he can say that Israel's collapse was caused by Jeroboam's offenses, a telescoping from the other direction. And, further, the Deuteronomist's standards by which the actions of Jeroboam are judged as sinful have this much in common with the standards presupposed by the Weidner Chronicle: they are cultic requirements and are anachronistically applied. The result is a certain distortion of history, but produced with a clear purpose, viz., to warn others of the dire consequences of neglecting the official cult of the day.

The practice of depicting reigns as "good" or "bad," which has been noted in the Akkadian "prophecies" as well as the Weidner

---

[92]When set in its tenth century, north Israelite context, Jeroboam's religious program in each of its details can be seen as an accommodation to the religious views and customs of his subjects. Rather than being an innovator who introduced "sinful" practices, as the Deuteronomist claims, Jeroboam was in fact more of an archaizer. For this view of matters, cf. the following: S. Talmon, "Divergences in Calendar-Reckoning in Ephraim and Judah," *VT* 8 (1958) 48-74; F. M. Cross, "The Priestly Houses of Early Israel," in the book cited above (n. 51) 195-215, esp. 198-99; B. Halpern, "Levitic Participation in the Reform Cult of Jeroboam I," *JBL* 95 (1976) 31-42; and H. Motzki, "Ein Beitrag zum Problem des Stierkultes in der Religionsgeschichte Israels," *VT* 25 (1975) 470-85.

Chronicle, is also characteristic of the Deuteronomist's whole historio-graphic enterprise. The reign of virtually every king is depicted in one way or the other, and prophetic oracles and legends have been liberally used to assist in the effort. In this regard, too, we find that the treatment of Jeroboam is paradigmatic for the rest of the work. Apart from the Ahijah traditions which the Deuteronomist has used to support his well-known prophecy-fulfillment scheme, we find in 1 Kings 13 a prophetic legend which employs a striking *vaticinium ex eventu* to depict the consequences of Jeroboam's "bad" reign. A son will be born to the house of David by the name of Josiah, according to a certain man of God, who will destroy Jeroboam's altar at Bethel and sacrifice upon it the priests of the *bāmôt* (vv 2-3). Although many scholars have claimed that this entire legend, which goes ahead to tell about an encounter between this same man of God and a prophet of Bethel, is a post-deuteronomistic addition to the Book of Kings,[93] a recent study by Lemke has persuasively argued that 1 Kings 13 is another "pivotal passage" in the Deuteronomistic History which, like other such passages, has an important place in the structure and theology of the whole work.[94] This passage, as Lemke has correctly noted, draws upon older prophetic traditions[95] which the Deuteronomist has creatively adapted for his own purposes. In particular, the prophetic criticism of the Bethelite cult becomes a condemnation of Jeroboam's altar at Bethel and a "prediction" that it would be destroyed by Josiah. This reworking of the prophetic tradition in the light of Josiah's activity at Bethel (2 Kgs 23:15) makes it possible for the Deuteronomist to claim that Josiah's action was another instance of the fulfillment of prophecy. Thus, the Deuteronomist uses the prophetic legend to show that "bad" reigns have predictable consequences, and the same is implied for "good" reigns.

In view of the Deuteronomist's overall purpose, the *vaticinia ex eventu* used in the prophecy-fulfillment scheme can be seen as an attempt to establish the credibility of a particular view of history. This was needed to legitimate the claims being made about the rightness of

[93]This was the view especially of earlier scholars such as Wellhausen, Benzinger, and Eissfeldt. More recently it has been espoused by Debus, *Die Sünde Jerobeams*, 35, n. 10.

[94]W. E. Lemke, "The Way of Obedience: I Kings 13 and the Structure of the Deuteronomistic History," in *Magnalia Dei: The Mighty Acts of God* (=G. E. Wright Memorial Volume), ed. F. M. Cross, W. E. Lemke, and P. D. Miller, Jr. (Garden City, NY: Doubleday & Company, 1976) 301-26.

[95]Two prophetic stories are combined in the chapter: one is about a man of God from Judah who came to Bethel and denounced the cult he found in that city (vv 1-10); the other is about an encounter between this same man of God and an old prophet of Bethel which illustrates the importance of obedience to the divine will, especially in the face of challenges (vv 11-32).

Josiah's program. Whereas the way of the *Unheilsherrscher* Jeroboam led to the ruin of the sister kingdom, the opposite way, symbolized by "David" and represented in the policies of Josiah, will lead to Judah's ultimate well-being.[96] The historiographic significance of the figure of "David" lies beyond the scope of this study, but the themes and literary patterns employed by the Deuteronomist suggest that David is portrayed as Israel's archetypal *Heilsherrscher,* much as Sargon of Akkad and other "ideal" rulers are remembered in Mesopotamian tradition.[97] With the juxtaposition of both typologies, the Deuteronomist's work was a summons to his contemporaries to learn from the past, to appropriate the lessons derived from "good" and "bad" rulers, and to respond with favor to the challenges offered by Josiah. "No king before him had turned to the Lord as he did, with all his heart and soul and strength, following the whole law of Moses" (2 Kgs 23:25a).[98]

Finally, we find that Jeroboam is not the only figure who has been cast in the mold of the *Unheilsherrscher* in the Book of Kings. The most notable case is that of Manasseh who, like Jeroboam, is held responsible for his own nation's ruin.[99] As Cross has observed, the account dealing

---

[96]Cf. the discussion of the theme of the faithfulness of David in the Book of Kings offered by Cross, "The Themes of the Book of Kings," which, as he puts it, "reaches its climax in the reform of Josiah. . . . We have been prepared for this climax. Josiah, as already predicted, becomes the protagonist of the drama, extirpating the counter-cultus of Jeroboam at Bethel" (p. 283).

[97]For now see B. Lewis's suggestive observations on "the career of the idealized ruler" comparing how later tradition remembered Sargon, Moses, David, and Cyrus (*The Sargon Legend,* 275-76).

[98]The latter part of the verse is from the hand of the exilic redactor, looking back as it does on the succession of rulers after Josiah.

[99]Cross rightly argues ("The Themes of the Book of Kings," 285-86) that this treatment of Manasseh must be attributed to the exilic redactor, not the Deuteronomist of the Josianic period. If it were the work of the latter, the sense of hope and optimism that pervades the account of Josiah's reign would not be present. To the same exilic hand that makes Manasseh into Judah's *Unheilsherrscher* must also be attributed the present form of Huldah's prophecy in 2 Kgs 22:15-20 and the appendage to the account of Josiah's reign in 2 Kgs 23:26-27. M. Smith, however, contends that the final fall of Jerusalem in 587 is not explained by the "sins of Manasseh" in Kings; rather, he thinks Kings "probably attributes [the calamity of 587] to the wickedness of *Zedekiah* (11 24, 19f.; according to the Targum, of Zedekiah and of Jehoiakim)" ("The Veracity of Ezekiel, the Sins of Manasseh, and Jeremiah 44, 18," *ZAW* 87 [1975] 14). However, in view of Smith's acknowledgement that the Book of Kings does use the "sins of Manasseh" to explain the defeat of Josiah (2 Kgs 23:26-27) and the rebellion of Jehoiakim and resulting disaster of 597 (2 Kgs 24:3-4), one may question whether his interpretation of 2 Kgs 24:19-20 is not too dependent on the evidence of the Targum.

with Manasseh in 2 Kings 21 "is modeled almost exactly on the section treating the fall of Samaria."[100] Manasseh's great wickedness, "not to mention the sin into which he led Judah" (v 16), will be answered by great disaster to come upon Jerusalem and Judah. Again, we find that Yahweh had spoken warnings through his servants the prophets, but to no avail. Manasseh is thus portrayed as Judah's *Unheilsherrscher*, however different this may be from other portraits in the Bible (cf. 2 Chronicles 33 where Manasseh is a repentant figure) or from more objective modern assessments of his reign.[101]

IV. CONCLUDING REMARKS

This study has called attention to the typology of the *Unheils-herrscher* in Mesopotamian and biblical historiography, especially as reflected in the traditions about Naram-Sin and Jeroboam. By high-lighting the main features of the typology in the two historiographical traditions, a number of similarities have been revealed. Both Naram-Sin and Jeroboam are cast in the role of the archetypal *Unheilsherrscher*. In both cases, the traditions emphasize the ruler's misfortune or condemna-tion and focus on a general calamity that overtakes the dynasty and nation, claiming that all is the result of certain religious offenses on the part of the king. The religious offenses that are alleged in each case vary from text to text, depending on the propensities of the scribe or tradent, and, in both cases, the cultic order presupposed by the allegations in some of the texts is anachronistically imposed on the time of the king. The typology is thus a complex of motifs by which great misfortune is understood according to a principle of retribution and, as such, lends itself to the interpretation of other events and rulers. Naram-Sin and Jeroboam, however, remain the archetypal figures. That this portrayal of matters conflicts sharply with other traditions, both early and late, that have been preserved about the two rulers is testimony to the literary conventions and tendencies in both historiographical traditions and a reminder to the modern historian that objective reconstructions must take into account the multi-faceted nature and functions of the native traditions.

As for the typology itself, its appearance in both Mesopotamian and biblical contexts in a variety of materials over a period of several centuries and its adaptation, by assuming changing literary forms, to the type and function of the material in which it occurs indicate something of its value to the native historiographers. It is used primarily to explain the misfortunes that befall royal dynasties and the great calamities that

[100]"The Themes of the Book of Kings," 285.
[101]See, e.g., C. D. Evans, "Judah's Foreign Policy from Hezekiah to Josiah," in the collection cited above (n. 71) 157-78, esp. pp. 166-69.

plague nations, especially invasions and revolutions that change peoples' destinies. When coupled with a schematic pattern of "good" and "bad" reigns, it assumes propagandistic functions, perhaps to legitimate religio-political programs which, in their own way, are designed to change the course of events, to break the pattern of misfortune and defeat.

The typology is thus a literary convention which, because of its association with the momentous experiences in the life of a people, would seem to belong as naturally in Israel as in Mesopotamia. Hence, it is surprising that the typology is not more widely diffused in the biblical traditions. Its occurrence in the deuteronomistic materials is no doubt due to the courtly interests and setting of the circle responsible for transmitting and preserving this historiographical tradition. Court scribes, because of the nature of their occupation, would have had occasion to draw upon and adapt for their purposes a wealth of ideas and literary patterns from neighboring cultural traditions, as many studies have established.[102] The typology of the *Unheilsherrscher* should be seen as another example of this phenomenon, indicating once again the value of studying the biblical traditions in their ancient Near Eastern context.

[102]See, e.g., Weinfeld, *Deuteronomy and the Deuteronomic School.*

MICAH AND THE PROBLEM OF CONTINUITIES AND DISCONTINUITIES IN PROPHECY

W. ROBERT McFADDEN

Bridgewater College

I. INTRODUCTION

Suggesting that one will discuss the Hebrew prophets and the book of Micah in the context of the continuities and discontinuities in ancient Near Eastern prophecy appears to be an audacious undertaking. Many commentators regard Micah as a compendium of literary units that span five centuries and as "a source book for observing the development of Hebrew thought."[1] The dating of many of the units within the book is still a major problem for those who would analyze the contents. At the same time, the term "prophecy" seems to cover different kinds of activity in the ancient Near East, including ecstasy-producing rituals and the delivering of oracles, and different kinds of literature, including perhaps both prophetic and apocalyptic genres of writing.[2]

---

[1]Rolland E. Wolfe, "Micah," *The Interpreter's Bible* 6 (ed. George A. Buttrick; New York: Abingdon, 1952-57) 900.

[2]Cf. the following comments regarding one genre of materials in the cuneiform texts: "The genre of Akkadian literature here called 'Prophecy' includes texts which are descriptions of the reigns of unnamed kings cast in the form of predictions" (A. K. Grayson and W. G. Lambert, "Akkadian Prophecies," *JCS* 18 [1964] 7); "The texts . . . show an essential affinity with biblical apocalyptics and should henceforth be considered in any investigation of the origins of this relatively late phenomenon in the spectrum of Biblical literary genres" (W. W. Hallo, "Akkadian Apocalypses," *IEJ* 16 [1966] 242); "The 'prophecies' must, I believe, be considered simply a peculiar part of the vast Mesopotamian omen tradition, from which the 'prophecies' . . . differ only because they lacked protases (i.e. a clause 'if such-and-such occurs')" (Robert D. Biggs, "More Babylonian 'Prophecies,'" *Iraq* 29 [1967] 117); "I think it best to maintain the general term 'prophecies' for these texts since the word does not necessarily imply Biblical prophecy. But the term 'apocalypses' does imply a very specific genre" (A. K. Grayson, *Babylonian Historical-Literary Texts* [Toronto: University of Toronto Press, 1975] 22, n. 35); and "Although we cannot yet rightfully speak of these texts as forming a genre, there can be little

The emergence of the literary prophets in the eighth century B.C.E. remains one of the intriguing mysteries of Israelite and Judean history. As one of those first literary figures, Micah will provide a focal point in this examination of both the uniqueness of the Classical Prophets and their relationship to the context in which they emerge. We begin with a discussion of prophecy in Hebrew history and in the ancient Near East as a means of gaining a better understanding of Micah.

II. PROPHECY IN THE BIBLE

Within the Bible itself, the common word for prophet, *nābî*, is used to refer to diverse personages. A young prophet, designated by Elisha, secretly anoints Jehu king over Israel. Jehu's companions at Ramoth-gilead ask him later, "Why did this mad fellow come to you?" (2 Kgs 9:11). The use of the term, "mad" or "frenzied," also occurs when Shemaiah charges, in a letter from exile in Babylon, that Jeremiah is a "madman who prophesies" in the house of YHWH (Jer 29:26).[3] The term *nābî* is also used, however, to refer to the outstanding leaders in the early history of the Hebrews: Abraham (Gen 20:7), Moses (Deut 34:10), Miriam (Ex 15:20), Deborah (Jg 4:4), and Samuel (1 Sam 3:20).

The term *nābî* is used most frequently by the dominant Deuteronomic and Ephraimite tradition regarding prophecy in Israel. It is a tradition that is expressed in a passage in Deuteronomy 18.[4] Divination and diviners are condemned, and prophets are recognized as consisting of both those who speak the word which YHWH has given them, and those who speak a word which YHWH has not given them.[5] Knowing which is which is not a simple matter.[6]

---

doubt that more and more texts of a similar nature will turn up" (Herman Hunger and Stephen A. Kaufman, "A New Akkadian Prophecy Text," *JAOS*, 95 [1975] 375). The comments above are cited to indicate the fluidity of the term prophecy. For a recent statement of the significance and meaning of the cuneiform texts involved, see W. G. Lambert, *The Background of Jewish Apocalyptic* (London: The Athlone Press, 1978).

[3]The term, "mad" or "frenzied," is also used in Hos 9:7. In contrast to Mic 3:8, where Micah claims to be filled with the Spirit of the LORD, here Hosea declares "the prophet is a fool, the man of the spirit is mad," and claims, as does Micah, that the prophets are misleading the people.

[4]For a discussion of the Ephraimite Tradition, see Robert R. Wilson, *Prophecy and Society in Ancient Israel* (Philadelphia: Fortress Press, 1980) 135-252. See pages 156-66 for a discussion of this passage (Deut 18) in the context of the Deuteronomic tradition. Cf. his article, "Early Israelite Prophecy," *Interpretation* 32 (1978) 3-16.

[5]Cf. Deut 13:1-5 and 2 Kgs 17:13-14.

[6]For a discussion of the issues, see A. S. van der Woude, "Micah in Dispute with the Pseudo-Prophets," *VT* 19 (1969) 244-60.

Moreover, there are some practices noted in the Bible which are related to divination, but which are not condemned. Joseph uses a cup for divining (Gen 44:4-5) and Saul cast lots (1 Sam 14:41-42). Before he fights the Philistines at Mount Gilboa, Saul consults dreams, the Urim and Thummin (sacred lots) and the prophets. Receiving no answer from YHWH, he then consults the medium at Endor (1 Sam 28:6-25). While consulting a medium was specifically prohibited by the Deuteronomists (Deut 18:11), it seemed that "casting the lots" was an accepted procedure to secure an answer from YHWH.[7]

Although the prophet Micah is a prophet in the Judean tradition,[8] he shares the Deuteronomic attitude toward divination. At one point, prophets, seers and diviners are all named as "those who lead my people astray" (Mic 3:5-7). One could see the major distinction to be between those who speak the Word of YHWH and those who do not, or between those who practice divination as in the other nations and those who prophesy in Israel according to accepted norms.

There are other phenomena subsumed under the term prophecy in the Bible. The phrase, "band of prophets," is used to describe the ecstatics that are prominent in the narratives about Samuel and Saul (1 Sam 10:5-6 and 10-13). Saul is instructed by Samuel to join momentarily one of these groups (1 Sam 10:6). Another similar story about Saul and a company of prophets (1 Sam 19:20-24) indicates again that dancing, music and frenzied behavior often characterized the bands of prophets.

In the cycle of stories about Elisha, the phrase "sons of the prophets" is used to refer to guilds of prophets.[9] It is assumed that a similar usage of the term occurs when Amos denies that he is a member of any such professional group (Amos 7:12-14).

It is also clear that there were "court prophets" (1 Kgs 22:6). King Ahab had four hundred of them available to give him advice before he went into battle, and most of them told him what he wanted to hear. Only the famous Micaiah[10] speaks the truth, having, as he claims, stood

---

[7]Note also that in 1 Sam 20:18-23, David and Jonathan shoot arrows. What they did may be related to the Mesopotamian divination technique of casting arrows, a practice known as belomancy. For a survey of divination in the Bible, see Hallo, "Akkadian Apocalypses," 231ff., and Burke O. Long, "The Effect of Divination upon Israelite Literature," *JBL* 92 (1973) 489-97.

[8]See Wilson, *Prophecy and Society*, Chapter 5, for a discussion of the Judean Traditions.

[9]"Now the sons of the prophets said to Elisha, 'See the place where we dwell under your charge is too small for us'" (2 Kgs 6:1).

[10]The name Micaiah means, "Who is like YHWH?" The name Micah is a shortened version of this. It is possible that the corpus of oracles in the book of Micah is attributed to the earlier ninth century prophet or, *vice versa*, that the

in the council of YHWH (1 Kgs 22:19-23).[11] Similar court prophets may
be found in the palaces of Esarhaddon and Ashurbanipal, kings of
Assyria in the seventh century B.C.E. They were known as "announcers"
(raggimu/raggintu) or "seers" (šabrū/šabrātu) by their contemporaries.
They were both men and women, and they gave oracles to the king. The
texts now surviving are either messages of assurance for the king, or
requests that would benefit the temples or groups with which these
persons were associated.[12] The existence of these texts would seem to
imply that court prophecy was commonly known outside Israel as well
as in Israel.

In addition, it is significant that Jeremiah directed some of his
preaching against a group or a class of prophets (Jer 23), and Ezekiel is
instructed to prophesy against the prophets of Israel who say "Peace"
when there is no peace (Ezek 13:2 and 10). There appear to have been
large groups of prophets in Israel and Judah throughout the period of the
Divided Monarchy. It is not clear that they were all court prophets or
that they were all members of guilds of prophets. There are those who
see the prophets emerging at the time of the monarchy and continuing
as a parallel institution.[13]

The writing prophets emerge in the second half of the eighth
century. While a major question for us is the similarities or differences

---

eighth century prophet has been placed in the ninth century by the Deuteronomic
historians (1 Kgs 22). Hallo has raised a similar question regarding the prophet
Jonah: "Perhaps Israelite tadition . . . [attached] the legend of the near-collapse
of Nineveh to Jonah, a prophetic contemporary of Jeroboam II or, conversely,
. . . [assigned] the Jonah of legend to the reign of Jeroboam (2 Kgs 14:25)"
(William W. Hallo and William K. Simpson, *The Ancient Near East* [New York:
Harcourt Brace Jovanovich, 1971] 132). Hallo also comments on the exegetical
problem in "On the Antiquity of Sumerian Literature," *JAOS* 83 (1963) 175,
n. 68. It is of interest to compare a similar view regarding Micah held by J. M. P.
Smith: "The appellation 'Morashtite' (1:1, Jer 26:18) is applied to Micah to
distinguish him from the many other bearers of his name; and particularly from
his predecessor, Micaiah ben Imlah, with whom he is confused in 1 Kgs 22:28,
where a phrase from his book is ascribed to the earlier Micaiah" (*The International
Critical Commentary* 23 [Edinburgh: T. & T. Clark, 1911] 17).

[11]For an understanding of the Council of YHWH within an ancient Near
Eastern context, see Max E. Polley, "Hebrew Prophecy within the Council of
Yahweh, Examined in its Ancient Near Eastern Setting," *Scripture in Context:
Essays on the Comparative Method* (Pittsburgh: Pickwick Press, 1980) 141-56.

[12]The translated texts are published in *ANET*[3], "Akkadian Oracles," 499-51.
The titles, "announcer" and "seer," and the significance of the texts are treated
by H. B. Huffmon, "The Origins of Prophecy," *Magnalia Dei: The Mighty Acts
of God* (ed. Frank M. Cross, et al.; New York: Doubleday, 1976) 175-76.

[13]Ibid., 178-80.

between the pre-literary and the Classical prophets,[14] no such distinction is made by the authors of Deuteronomy 18. By the same token, they make no distinction between seer and prophet; only in 1 Sam 9:9 is it said that "he who is now called a prophet was formerly called a seer."[15]

III. THE CLASSICAL PROPHETS

Modern commentators see the Classical Prophets as a separate and important aspect of prophecy in the ancient world. If their role in Israel and Judah is to be fully appreciated, two significant factors must be understood—the place of "prediction" and the contrast with divination.

Although some writers still hold that the prophets received supernatural revelation which enabled them to write about future persons, places and events,[16] it is generally assumed today that the Classical Prophets were concerned with the relevance of the Word of YHWH for the conditions and circumstances in their own time.[17] As has often been pointed out, they were "forthtellers" of the will of God, not "foretellers"

---

[14]See a recent article which discusses the emergence of classical prophecy, and gives attention to the use of writing as a medium of expression: Menahem Haran, "From Early to Classical Prophecy: Continuity and Change," *VT* 27 (1977) 385-97. Note also the comment by John S. Holladay, "The explosive emergence of the so-called 'writing prophets' in the history of Israel is one of the great historical mysteries of Old Testament scholarship" ("Assyrian Statecraft and the Prophets of Israel," *HTR* 63 [1970] 29).

[15]Huffmon sees no basis for making a role distinction between "seer" and "prophet" on the basis of the words alone. Both terms are applied to Samuel in 2 Chr 16:1-10 where Samuel and Hanani are the only persons given the title "seer" ("Origins of Prophecy," 179).

[16]For example: "Certainly he [Micah] received revelations concerning the Babylonian captivity and the subsequent restoration, just as Isaiah did (and for this reason it is customary for some critics to deny the authenticity of such passages in both prophets)" (Gleason L. Archer, Jr., "Micah," *The New Bible Commentary Revised* [ed. D. Guthrie, *et al.*; London: Inter-Varsity Press, 1970] 752).

[17]"The basic presupposition of Biblical criticism is that the Bible, whatever else it may be, is a collection of human documents written by human authors in human language and therefore subject to the same canons of historical and literary investigation as all other books" (John H. Hayes, *Introduction to the Bible* [Philadelphia: Westminster Press, 1971] 11). A theological corollary of this is expressed very well in the following: "The task of the genuine prophet was not to predict but to confront man with the alternatives of decision" (Martin Buber, *Pointing the Way* [New York: Harpers, 1957] 197), cited by Hallo, "Akkadian Apocalypses," n. 26; republished in *On the Bible: Eighteen Studies* (ed. Nahum N. Glatzer; New York: Schocken, 1968) 177.

of future events.[18] In Exodus 7:1, the term "prophet" applies to one who speaks on behalf of another. As Aaron spoke for Moses, so Moses spoke for YHWH.[19] The Classical Prophet was one who faithfully presented the Word of YHWH.

Micah is noted for having predicted the destruction of Jerusalem in his day (Mic 3:12). He was remembered and quoted in this regard one hundred years later by the elders of Jerusalem who used the information to save the life of Jeremiah (Jer 26:16-19). The fact that Jerusalem was not destroyed by the Assyrians in Micah's time does not detract from the reputation of the prophet, and does not affect the message of judgment and salvation in the book in its canonical form. Micah's demand for social justice and faithfulness to YHWH, and an acknowledgment of YHWH's grace, are of central concern, and punishment for gross inhumanity is a consequence.

In addition to making a distinction between prediction and setting forth the will of YHWH, it is important to make a contrast between Israelite and Mesopotamian cultures. Whereas divination practices are only occasionally noted in the Bible, they dominate the literature and culture of Mesopotamia.

Oppenheim is not alone in pointing out that the significance attached to divination in Mesopotamia by scholars is supported by a large number of omen collections and related cuneiform texts. His own judgment is that "there can be little doubt that Akkadian divination . . . was considered a major intellectual achievement in Mesopotamia and surrounding countries."[20] The practice of extispicy (the prediction of the future based on the examination of the viscera of animals) and the practice of hepatoscopy (the examination of the sheep's liver to predict the future) were highly developed arts. Other related practices are also known from the cuneiform texts.[21]

The omen handbooks make it clear that divination was a craft that required years of training and apprenticeship. The art was seen as

[18]See, for example, Johannes Lindblom, *Prophecy in Ancient Israel* (Philadelphia: Fortress Press, 1962) 1.

[19]A similar passage is to be found in Exod 4:15-16: "He shall speak for you to the people; and he shall be a mouth for you, and you shall be to him as God."

[20]A. Leo Oppenheim, *Ancient Mesopotamia* (Chicago: University of Chicago Press, 1964) 206.

[21]Hallo contrasts the *Weltanschauung* of Mesopotamian divination ("a symptomatic association between events") with the causal relationship between phenomena assumed by modern science. This Mesopotamian world view was expressed in numerous techniques that were employed by the diviners. In addition to extispicy and hepatoscopy, which were favored by the kings who could afford animal sacrifices, there were numerous other mantic practices. For Hallo's explanation of the worldview and a description of the divinatory techniques, see "The Prediction and Control of Events," *ANEH*, 158-63.

necessary and effective in averting evil and securing the well-being of the nation or of the individual.[22] It is worth noting that divination in Mesopotamia and prophecy in Israel are not only phenomena to be compared, but marks of religion and philosophy that distinguish one culture from another.[23]

Strangely enough, there is only one reference to the practice of hepatoscopy in Mesopotamia in the Bible. Ezekiel writes, "For the king of Babylon stands at the parting of the way, at the head of the two ways, to use divination; he shakes the arrows, he consults the teraphim, he looks at the liver" (21:21).[24] Just as interesting is the fact that there are no examples of Mesopotamia omen texts or extispicy reports in *ANET*.[25] Yet the differences between prophecy and divination remain the major contrast between Israelite and Mesopotamian religio-cultural expression. Each was as important to its own culture as science is to our culture today, and as pervasive in daily life.

As important as this contrast is, there are some scholars who make the judgment that forerunners of the Classical Prophets are found in Mesopotamian cultures as well as within Israel. The Mari "prophets" have been cited most often in recent years to substantiate this claim. Although nearly one thousand years earlier, these prophetic texts are worth noting because they constitute the largest collection of texts that are available for comparative study.

[22]Oppenheim, *Ancient Mesopotamia*, 207.

[23]"The Biblical prophets derided the arts of the Mesopotamian diviners for, alone among cuneiform literary genres, the literature of divination had no precise parallels in Biblical or other Near Eastern writings, just as Biblical prophecy, alone among Biblical genres, is unparalleled in cuneiform" (Hallo, *ANEH*, 158).

[24]See n. 7 for a reference to casting arrows, a practice known as belomancy. Oppenheim makes the comment that "the throwing of lots . . . had no cultic status in Mesopotamia" (*Ancient Mesopotamia*, 208).

[25]The same is true for *Documents from Old Testament Times* (ed. D. Winton Thomas; London: Thomas Nelson and Sons, 1958), and *Near Eastern Religious Texts Relating to the Old Testament* (ed. Walter Beyerlin; Philadelphia: Westminster, 1978). In his review of the latter book, H. W. F. Saggs writes, "The editor of the Mesopotamian texts states his principles of selection in terms which indicate that whilst he is conscious of the considerable contrast between Mesopotamian and Israelite religion, he does not propose to investigate or even to illustrate this" ("Review of Walter Beyerlin, *Near Eastern Religious Texts Relating to the Old Testament*," *JTS* 31 [1980] 105-6). Saggs adds, "The editor of the Egyptian section, on the other hand, is very cautious in his attitude to parallels, and gives 'a warning . . . against over-hasty conclusions from real or apparent consonances' (p. 1). He also emphasizes that whole areas of the essence of Egyptian religious thought have been omitted" (p. 106).

IV. PROPHECY AT MARI

Among the thousands of letters recovered from the palace archives of Zimri-Lim (ca. 1780-1760 BCE) at Mari are twenty-three texts that have been classified as prophetic sayings. These sayings were sent to the king by official and unofficial members of the court, by persons both within Mari and from the environs, by both men and women, and from both professional and nonprofessional recipients.[26] Many of the messages relate to temples and the interests of those connected with them, while others relate to the king—his safety and his success in battle. The messages are said to have been inspired by various gods worshipped in the temples in and around Mari. The reports have come *via* dreams, visions, and persons said to have had an ecstatic experience, or to have been in a trance.[27]

The prophetic sayings of Mari are significant because they are quite different from the usual omen literature and extispicy reports. One translator of the texts regards them as "certainly parallel to the proclamations of the official Israelite *nĕbî'îm* [prophets],"[28] that is, those court prophets of the Israelite kings who were condemned by Micah and the Classical Prophets. "They cry 'Peace' when they have something to eat, but declare war against him who puts nothing into their mouths" (3:5). They are messages which have been received through personal experiences, not through the analysis of external, public phenomena. Moran groups the texts according to the recipients of the "revelations": private persons, ecstatics, those designated by the term *āpilum* ("Answerer"), and a prophetess.[29] Hallo sees them distinguished by the fact that they are private messages which did not become part of the literary tradition as did the oracles of the Hebrew prophets.[30]

---

[26]"Although both Ellermeier . . . and Huffmon . . . divide the recipients of these divine communications into cultic and lay, a happier division is simply professional and non-professional. . . . The principal professional recipients are the 'ecstatic' (*muḫḫûm*—male; *muḫḫûtum*—female) and the 'answerer' (*āpilum*—male; *āpiltum*—female)" (John F. Craghan, "Mari and Its Prophets: The Contributions of Mari to the Understanding of Biblical Prophecy," *BTB* 5 [1975] 38).

[27]"In using the term 'possession' we touch upon the difficult question of the psychic state of these prophets . . . Thus, it could be used of a trance, and it is trance that seems to answer best to all the data" (W. L. Moran, "New Evidence from Mari on the History of Prophecy," *Biblica* 50 [1969] 27). Moran has translated the relevant texts in *ANET*[3], 629-32.

[28]Hartmut Schmökel, "Mesopotamian Texts," *Near Eastern Religious Texts Relating to the Old Testament*, 123.

[29]W. L. Moran, "Divine Revelations," *ANET*[3], 629-32.

[30]Oral comment.

Various attitudes have been expressed regarding the relationship of the Mari sayings to the prophecy of Israel. Huffmon believes that the Mari documents represent prophetic sayings which can be dated several hundred years earlier than the prophets in Israel. This is true because a prophet is "a person who through non-technical means receives a clear and immediate message from a deity for transmission to a third party."[31] That definition places the "prophet" in striking contrast to the diviner who uses mechanical means and makes possible conceptual continuity between the Mari prophets and the prophets of Israel.[32] Huffmon believes that the prophetic oracles had only marginal standing in the court at Mari because "the royal official . . . often advises the king to have a proper extispicy made, i.e. to resort to learned divination."[33] Nevertheless, these prophetic sayings were significantly different from the usual divination.[34]

Malamat sees the strongest connection between the Mari prophecies and the early Israelite prophets. He believes that the Mari prophecies existed alongside the standard divination practices. He claims that "the diviner-prophets of Mari were imbued with the consciousness of mission and took their stand before the authorities in a spontaneous manner and upon the initiative of their god."[35] He describes this as a phenomenon of "intuitive divination" and believes that it is closer to what one finds in Israelite prophecy than anything else in the ancient Near East. He concludes that "prophecy in Mari represents the early budding of the later, brilliant prophetic flowering in Israel."[36]

A mitigating position is taken by Hayes. He points out that "the texts do show that the Mari spokesmen, like the Hebrew prophets, made the matters of the king and the policies of state their personal concern and that they had no hesitation about intervening in royal affairs."[37]

---

[31]Huffmon, "The Origins of Prophecy," 172.

[32]Huffmon translates *muḫḫū/muḫḫūtu* as "ecstatic" and *āpilu/āpiltu* as "answerer." A third title, *assinnu*, is of uncertain meaning and is later associated as a singer with the cult of Ishtar (ibid., 173). He also notes that persons bearing titles apparently at times received royal support.

[33]Ibid., 174.

[34]Note the following interesting observation made about the early prophets in the Samuel and Saul narratives: "While the initial impression given by these early prophets is crude and primitive, it is likely that they had already separated themselves rather sharply from religious functionaries who used omens and lots" (Norman K. Gottwald, *All the Kingdoms of the Earth* [New York: Harper and Row, 1964] 53).

[35]A. Malamat, "Prophetic Revelations in New Documents from Mari and the Bible," *VTSup* 15 (1965) 208.

[36]Ibid., 209.

[37]John H. Hayes, "Prophetism at Mari and Old Testament Parallels," *ATR* 49 (1967) 402.

The conclusions of Hayes form a good consensus regarding the Mari texts. Hayes observes that the sayings are "the clearest non-biblical antecedent to the intuitive prophecy of ancient Israel," that they come from "within West Semitic circles," and that the prophetic figures at Mari and in Israel are similar in their appeal to deity, sense of mission, form of address, and concern with salvation and conditional judgment both for Zimri-Lim and neighboring states.[38] The last conclusion recognizes the distinction between early and late Hebrew prophecy. "Israelite prophetism's proclamations of unconditional judgment and high ethical and theological concerns are not to be found in the Mari texts, but these were scarcely present in early Israelite prophecy either."[39]

V. SOCIETY AND PROPHECY

The most recent approach to the study of prophecy in ancient Israel is Wilson's attempt to silhouette the role of the prophet in society. His method for doing this is to examine anthropological data describing the role of prophets in primitive societies and relating that to the ancient Near East. Despite the complexity of both the biblical and the anthropological data, Wilson finds conceptual models that allow intercultural comparisons and illumine the relation of prophecy and society.

Instead of using such terms as prophet, shaman, witch, sorcerer, medium, diviner, mystic or priest, Wilson uses the term "intermediary" for those persons who carry out the functions of "intermediation," that is, communication between the natural and the supernatural.[40] Current anthropological studies indicate that such intermediaries have "support groups," that is, they do not function strictly as individuals. Furthermore, their behavior is "stereotypical behavior." For instance, if an intermediary is an ecstatic, his behavior follows predictable patterns in the society of which he is a part. Even uncontrollable behavior is part of the larger pattern, for stereotypical behavior patterns dictate that uncontrolled behavior is the way that spirit possession begins. All intermediaries need a support group. Such a societal group influences how "prophets" are created or chosen, how they shape their behavior, and how they function in society.

Further, Wilson makes a distinction between "peripheral" intermediaries who operate on the fringes of the centers of power, wishing to bring about change from outside the establishment, and those whom he calls "central" intermediaries who operate within the power base, helping to maintain social order and to regulate the pace of social change.[41] It is

---

[38]Ibid., 408-9.
[39]Ibid., 409.
[40]Robert R. Wilson, *Prophecy and Society*. See the discussion on pages 21-32.
[41]Ibid., 88.

clear that Wilson can use these models to talk about the role of the Mari prophets in their society or the role of the Hebrew prophets in their nation.

The use of such an apparatus along with an examination of the evidence results in the conclusion that Micah was a peripheral intermediary and that he directed strong criticisms against the central intermediaries in Jerusalem.[42] We shall suggest later that his support group may be seen to be the "elders of the land" at Moresheth, his home city. By a similar analysis, Wilson sees the Mari prophets as peripheral intermediaries.[43] The overall conclusion is inevitable in light of what we have already said. In the end, the central intermediaries at Mari were the diviners.

Wilson's approach means that the Classical Prophets can be viewed as either peripheral or central intermediaries, and that earlier Israelite prophets may be seen the same way. Ahijah, for example, is seen as a peripheral intermediary while Shemaiah is perceived as a central intermediary.[44] Such a perspective tends to blur the sharp distinction that is made by some between the Classical Prophets and the earlier prophecy of Israel and Mari.

VI. DISCONTINUITY AND CONTINUITY

In contrast to what we have been implying, continuity and development, Orlinsky argues that canonical prophecy is "a uniquely Israelite phenomenon."[45] The Classical Prophets did not emerge anywhere other than in Israel, and there is a sharp discontinuity between them and all other forms of prophecy and divination.

Orlinsky terms the early prophetic individuals in Israelite society "seer-priests" because the persons usually functioned as priests and the term avoids the confusion which results if the term divination is used to designate early Israelite prophecy. Orlinsky recognizes the existence in the Bible of different words for these seer-priests, i.e., visionary, man of God, seer, prophet.[46] One should not be misled, however, by different terms for the same phenomenon. And what is true for early Israel is also true for Mesopotamia. The various titles given to recipients of messages

---

[42]Ibid., 274-76.

[43]Ibid., 110.

[44]Ibid., 184-87.

[45]H. M. Orlinsky, "The Seer in Ancient Israel," *OrAnt* 4 (1965) 153-74; reprinted with modifications as "The Seer-Priest," *The World History of the Jewish People* 3 (ed. Benjamin Mazar; Tel Aviv: Jewish History Publications Ltd.; New Brunswick: Rutgers University Press, 1971) 268-79. The quotation is from "The Seer-Priest," p. 279.

[46]Orlinsky, "The Seer-Priest," 269.

for the king do not change the fact that they are part of the pattern of divination, that is, that they are all "seer-priests."

Orlinsky sees many contrasts between the seer-priests and the Classical Prophets. The seer-priest was a member of a guild, he learned his craft, he was usually associated with a holy place, his sons occasionally followed him in his trade, he practiced a craft, and was paid a fee for his services, he predicted the future and attempted to control it, and he performed miracles.[47] Micah, in contrast to the seer-priest, was an individualist. As one of the Classical Prophets, he did not learn prophecy as the member of a guild. He had a calling, he did not make his living by practicing his "art," he opposed divination and miracle-making, he did not try to control the future, and he called for his people to return to YHWH. The two classes are distinctly different.

One implication of the argument is that "since divination was a universal craft, recognized in all countries and cultures of the ancient world, it is not surprising that the activities of the Israelite seer sometimes ranged beyond the Israelite population and border."[48] For example, Elisha is sought in order to give his services to Naaman of Syria.[49] One cannot imagine Micah being requested to give his services to a foreign dignitary!

In a similar argument, Orlinsky suggests that the conflict between Elijah and the prophets of Baal was not so much an ethical-monotheistic question as it was a showdown over which group of seer-priests was going to have the dominant place in northern Israel. It was a clash between the vested interests of the seers of Baal and the seers of YHWH, not a clash of principles.[50]

Holladay also sees the Classical Prophets as radically different from the earlier Hebrew prophets, but from a different perspective. He adds the point that the essential difference lies in the audience to which the prophets addressed themselves. The pre-literary prophets were primarily court prophets, while the canonical prophets were "popular prophets." He writes, "there is not one single indication of a prophetic oracle being delivered to anyone outside the royal court prior to the time of Amos"[51] unless one takes into account the most legendary sections of the Elijah-Elisha cycles of narratives.

Thus, in an examination of the major sections of Micah, one finds that the major oracles are addressed to "all peoples" (1:2), the "heads of

[47]Ibid., 271. Cf. "The Seer in Ancient Israel," 155-56.

[48]Orlinsky, "The Seer in Ancient Israel," 159.

[49]2 Kgs 5.

[50]Orlinsky, "The Seer-Priest," 278.

[51]J. S. Holladay, "Assyrian Statecraft and the Prophets of Israel," *HTR* 63 (1970) 35.

Judah and rulers of the house of Israel" (3:1), and "his people" (6:2-3). According to Holladay, the audience of Micah makes him one of the Classical Prophets and sets him apart from all the court prophets of an earlier period.

Although many additional scholars would also see the literary prophets as being unique,[52] that point of view is not shared unanimously. Weinfeld has argued that the canonical prophetic literature, like "law, epic, historiography, psalms, and wisdom," is not the unique creation of Israel, but that "basic forms as well as basic motifs of classical prophecy are rooted in the ancient Near-Eastern literature."[53] In order to illustrate this line of reasoning, Weinfeld selects a number of motifs and then cites relevant Near Eastern literature that he believes supports his thesis.

Many of the themes he selects for treatment seem to relate more easily to the pre-classical Hebrew period than to the canonical literature, e.g. when he describes the ecstatics of Israel and the ecstatics of other countries. He also selects the motifs of the prophet as messenger, "signs and portents," "purification of the mouth,"[54] salvation oracles (oracles of encouragement which promise the defeat of one's enemies), the idea of false prophets, and "dream and vision." Comparisons are frequently made with the Mari prophets. Three of the motifs selected relate directly to canonical Micah among others; the three motifs are "the *rîb* pattern," "morality vs. cult," and the "violation of morality as cause for destruction." We can pick out the Micah references for descriptive purposes.

It has been argued for a long time that the lawsuit pattern was taken over and used by the prophets. Micah 6:1-8 is always given as one of the examples of a lawsuit presentation. Although Weinfeld recognizes that the prophets gave the concept literary embellishments, he cites examples to show that the prototypes of this form of oracle were not the creative work of the prophets themselves. The use of the lawsuit pattern has been

---

[52]"It may be true that almost everywhere some sort of revelation is regarded as the primary source of religious truth. Yet the supernatural means by which such truth is communicated are omens, dreams, divination, inferences from strange happenings, utterances of shamans and priests. The biblical prophet is a type *sui generis*" (Abraham J. Heschel, *The Prophets* [New York: Harper and Row, 1962] 473).

[53]Moshe Weinfeld, "Ancient Near Eastern Patterns in Prophetic Literature," *VT* 27 (1977) 178.

[54]Ibid., 180. Weinfeld quotes from a translation given by Albrecht Goetze, "An Old Babylonian Prayer of the Divination Priest," *JCS* 22 (1968) 25, the following: "O Šamaš! I am placing in my mouth pure cedar (resin) . . . I wiped my mouth with . . . cedar (resin) . . . Being (now) clean, to the assembly of the gods I shall draw near." He compares this with Isaiah 6, suggesting that Isaiah also "undergoes a purification ceremony before undertaking his mission."

seen as a way to show the relation of the prophets to the tradition of the covenant and Mosaic Yahwism.[55] The prophets are, in effect, calling the people of Israel to judgment for having broken the covenant with YHWH. The *rîb* pattern has been employed to link the prophets and the covenant tradition since that is not spelled out by the prophets themselves.

Opinion regarding the use of the *rîb* pattern is not unanimous, however. It may not be the usual thing, as in Micah, to call the mountains and the "foundations of the earth" as witnesses in the trial. It also appears that the trial begins in Micah but is never completed; there is no sentencing or announcement of punishment.[56] In dealing with a similar and prototypical passage in Deuteronomy 32, Mendenhall believes that the legal metaphors have simply been transferred from the normal political-legal procedures of the day. Contrary to Wright, Mendenhall does not see Deuteronomy 32 as a lawsuit at all.[57]

Clements reviews the materials relating the *rîb* pattern to the prophets and draws a similar conclusion: it is not necessary to resort to ancient Near Eastern treaties to explain the prophetic oracles. "The creative possibilities of Israel's own religious life" can inspire the writings.[58] It is possible that Micah was using language that would have been commonplace for those with whom he wished to communicate, and to set forth the *rîb* pattern as necessary to explain the origin of the unit (6:1-8) is not to appreciate the genius of Micah himself.

The same unit in Micah contains another motif for which Weinfeld observes Near Eastern precedents—the theme that social justice is more significant than sacrifice ("morality vs. cult"). Weinfeld quotes the Egyptian papyrus, "Instruction to King Merikare," to the effect that sacrifices are not advised to achieve righteousness. "Make firm your place (= grave) with uprightness and just dealing for it is on that which their hearts rely; more acceptable is a loaf of the upright than the ox of the wrongdoer."[59] There are other quotations from Egyptian sources and

---

[55]See a summary discussion of the "Prophets and the Covenant" in R. E. Clements, *Prophecy and Tradition* (Atlanta: John Knox Press, 1975) 8-23.

[56]H. B. Huffmon, "The Covenant Lawsuit in the Prophets," *JBL* 78 (1959) 287. Huffmon actually says that the "sentencing" is expressed in a unique way in Mic 6:8. See also his questions about the "witnesses" on p. 291.

[57]Cf. G. Ernest Wright, "The Lawsuit of God: A Form-Critical Study of Deuteronomy 32," *Israel's Prophetic Heritage* (ed. Bernhard W. Anderson and Walter Harrelson; New York: Harpers, 1962), 26-67, and George E. Mendenhall, "Samuel's 'Broken Rib': Deuteronomy 32," *No Famine in the Land* (Festschrift John L. McKenzie; ed. J. W. Flanagan and A. W. Robinson; Missoula: Scholars Press, 1975) 63-74.

[58]R. E. Clements, *Prophecy and Tradition*, 21.

[59]Weinfeld, "Ancient Near Eastern Patterns," 190. Cited from *ANET*[3], 417.

from the psalms and proverbs of Israel. Weinfeld concludes that the notion that justice was better than the sacrifices was developed, not created, by the canonical prophets, for "this was already stressed by the Egyptians and also by the Psalmists and wise men in Israel."[60]

The last motif that Weinfeld discusses is the idea that the "violation of morality is a cause for destruction." In suggesting that this theme is also found prior to the writing prophets, he compares, among others, an inscription of Esarhaddon to a passage in Micah. The Esarhaddon inscription[61] reads:

> the people living in it (Babylon) answered each other Yes, (in their heart): No; they plotted evil . . . they (the Babylonians) were oppressing the weak/poor and putting them into the power of the mighty, there was oppression and acceptance of bribe within the city daily without ceasing; they were robbing each other's property; the son was cursing his father in the street . . . then the god (Enlil/Marduk) became angry, he planned to overwhelm the land and to destroy its people.

The translation is Weinfeld's and is given as it is found in the article.

Immediately following the Esarhaddon inscription, Weinfeld writes, "This passage reminds us especially of the prophecy of Micah 7:1 ff.:

> there is no upright man, people hunt each other, the officer and the judge ask for [a] bribe, the son despises the father, the daughter rises against her mother . . . "[62]

Weinfeld's conclusion, that moral behavior was also seen in Mesopotamia as a necessary condition for survival, means that while the canonical prophets developed the idea of collective responsibility, they certainly did not originate the concept.[63] (However, in this particular example, the quotation from Micah may actually precede in time the inscription of Esarhaddon if Mic 7:1ff. is assigned to the end of the eighth century B.C.E.)

---

[60]Ibid., 193.

[61]Ibid., 194. The Esarhaddon inscription is to be found in Riekele Borger, *Die Inschriften Asarhaddons, Königs von Assyrien,* AfO Beiheft 9 (1956) 12-13.

[62]Ibid., 194. The Micah quotation is actually several quotations from chapter 7. The parts of the verses, as found in the RSV translation, are identified as follows: 2bc . . . and there is none upright among men; they lie in wait for blood, . . . ; 3b . . . the prince and the judge ask for a bribe, . . . ; 6a . . . for the son treats the father with contempt, the daughter rises up against her mother . . .

[63]This specific conclusion is challenged by Hallo who finds that the cuneiform texts overwhelmingly stress only *royal* responsibility. See his comments in B. J. Bamberger (ed.), *The Torah: A Modern Commentary,* 3: *Leviticus* (New York: Union of American Hebrew Congregations, 1978) xxviii.

The arguments of Weinfeld, that these three key themes of Micah (and the Classical Prophets) are rooted in non-Israelite texts of the ancient Near East, appear to be inconclusive. Although there may be points of contact, an overall pattern of development from early to literary prophecy is missing, and the Classical Prophets still seem to be a class *sui generis*.

Two analogies may point the direction for future reflection. Our definitions of politician and statesman include perceiving the politician as one who gains political office for selfish reasons and operates with short-term interests in mind; we perceive the statesman as one who exerts influence for the well-being of society and who works to achieve that which is best for the present and the future. An image from modern warfare is also useful: the nuclear weapons have things in common with earlier explosive bombs, but the differences in consequences result in radically new concepts of strategy.

One author wrote about the prophets of Israel: "In the great poetic sermons of the literary prophets, the differences of degree unmistakably merge into a significant difference of kind."[64] He might have been talking about politicians and statesmen or about weapons of mass destruction. In turn, these contemporary models may spark new ideas about the relation of prophecy in the ancient Near East to the prophetic giants of Israel. The issues of continuity and discontinuity remain.

VII. CONTINUITY AND DISCONTINUITY IN MICAH

In an article surveying recent commentaries on the book of Micah, Jeppesen divides the writers into two groups, those that assume authentic Micah material only in the first three chapters of the book, and those that assume that most of the book belongs to Micah or is to be found within the provenance of the eighth century B.C.E.[65] Chapter 3 ends with the prediction of the destruction of Jerusalem, which many see as a climax of an authentic Micah oracle of judgment against the rulers and leading citizens of the city.

> Jerusalem shall become a heap of ruins, and the mountain of the house a wooded height (3:12b).

Chapter four begins with a statement of hope and restoration, which many consider to be a post-exilic unit along with later sections.

> It shall come to pass in the latter days that the mountain of the house of the LORD shall be established as the highest of the mountains, and shall be raised up above the hills; and peoples shall flow to it . . . (4:1).

[64]H. M. Orlinsky, *Ancient Israel* (Ithaca: Cornell University Press, 1954) 148.
[65]K. Jeppesen, "New Aspects of Micah Research," *Journal for the Study of the Old Testament* 8 (1978) 4.

We propose to examine the possibility that the oracle which begins chapter four is in continuity with the oracle that ends chapter three, and suggest a few things to be considered in discussing the issue.

Regardless of how they handle the book's structure and individual units within the book, many commentators see 'judgment and salvation' as a basic theological theme. Thus Childs would see three repetitions of the theme in the canonical book: judgment in 1:2-2:11 followed by salvation in 2:12-13; a comparatively shorter section on judgment in chapter three followed by a comparatively longer section on salvation in chapters four and five; and then 6:1-7:7 (judgment) followed by 7:8-20 (salvation). Childs argues that this division is also supported by the fact that each section is introduced by the call to "hear" what the LORD would say to the people of Israel.[66]

Mays holds that the book falls into two main divisions, but sees judgment and salvation as a basic theological theme, whether considering Israel in the context of universal history or Israel alone.[67] In contrast to Mays, who considers only the first three chapters authentic Micah material, Allen assigns most of the book to Micah, and proposes a structure of the book with judgment and salvation as alternating motifs throughout.[68] Even though Allen believes that Micah 4:1-4 is an oracle that antedates both Micah and Isaiah,[69] he proposes in his outline that 3:1-12 and 4:1-4 are related as oracles of "long doom" and "short hope" or as Jerusalem's punishment over against Jerusalem's positive role.[70]

White has discussed the relevancy of the "typology of exaltation" to the Deutero-Isaiah message, and it is possible to consider his essay in regard to this material.[71] White acknowledges that the exaltation of a god is usually celebrated in connection with a nation's triumph over its enemies, but argues that both cuneiform texts and Israelite literature see defeat (past history) and victory (salvation prophecy) linked together at

[66]Brevard S. Childs, *Introduction to the Old Testament as Scripture* (Philadelphia: Fortress Press, 1979) 431.

[67]James L. Mays, *Micah: A Commentary* (Philadelphia: Westminster Press, 1976) 4-12. "The first section is concerned with universal history, with the nations and their power as the context in which YHWH's reign will be established" (p. 4). "The second is concerned directly and intimately with the relationship between YHWH and Israel, with judgment and salvation as God's struggle for the soul of his people" (p. 9).

[68]Leslie C. Allen, *The Books of Joel, Obadiah, Jonah and Micah* (NICOT; Grand Rapids: Eerdmans, 1976). The section on Micah is to be found on pages 238-427. See page 256 for a statement that "the God who destroys is also the God who delivers."

[69]Ibid., 251.

[70]Ibid., 260-61.

[71]John B. White, "Universalization of History in Deutero-Isaiah," *Scripture in Context*, 179-95.

times. In other words, "both Ezekiel and Deutero-Isaiah make it clear
that Israel's defeat is not due to Marduk, but to Yahweh's own punishment of his people."[72] Further, a cuneiform text known as "The Prophetic
Speech of Marduk" is available and "serves as an interesting example of
the deity's bringing about the defeat of his own people and then
announcing their subsequent salvation and rebuilding."[73]

The basic point which White makes that is relevant to the Micah
passage is that YHWH's exaltation is announced "in spite of the nation's
current plight" and "the image of divine exaltation is cast into an
eschatological framework which celebrates Yahweh's future intervention
based upon the continuity of his past grace."[74]

Judah was almost completely devastated by the end of the eighth
century as a result of the Assyrian King Sennaherib's campaign there. In
light of this near collapse of Judean civilization, it is not untenable that
Micah had a vision of the future when Jerusalem would not be humbled
by other nations and when warfare would not be an overwhelming
reality in daily life. Micah may have been sensitive to the plight of the
refugees as well as to the injustices in Jerusalem.[75] Amos reinterpreted
the concept of the "Day of the LORD" in his writing (Amos 5:18-20),
seeing it as a day of darkness and not as a day of light. So too Micah
might have reinterpreted the "Day of YHWH," seeing it in the future
when the horrors of war in his own day had passed.

The judgment and salvation sequence in Micah may arise necessarily
out of his own experience. In the passages under consideration, Micah
announces that "the mountain of the house shall become a wooded
height" (3:12) and immediately following that "the mountain of the
house of the LORD shall be established as the highest of the mountains"
(4:1). It may be that these two passages are deliberately connected in a
sequence of judgment and salvation by use of the image of "the
mountain of the house of YHWH."

Another possible way to link the two oracles is suggested by a recent
essay on the background of Micah.[76] Little is known about the prophet

---

[72]Ibid., 183.

[73]Ibid., 183-84. For the Speech of Marduk, he cites A. K. Grayson and W. G.
Lambert, "Akkadian Prophecies," *JCS* 18 (1964) 7-23; and Rykle Borger, "Gott
Marduk und Gott-König Šulgi als Propheten: Zwei prophetische Texte," *BiOr* 28
(1971) 3-24.

[74]Ibid., 189.

[75]See the article in this volume by Stephen Stohlmann, "The Judean
Exile after 701 B.C.E." (pp. 147-74). He not only aruges for an "exile" at that time,
but communicates also a picture of the devastation in Judea that resulted from
Sennaherib's campaign, and the large number of Judeans made homeless by
the war.

[76]Hans Walter Wolff, "Micah the Moreshite—The Prophet and His Back-

Micah himself. Wolff argues that we may learn some things by correlating the title of the book which refers to "Micah of Moresheth" (1:1) and the passage in Jeremiah which reads, "And certain of the elders of the land arose and spoke to all the assembled people, saying, 'Micah of Moresheth prophesied in the days of Hezekiah king of Judah, and said to all the people of Judah . . .' " (26:17-18).

Wolff conjectures that the phrase "of Moresheth" identifies Micah to the elders as someone outside of Jerusalem; Wolff suggests, moreover, that the words of Micah may have been handed down among the "elders of the land" and, yet another implication, that Micah himself may have been one of the "elders of the land." He may have been such an elder not only at Moresheth, but also a member of a larger social and class grouping known as the "elders of the land." Wolff notes that "the 'elders of the land' (Jer 26:17) are identical with the 'elders of Judah' (1 Sam 30:26). They convene in Jerusalem not only on the occasion of great festivals but also at the directive of the king (2 Kgs 23:1)."[77]

Micah's attack on "you heads of Jacob and rulers of the house of Israel" (3:1 and 3:9) would suggest to Wilson a charge leveled by a peripheral intermediary against the central intermediaries, and to Wolff, a conflict between the old local jurisprudence and official juridical circles in the city of Jerusalem. In either definition of the social relationships, it is clear that Micah's support group consists of the elders of Moresheth. Wolff uses this line of reasoning to ask another question on a related topic: "For the judgment of the passages of the Book of Micah, the authenticity of which is questioned, the following criterion will be useful: Can they be interpreted as having come from the linguistic sphere of an elder in a Judean country town in the last third of the eighth century B.C.?"[78]

With this question in mind, we can look again at the prophecy of salvation unit in Micah 4:1-4. The first three verses of the unit appear almost verbatim in Isaiah 2:2-4. Mays and Wilson agree that the passage was an independent oracle which was incorporated into both Isaiah and Micah by their redactors.[79] Allen agrees that the unit was an independent oracle, but believes that it antedates both Micah and Isaiah.[80]

Verse four of the unit, "they shall sit every man under his vine and under his fig tree, and none shall make them afraid," may be an

---

ground," *Israelite Wisdom* (Festschrift Samuel Terrien [ed. John G. Gammie, *et al.*; Missoula: Scholars Press, 1978] 77-84).

[77]The article reads 1 Sam 30:36, a typographical error, and 1 Kgs 23:1, also a typographical error.

[78]Ibid., 83.

[79]Mays, *Micah: A Comentary*, 95, and Wilson, *Prophecy and Society*, 275.

[80]Allen, *The Books of Joel, Obadiah, Jonah and Micah*, 251, 323.

idiomatic expression which was used at the end of the eighth century, and which was an integral part of the original oracle. Perhaps the expression has an affinity with the words of Rabshakeh, the representative of Sennaherib: "Make your peace with me and come out to me; then every one of you will eat of his own vine, and every one of his own fig tree . . ." (2 Kgs 18:31-32). The phrase also appears in a passage describing the reign of Solomon: "Judah and Israel dwelt in safety . . . every man under his vine and under his fig tree' (1 Kgs 4:25), and in a vision of Zechariah: "In that day, says the LORD of hosts, every one of you will invite his neighbor under his vine and under his fig tree" (3:10).

If this expression of speech was known in the eighth century, rather than originating later, it could be argued that it was a part of the original oracle. It might be argued further that the oracle first was in the Micah corpus and that this expression was deleted, for whatever reason, when the oracle was taken over and added to the materials associated with Isaiah. If such were the case, it would strengthen the argument that the oracle of hope is in continuation with the oracle of doom that precedes it.

In summary, it may be that, in a time of severe crisis, when Judean society was in danger of collapse from within and without, an elder of Moresheth explained both to those still secure in their way of life and to those who had become refugees, that YHWH was not only bringing about the crisis, but would resolve it.

THE JUDAEAN EXILE AFTER 701 B.C.E.

STEPHEN STOHLMANN

Concordia College

I. INTRODUCTION

Normally the term exile in OT studies calls to mind the sixth century Babylonian exile or less frequently the eighth century Israelite exile. Both of these exiles were treated somewhat similarly by the biblical authors: both were regarded as chronological turning points in the history of Israel; both marked the end of independent national entities; both marked the beginning of new phases in the history of Israel. There is a continuity with the past after these chronological turning points in Israel's history; but they mark a break with that past as well.

According to Assyrian sources there was also a third exile. This exile does not receive the same treatment by the biblical authors as the other two exiles. It was not regarded as a chronological turning point in Israel's history. It did not mark the end of a national entity. It did not begin a new phase in Israel's history. This exile from Judah took place after Sennaherib's 701 campaign. The number of Judaeans claimed to have been brought out and counted as booty in Sennaherib's annals is almost ten times the number of Israelites claimed to have been deported by Sargon II in the eighth century from Israel and perhaps 15 times as many as those deported from Judah in the sixth century by the Babylonians.[1] This comparison leads to some questions. Did such an exile really take place? If it did take place, why are the biblical sources silent about this exile? Is the number of deportees a case of Assyrian exaggeration? Even if exaggerated, do not the Assyrian sources indicate that an exile took place?

Scholars have pointed out several peculiarities about Sennaherib's account of this Judaean campaign. 1. Hezekiah receives less severe treatment than one would expect. He is not deposed as king. Why? No satisfactory historical answer is available. The Bible states that it is because the Lord miraculously delivered Jerusalem from the Assyrians.

---

[1]For Sargon II's 27,290 from Samaria, see James B. Pritchard, *Ancient Near Eastern Texts Relating to the Old Testament* (Princeton: Princeton University Press, 1969) 285. For the Babylonian exile compare the figures in Jeremiah 52:25-30 and II Kings 24. Josephus claims 13,832 (*Antiquities* X:6:3 and 7:1).

2. Judah is not turned into an Assyrian province nor is Jerusalem occupied. The annals claim the city was besieged and exit from it denied, but they do not claim its capture.[2] 3. The annals are not arranged in completely chronological order. They recount the restoration of Padi, king of Ekron, before the campaign against Judah. Yet Padi was imprisoned by Hezekiah in Jerusalem and so could not have been restored until after the Judaean campaign. 4. If 200,150 Judaeans were deported as the annals claim, then one would expect Judah to have lost its independence. Because it didn't, some have argued that there was no large deportation at this time.[3] 5. The annals state that Hezekiah made submission by sending his tribute and his messengers to Nineveh. He himself did not go. This is highly unusual. Again we don't know why he was not required to go in person to submit.[4] Does this mean that the annals are not to be trusted at all?

The major biblical source (2 Kings 18-20 and Isaiah 36-39) also presents some difficulties. 1. Why does the account of Hezekiah's submission and payment come first and then the account of the demand for Jerusalem's surrender and its miraculous deliverance? 2. Why does the amount of tribute differ from the annals?[5] 3. Is the biblical account referring to one campaign of Sennaherib or telescoping the accounts of two different campaigns?[6] 4. Why, if there was an exile, is it not

[2]Cf. 2 Kgs 19:31-32. See also H. H. Rowley, "Hezekiah's Reform and Rebellion," *Men of God* (London: Thomas Nelson and Sons, 1963) 120.

[3]Edward Kissane, *The Book of Isaiah* 1 (Dublin: Brown and Nolan Ltd., 1941) xiii.

[4]D. D. Luckenbill, *Ancient Records of Assyria and Babylonia* 2 (New York: Greenwood Press, 1975) 143. See also Moshe Elat, "The Political Status of the Kingdom of Judah within the Assyrian empire in the 7th century B.C.E.," *Lachish* 5 (Tel Aviv: Gateway Publishers Inc., 1975) 61.

[5]2 Kings has 300 talents of silver and the annals 800 talents of silver. See Luckenbill, *AR* 2, 121. R. E. Clements (*Isaiah and the Deliverance of Jerusalem* [JSOT Supplement 13; Sheffield: JSOT Press, 1980] 19-20) suggests the stability of the Davidic dynasty as a reason for Hezekiah's survival. He later states: "The need to retain some degree of political stability without the cost of maintaining a substantial Assyrian force in Judah adequately explains the terms that were offered and accepted" (p. 62).

[6]An answer to this question is outside the scope of this paper. However, I assume only one campaign in 701. For discussion see K. A. Kitchen, *The Third Intermediate Period in Egypt (1100-650 B.C.)* (Westminster: Aris and Phillips Ltd., 1973) 385-88, especially footnotes 824 and 833. Also, by the same author, "Late Egyptian Chronology and the Hebrew Monarchy," *JANESCU* 5 (1973) 225-33. See also Anson Rainey, "Tarhaqa and Syntax," *Tel Aviv* 3 (1976) 38-41; and Clements, *Isaiah*, 62 and 92. For a recent defense of the two campaign theory see William Shea, "One Invasion or Two?" *Ministry* (March, 1980) 26-28. The real question concerns whether Tirhakah was at Eltekeh, or did he come later with a second force? Or was he both at Eltekeh and at a second battle with

mentioned? We cannot hope to answer all the questions we have raised. Instead, given the difficulties of the sources, we shall attempt to discover whether there was an exile after Sennaherib's campaign in 701 and what can be learned about it if there was one.

II. SENNAHERIB'S JUDAEAN CAMPAIGN

Sennaherib regarded his campaign against Judah very highly. He had the siege of Lachish depicted in relief on the walls of his "Palace without a Rival" in Nineveh. He claims in the annals to have shut up Hezekiah in Jerusalem "like a bird in a cage," an expression used only one place else in Assyrian inscriptions. One of his bull inscriptions summarizes the campaign in this way:

> I devastated the wide province of Judah: the strong proud Hezekiah, its king, I brought in submission to my feet.[7]

The number of captives from Judah is exceeded in the annals only slightly by the number of captives taken from Babylonia in the first campaign. Therefore,

> The conquest of Lachish was of singular importance; it may even have been Sennacherib's greatest military achievement prior to his construction of the royal palace. At any rate no other campaign of Sennacherib was recorded in a similar fashion.[8]

What Ussishkin says here of Lachish would also be true of the whole campaign against Judah.

The annals describe the campaign as taking place in three stages.[9] First, Sennaherib marched against Luli, king of the Sidonians (which

---

Sennaherib? Kitchen (*The Third Intermediate Period*, 385) places Tirhakah at Eltekeh and thinks he marched a second time to Hezekiah's relief while Sennaherib was at Lachish. Elat ("The Political Status," 62-63) places Eltekeh at the end of the Assyrian campaign, arguing the annals are not in chronological order. Nadav Na'aman ("Sennaherib's Campaign to Judah and the Date of the LMLK Stamps," *VT* 29 [1979] 65) argues that the Egyptian army at Eltekeh was led by a Delta prince and that Tarhaqa led a second expedition later which is mentioned in 2 Kgs 19:9.

[7]Luckenbill, *AR* 2, 148. For a newer translation see Elat, "The Political Status," 61 n. 1 and Anson Rainey, "The Fate of Lachish during the Campaigns of Sennacherib and Nebuchadnezzer," *Lachish* 5, 52. Tiglath-pileser III's annals used the same expression to describe the king of Ura in Muṣurni. Cf. John Geyer, "2 Kings 18:14-16 and the Annals of Sennacherib," *VT* 21 (1971) 604 n. 60.

[8]David Ussishkin, "Answers at Lachish," *BARev* 5 (1979) 31.

[9]Na'aman ("Sennaherib's Campaign," 64-65) indicates the division is geographical and chronological. The three stages appear to me to be that, but not necessarily the details within each stage. Cf. Clements, *Isaiah*, 19.

included Tyre). Luli fled to Cyprus and Sennaherib installed Ethbaal in his place.[10] Various vassals of the west then rushed to pay homage and tribute. The second part of the campaign was directed against the Philistine rebels. Sidka, king of Ashkelon, his gods and his family were deported to Assyria and Sharruludari was appointed king in his place. Four cities belonging to Ashkelon were besieged and sacked. An Egyptian and Ethiopian army marching to the aid of Ekron was defeated at Eltekeh. Ekron fell, its rebels were executed, and Padi was restored to his throne.[11]

The third part of the campaign was directed against Hezekiah and Judah. The Oriental Institute Prism describes the campaign in the following way:

> As to Hezekiah, the Jew, he did not submit to my yoke. I laid siege to 46 of his strong cities, walled forts and to the countless small villages in their vicinity, and conquered (them) by means of well-stamped (earth-)ramps, and battering rams brought (thus) near (to the walls) (combined with) the attack by foot soldiers, (using) mines, breeches as well as sapper work. I drove out (of them) 200,150 people, young and old, male and female, horses, mules, donkeys, camels, big and small cattle beyond counting, and considered (them) booty. Himself I made a prisoner in Jerusalem, his royal residence, like a bird in a cage. I surrounded him with earthwork in order to molest those who were leaving his city's gate. His towns which I had plundered, I took away from his country and gave them (over) to Mitinti, King of Ashdod, Padi, King of Ekron, and Sillibel, King of Gaza. Thus I reduced his country, but I still increased the tribute and the *katru*-presents (due) to me (as his) overlord which I imposed (later) upon him beyond the former tribute, to be delivered annually. Hezekiah himself, whom the terror-inspiring splendor of my lordship had overwhelmed and whose irregular and elite troops which he had brought into Jerusalem, his royal

---

[10]Luckenbill, *AR* 2, 118-19. For a relief depicting the flight of Luli and the temple of Melkart see R. D. Barnett and Amleto Lorenzini, *Assyrian Sculpture in the British Museum* (Toronto: McClelland and Steward Ltd., [1975] 28). Cf. H. J. Katzenstein, "Eloulaios (Luli), King of the Sidonians," *The History of Tyre* (Jerusalem: The Shocken Institute for Jewish Research, 1973) 220-58. On the reliefs see especially 253-54. The relief is dated 690 B.C.E. by Barnett ("Phoenecia and the Ivory Trade," *Archeology* 9 [1956] 91 and Figure 9).

[11]Luckenbill, *AR* 2, 118-20. For a reconstruction of the third campaign of Sennaherib see Hayim Tadmor, "Philistia under Assyrian Rule," *BA* 29 (1966) 97. For the Judaean part of the campaign see Na'aman, "Sennaherib's Campaign," 86. On the battle of Eltekeh see note 6 above; and H. H. Rowley, *Men of God*, 109; and Andre Parrot, *Ninevah* [sic] *and the Old Testament* (New York: Philosophical Library Inc., 1955) 60. Tadmor ("Philistia," 97) argues that Eltekeh was not a total defeat for Egypt because no booty was taken by the Assyrians, no captives are recorded as being taken and there was no pursuit of the Egyptians by the Assyrians.

residence, in order to strengthen (it), had deserted him, did send me, later, to Nineveh, my lordly city, together with 30 talents of gold, 800 talents of silver, precious stones, antimony, large cuts of red stone, couches (inlaid) with ivory, *nimedu*-chairs (inlaid) with ivory, elephant-hides, ebony wood, boxwood (and) all kinds of valuable treasures, his (own) daughters, concubines, male and female musicians. In order to deliver the tribute and to do obeisance as a slave he sent his (personal) messenger.[12]

The Oriental Institute Prism together with the Taylor cylinder, virtually a duplicate, represent the final edition of the royal annals.[13] The Rassam cylinder, written after the third campaign, is several years earlier. It should be more historically reliable because it was written closer to the events described.[14] However, the Rassam cylinder has never been fully translated because its account differs so little from the two later accounts.[15]

There is an important difference at the end of the Rassam cylinder. It concerns the booty taken from the third campaign. The Oriental prism and Taylor cylinder list the booty as 30 talents of gold and 800 talents of silver, various types of gems, ivory couches and chairs, various kinds of wood, Hezekiah's daughters, his harem, and his male and female musicians.[16] To this the Rassam cylinder adds the following: various types of clothes, war materials consisting of iron, chariots, shields, lances, armor, iron daggers, bows and arrows and spears. Then it concludes by stating that the captives from all of the third campaign

[12]Oppenheim, *ANET*, 288.

[13]Luckenbill, *AR* 2, 115. For a discussion of the sources for Sennaherib see Julian Reade, "Sources for Sennaherib: The Prisms," *JCS* 27 (1975) 189-96. See also A. K. Grayson, "The Walters Art Gallery Sennaherib Inscription," *AfO* 20 (1963) 83-96. This is apparently a copy of a victory stele erected in the plain of Halule by Sennaherib. It arranges his campaigns into four against Chaldaea (campaigns 1, 4, 6, 8 of the annals) and three against Elam (campaigns 6, 7, and 8 of the annals). It omits campaigns 2, 3 and 5 of the annals. It is dated 690 B.C.E., the limmu of Nabu-kittu-uṣur.

[14]A. T. E. Olmstead (*Assyrian Historiography*, University of Missouri Social Science Studies 13:1 [Columbia: University of Missouri Press, 1916] 8, 64-65) says the latest edition of Sennaherib's annals is not very different from the earlier editions (53), an opinion which needs some modification in the light of the recent join (see below n. 35). He also points out that Assyrian official documents tell only what benefits the king. Leo Honor (*Sennacherib's Invasion of Palestine* [New York: Columbia University Press, 1926] 28) states that the Rassam cylinder should be used for the third campaign because it is the earliest (cf. note 15).

[15]Luckenbill (*AR* 2, 136) dates Rassam 700 B.C.E. Cf. Hayim Tadmor, "Philistia," 96 n. 38. On the relation of later editions to earlier editions of the annals see Louis Levine, "The Second Campaign of Sennacherib," *JNES* 32 (1973) 312.

[16]*ANET*, 288.

were "divided like sheep among my whole camp (army), as well as my governors and the inhabitants of my large cities."[17]

We can now answer at least one of our opening questions. Was there an 8th century Judaean exile after the 701 campaign? Yes, there was. The exiles included Hezekiah's daughters, wives and musicians plus unnumbered captives from the whole of the 3rd campaign divided up in three ways according to the Rassam cylinder. But what about the figure of 200,150 people from the 46 walled cities and the small towns in their neighborhood? Here we find a difference of opinion among scholars.

Some say the number is grossly exaggerated.[18] Olmstead, for example, thought the scribe had exaggerated an original 150 prisoners into 200,150 just as 1235 sheep in Sargon's display inscription became 100,225 sheep in his annals.[19] Ungnad could not accept the idea that the number of captives from Judah was almost the same as the number of captives taken from Babylonia in the first campaign. He also noted that Sargon's total number of prisoners from a greater number of villages was much smaller (140 or 146 villages and 6,170 or 20,170 captives depending on the version). Unlike Olmstead, however, Ungnad felt that one should not consider the huge number as just an Assyrian exaggeration. Rather, he felt it should be explained on the basis of Assyrian scribal practice. He concluded that the scribe had originally meant 2,150 prisoners. The text has 2 *me lim* 1 *me* 50. Ungnad suggested, that the 2 *me lim* probably was originally 2 *lim* just as the above mentioned 1235 sheep in Sargon's display inscription became 100,225 sheep—by the addition of a *me* before *lim* in the annals.[20] Borger, however, regarded Ungnad's view as orthographically improbable.[21]

[17]Luckenbill, *AR* 2, 136.

[18]R. Kittel, *A History of the Hebrews* 2 (London: Williams and Norgate, 1896) 369; and Ernest Nicholson, "The Centralization of the Cult in Deuteronomy," *VT* 13 (1963) 385. R. W. Rogers ("Sennacherib and Judah," *Studien zur Semitischen Philologie und Religionsgeschichte Julius Wellhausen gewidmet.* [Giessen: Alfred Töpelmann, 1914] 321) makes the following statement: "It is indeed not probable that there were 46 cities with walls in the Shephelah, or that there was a population of 200,150 outside Jerusalem in this small district, nor do later events make it probable that the king's successes were of so overwhelming a nature."

[19]Olmstead, *Historiography*, 8. See also his *History of Assyria* (New York: Charles Scribner's Sons, 1923) 305.

[20]Professor Hallo supplied the text reading. A. Ungnad, "Die Zahl der von Sanherib deportierten Judäer," *ZAW* 18 (1942-43) 199-201. Na'aman ("Sennacherib's Campaign," 85) agrees with Ungnad: "The actual number of prisoners and quantity of booty being smaller by far." John Bright (*A History of Israel* [2d ed.; Philadelphia: Westminster Press, 1972] 284 n. 49) also quotes Ungnad favorably.

[21]Riekele Borger, *Babylonisch-Assyrische Lesestücke* (Roma: Pontificum

Still another view was presented by Martin Noth. He felt the number simply meant that the whole land of Judah had fallen into Sennaherib's hands.[22] At least this view seems to reflect the Biblical statement in 2 Kgs 18:13: "Sennacherib, king of Assyria, came up against all the fortified cities of Judah and took them." Are these suggestions the only possibilities? Is there another way to interpret this seemingly improbable figure of 200,150 Judaeans? Several scholars have noted what they regarded as a significant omission from the annals in their account of the third campaign against Judah. The word *ašlul* which is the word usually used for deportation is missing.[23] Instead, the annals say only that the 200,150 were "brought away . . . and counted as spoil."[24] Based on this omission as well as a study by Dougherty (see below), Albright argued that the residents of these towns were not deported at all but only reckoned as subjects of Assyria. Dougherty's study had noted that the annals also do not say the 46 walled cities were "destroyed, torn down, and turned into mounds." Hence he concluded the cities were not completely destroyed.[25] However, does the lack of the term *ašlul* (or the

---

Institutum Biblicum, 1963) 112. B. Mazar ("The Campaign of Sennacherib to the land of Judah," *Eretz Israel* 2 [1953] 173 n. 14) also rejects Ungnad's view.

[22]Martin Noth, *The History of Israel* (New York: Harper & Row, 1960) 268.

[23]Robert W. Rogers, *A History of Babylonia and Assyria* 2 (New York: Eaton and Maine, 1900) 199.

[24]Luckenbill, *AR* 2, 121. There is some disagreement about the translation of *ušeṣamma* here. Oppenheim (*ANET*, 288) translates "drove out," as does G. Ernest Wright (*Isaiah* [The Layman's Bible Commentary; London: SCM Press Ltd., 1964], 77). R. Barnett, (*Illustrations of Old Testament History* [London: British Museum Publications Ltd., 1977] 60) follows Luckenbill's translation of "brought away." Parrot's "I captured and removed . . . I took as plunder" is obviously a paraphrase (*Nineveh*, 53). Y. Aharoni's "I deported from among them" is also a paraphrase (*The Land of the Bible* [Philadelphia: Westminster Press, 1979] 389). H. R. Hall (*The Ancient History of the Near East* [London: Methuen and Co., 1913] 483) says that the word probably means, "the whole country's population was regarded as spoil, though we are not told that they were carried into captivity, as it is sometimes supposed." He stated that ten times the number of Sargon's deportees from Samaria is not possible when such a large captivity is not mentioned in Hebrew sources. Wright (*Isaiah*, 77) says 200,150 is "a figure which may well represent the approximate population of Judah at that time." Rowley (*Men of God*, 105) echoes Wright but thinks 200,150 is a generous estimate. A similar view is expressed by John Gray, *I and II Kings*. (2nd ed.; OTL; Philadelphia: Westminster Press, 1970) 673-74.

[25]W. F. Albright, "The Fourth Joint Campaign of Excavations at Tell Beit Mirsim," *BASOR* 47 (1932) 14. Raymond Dougherty, "Sennacherib and the Walled Cities of Judah," *JBL* 49 (1930) 160-71. For a critique of this view and a history of its development see Rainey, "The Fate of Lachish," 49-51. Cf. n. 63.

lack of a specific mention of total destruction) in the annals mean there was no deportation? On the contrary, I would suggest this phrase refers to something else.

This particular sequence of terms—"brought away . . . and counted as spoil"—occurs several times in Sennaherib's inscriptions. It occurs seven times in the various accounts of the first campaign. It is used of the captives and spoil from Merodach-baladan's palace in Babylon, of the captives and spoil from several cities in Babylonia (Erech, Nippur, Kish, Hursagkalam(m)a, Kutha and Sippar) and of the captives and spoil from the Arabs, and the Aramean and Chaldean tribes. Significantly, it is only at the end of the account of the campaign that the number of prisoners is given and the statement is made that they were carried off to Assyria.[26] This indicates two things. Contrary to Albright, this phrase does not exclude deportation just because of the lack of *ašlul*. Secondly, the various accounts of the first campaign indicate a time lag between the bringing out and reckoning as spoil and the deportation to Assyria. The reckoning as spoil took place right after conquest. Deportation in this case took place only at the end of the campaign.

Only one account of this campaign differs from this pattern. A bull inscription written after the sixth campaign says of the goods and people of the palace of Merodach-baladan and of the various cities of Babylonia —"I captured and carried off their spoil."[27] Here deportation is clearly meant. However, this is written and summarized several years after the first campaign. By that time, deportation would have already taken place so there was no need for the scribe to note the time lag between reckoning as booty and actual deportation.[28] Therefore the reckoning as

[26]Luckenbill, *AR* 2, 116-47.

[27]Ibid., 141.

[28]I understand the phrase *šallatiš amnû* in the following way. The mention of a number with the phrase indicates to me a two-fold process—a count (which no doubt the annals regularly round off and inflate) and a "reckoning" of those counted as "booty" or "inhabitants" of the land depending on the individual situation. If there was no actual count, why do the Assyrian reliefs often depict the scribes writing down the booty as the Assyrian soldiers bring it in and pile it up before them? Cf. R. Barnett and A. Lorenzini, *Assyrian Sculpture*, pls. 11, 53, 54, and 68. Isa 33:18 also mentions a scribe as the weigher of the tribute. Finally, one could cite the practice mentioned on page 155 of "counting" resettled refugees into the hands of the local Assyrian governor. One should not be bound to a literal interpretation of the number 200,150. Yet the relief scenes of the scribes recording the booty and the mention of a number together with the term suggests the keeping of some kind of count or record. If this was done for booty, why not also for prisoners? Cf. B. Oded, "The Implementation of Mass Deportation in the Assyrian Empire," *Shnaton* 2 (1977) xvi. The English summary says: "One of the most important activities in the process of deportation was recording

booty was intended for future deportation. Deportation itself took place only after the end of the campaign.

However, this was not the only possibility. The Nebi Yunus inscription says of the first campaign, "The whole of his land I conquered and counted as booty."[29] This is obviously exaggerated but it also seems to indicate that the reckoning as booty referred to everyone in the conquered territory. Was it likely that everyone was deported? No, but everyone was reckoned or counted for the purpose of future deportation.

In the accounts of the second campaign against three cities of the Kassites the phrase occurs twice. Again the same bull inscription says "I captured, I carried off their spoil," whereas the other two texts use the other phrase. Again, because he is writing much later the scribe simply mentioned the deportation and ignores the time lag.[30] There then follows an account of the rebuilding of one of the captured cities (Bit Kilamzah) as an Assyrian fortress and the settlement in it of deportees from other lands. Refugees from the Kassites and Iasubigallai were also then settled in the other two cities. These refugees were then placed (lit. counted) into the hands of the governor of Arrapha. We are not told what happened to the original population after their being reckoned as booty. Is it not fair to assume the original inhabitants were deported? This would mean some time must have gone by before the fortress was built and the new settlers brought in and also for the deportation of at least some of the original inhabitants.[31] The theory that the purpose of the captive count was for future deportation fits here, though the accounts of the second campaign do not give it any specific support. They do not disprove it either.

When we come to the account of the third campaign, we find some interesting parallels and differences with the first two campaigns. Like the first campaign we are told of the deportation of the captives (in the Rassam cylinder) at the end of the campaign. Unlike the first campaign the number of captives is given as part of the bringing out and counting as booty, not at the end of the campaign. Unlike the second campaign, we are not told of subsequent resettlement of the conquered territory.

---

the spoils—men and animals—and reporting the number of captives and their situation from time to time. There are many examples of this in both the pictorial material and the inscriptions." He further states deportation took place in family groups.

[29]Luckenbill, *AR* 2, 154.

[30]Ibid., 117, 135 and 141.

[31]Ibid., 117-18, 135-36. Edwin R. Thiele (*The Mysterious Numbers of the Hebrew Kings* [Grand Rapids: Eerdmans, 1965] 146) notes that Sargon II did not deport anyone from Samaria until after 720, a time lag of two years between conquest and deportation, though soon after the Samaria revolt of 720.

This means two things. There was a deportation of the captives. However, the 200,150 Judaeans counted as booty represent the total population of the 46 walled cities and numerous villages. Their population was reckoned at the time of their capture for future deportation. The actual deporting began at the end of the campaign, as with the first campaign. Unlike the first campaign, not all of those counted were deported because there was a time lag between the reckoning in the third campaign and the deportation at the end of the campaign. In the first campaign the totaling comes at the end of the campaign when deportation takes place. The number there is intended to represent the number of those deported. The number of Judaeans represents the population of the captured cities and towns reckoned for future deportation. Only some of these Judaeans were deported, not all, because we are not told of a subsequent resettlement of Judah by peoples from other lands.[32]

Further evidence of the time lag between captive count or reckoning for deportation and deportation itself I find in 2 Kgs 18:31-32.

> Make your peace with me and come out to me. Then every one of you will eat of his own vine and every one of his own fig tree, and every one of you will drink the water of his own cistern; until I come and take you away to a land like your own land.

Note the sequence. Make your peace and *come out to me*. Eat *your own* food *until* I come to take you away. This I contend means that the Rabshakeh was proposing to take the captive or booty count of the people of Jerusalem who would then go home, eat their own food, and drink the waters of their own cistern until he came back for the purpose of deportation.[33] This is supported by the fact that Hezekiah's wives,

---

[32]H. G. May ("The Ten Lost Tribes," *BA* 6 [1943] 55-60) argued that only a few northerners of the 27,290 were actually deported by Sargon II. The rest, he thought, stayed put in Palestine. See also J. A. Brinkman, ("Merodachbaladan II," *Studies Presented to A. Leo Oppenheim* [Chicago: Oriental Institute, 1964] 21-22). Sargon II deported the captives of Kummuhu to Babylonia, but Babylonia was not conquered until after Kummuhu! Obviously there was a time lag here between conquest and deportation. Cf. Luckenbill, *AR* 2, 21.

[33]Bright (*History*, 299) argues that the Rabshakeh's speech exhibits an accurate knowledge of contemporary Assyrian military and deportation practices. He regards it as composed while the memory of the invasion was fresh in the author's mind. See also B. Childs, *Isaiah and the Assyrian Crisis* (SBT 3: Naperville, Il.: Alec R. Allenson, 1967) 77-81 for a form critical analysis of the speech. Cf. W. von Soden ("Sanherib vor Jerusalem 701 v. Chr.," *Antike und Universalgeschichte* [Münster: Aschendorff 1972] 43-51, esp. 48) for further comments on the Rabshakeh's speech reflecting knowledge of Assyrian practices regarding deportation. Also, W. Hallo, "From Qarqar to Carchemish," *BA* 23 (1960) 59; reprinted in BAR 2 (1964) 184; H. W. F. Saggs, "The Nimrud Letters,

daughters, and musicians were sent to Nineveh after Sennaherib had returned there, not during or even at the end of the campaign.

Therefore during the campaign captives were brought out and reckoned as booty. The reference to 200,150 Judaeans (i.e. people of the captured walled cities and nearby villages) represents this activity. Deportation began at the end of the campaign. Then the Judaean captives were divided among the army, the governors of the provinces, and the inhabitants of the large cities and deported. But not all of the 200,150 were deported, because there is no evidence of Assyrian resettlement of the conquered territory.[34] If not all were deported, what happened to them? Is it not possible some of them were counted into the hands of the vassal kings of the 3 (or 4) Philistine cities to whom the conquered territory was given by Sennaherib (as per the second campaign's governor of Arrapha)? This is one possibility. Another possibility will be discussed shortly.

Before that, we need to discuss another fragment of an inscription of Sennaherib about this third campaign. The fragment helps to interpret the "46 walled cities" of the annals. Is that number possible for tiny Judah?

A recent join of two fragments of tablets has given us this fragmentary account of the third campaign. It describes the siege and conquest of the Judaean fortress of Azekah followed by the siege and conquest of an unnamed Philistine royal city.[35] There are several points

---

1952—Part II," *Iraq* 17 (1955) 47; H. W. F. Saggs, "The Nimrud Letters, 1952—Part III," *Iraq* 18 (1956) 55.

[34] By contrast the annals specifically say of Sidka of Ashkelon, "I tore away and brought to Assyria." The annals also say of the four cities of Ashkelon conquered by Sennaherib, "I carried off their spoil" (Luckenbill, *AR* 2, 119). Assyrian names do appear on two cuneiform tablets from Gezer found by R. A. S. Macalister. Macalister felt they indicated the presence of an Assyrian garrison at Gezer. The tablets concern the sale of real estate and one of the sellers is a Nathaniah. The tablets were dated by Macalister to 649 and 648 B.C.E. R. A. S. Macalister, *The Excavation of Gezer 1902-1905, 1907-1909* 1 (London: John Murray, 1912) 22-29 (see frontispiece for photos of the tablets). A relief depicting the siege of Ga-az-ru, probably Gezer, has been found from the time of Tiglath-pileser III. This would indicate it was conquered and resettled as part of the northern conquest, not the southern conquest by Sennaherib. However, some royal stamped jar handles were also found there. Does this mean Hezekiah had control of Gezer for a while? See W. G. Dever, "Gezer," *Encyclopedia of Archeological Excavations in the Holy Land* 2 (London: Oxford University Press, 1976-78) 428-43. Dever regards them as indicative of control by Josiah.

[35] Nadav Na'aman, "Sennacherib's Letter to God on his campaign to Judah," *BASOR* 214 (1974) 25-39. See also his "Sennacherib's Campaign," 61-62. Hayim Tadmor, "The Campaign of Sargon II of Assur: A Chronological-Historical Study," *JCS* 12 (1958) 22-40 and 77-100 and "Philistia," 94. Tadmor published

to be made from this new join. First, according to Na'aman, the fragment is part of the original account of the third campaign written soon after it had ended, from which the later accounts (Rassam, Taylor and Oriental Institute) were excerpted. He bases this conclusion on the greater detail devoted to the siege and capture of individual cities in this fragment.[36] Second, the fragment clearly states, "I carried off the spoil," referring to the capture of Azekah. This proves there was an exile from Judah after the 701 campaign. It involved captives from Azekah, from Jerusalem (Hezekiah's wives, daughters and musicians) and from Lachish (based on the relief of Lachish, see below). Third, Na'aman argues that the unnamed royal Philistine city can only be Gath. This is based on his reconstruction of the third campaign from the annals, the Bible and the new join. This conquest of Gath and Azekah opened up the northern approach through the Shephelah to Jerusalem. Sennaherib then moved south to Lachish. This march from Gath to Lachish is reflected in Mic 1:10-17 which begins the list of threatened or captured towns with Gath and ends at Lachish, Jerusalem being in the middle of the list.[37] Whether

---

the second part of the join relating it to the 712 campaign of Sargon II against Ashdod. Hence Katzenstein assumes Azekah was taken by Assyria in 712 in his *History of Tyre*, 246. This must now be changed. The first piece had been published by G. Smith and associated with Azriyau of Yaudi against Tiglath-pileser III. Na'aman joined the two fragments and in his first article argued that the fragments were from a letter to his God by Sennaherib about the third campaign. His reason for dating the join to Sennaherib is that Azekah is said to be between "my border and the land of Judah," which could not have been said until after the 712 conquest of Ashdod. In the second article Na'aman changed his mind about the fragment being part of a letter to his God. Instead, he now regards the join as from the original account of the third campaign written soon after its completion ("Sennacherib's Campaign," 63 n. 4). Cf. Aharoni, (*The Land*, 391-92).

[36]Grayson ("The Walters," 87-88) notes that the Walters Art Gallery Sennaherib Inscription in the 7th campaign lists 16 Elamite cities as conquered which previously were not mentioned in any other Sennaherib inscription, in addition to listing the Elamite cities previously known as conquered in the 7th campaign. This additional detail about individual cities in a non-annal account would seem to be somewhat comparable to the new join of Sennaherib.

[37]Na'aman, "Letter to God," p. 31-32 and "Sennaherib's Campaign," 86. There is therefore no need to amend the Micah text to read Giloh for Gath as, for example, James L. Mays does (*Micah* [OTL; Philadelphia: Westminster Press, 1976] 56). Shea argues the unnamed Philistine city is Ekron because he believes Gath had been previously destroyed by Uzziah based on 2 Chr 26:6 and Amos 6:2. Also, he claims the god name Anshar is not used by Sennaherib before 689 when he destroyed Babylon. He therefore argues the join can refer only to a second campaign of Sennaherib against Judah near the end of Hezekiah's rule in 688 ("One invasion or two?" 28). However, this would mean there were two sieges of

Gath is the unnamed Philistine royal city or not, one of the 46 walled cities of Hezekiah was a Philistine royal city. Therefore the 46 walled cities are not just Judaean walled cities, but also those walled cities in the territory of Philistia previously conquered by Hezekiah (2 Kgs 18:8 "He smote the Philistines as far as Gaza, from watchtower to fortified city"). The captive count from these 46 walled cities also includes the population of the territory of Philistia directly under Hezekiah's rule, as well as that part of Judah conquered by Sennaherib. Also, 1 Chr 4:39-41 states that there was a migration of Simeonites from Judah into Philistine territory during the time of Hezekiah. No doubt this migration took place after Hezekiah's conquest, so that there were some Judaeans from Simeon living in the newly conquered Philistine territory when Sennaherib attacked.[38]

We can now list the following walled cities of the 46 said to have been conquered by Sennaherib. Lachish and Libnah (2 Kgs 19:8 and Lachish relief [see below]) Azekah and Gath? (from the new join), Mareshah, Adullam, and possibly Moreshath Gath (from Micah 1 and 2 Chr 11:5-10) if the same Gath is meant in the two texts. Since this means five cities of the eleven in Micah 1 were definitely fortified (Gath, Adullam, Mareshah, Lachish, Jerusalem), and a sixth possibly (Moreshath Gath), it is possible that the other five, so far unidentified, were also fortified. To this we can add the following archeological sites—Tell Judeidah and Tell Sheikh el ʿAreini—based on the association of destruction levels with *lmlk* stamps. Other sites suggested by archeology include Beersheba II and Arad VIII and perhaps Tell Beit Mirsim.[39] Some have argued that Isa 10:27-32 also refers to this campaign. However, Hallo and others have argued that this list of thirteen towns in Benjamin refers to the Syro-Ephraemite war.[40] This gives a total of eight

---

Ekron by Sennaherib as well as the two campaigns against Hezekiah and Jerusalem and two sieges of Lachish, the first of which was unsuccessful and the second successful. This is impossible because the Lachish prisoners are depicted working on Sennaherib's palace which was finished and dedicated in 694, six years before Shea's proposed conquest of Lachish! In short, two campaigns of Sennaherib against Judah and Hezekiah are simply impossible to defend.

[38]Bustenay Oded, "Judah and the Exile," *Israelite and Judean History* (ed. John Hayes and J. Maxwell Miller [Philadelphia: Westminster Press, 1977] 444-45). Chronicles mentions the movement of Philistine settlers into Judaean territory during the reign of Ahaz (2 Chr 28:18).

[39]See Na'aman ("Sennacherib's campaign," 83) for his discussion of Micah 1. He does not accept Tell Beit Mirsim (p. 74). Cf. Rainey, "The Fate of Lachish," 49 and Aharoni, *The Land*, 392.

[40]Aharoni (*The Land*, 393) suggests that the list of towns in Isaiah 10:28-32 may refer to an Assyrian force from Samaria which advanced from the north against Jerusalem in 701 B.C.E. Na'aman ("Sennacherib's Campaign," 69 and 86)

walled cities definitely identified (Lachish, Libnah, Azekah, a royal Philistine city [probably Gath], Adullam, Mareshah, Tell Judeidah and Tell Sheikh el ʿAreini) as conquered by Sennaherib in his 701 campaign. Another six can probably be identified (the other six towns of Micah 1), while another 3-16 are questionable but not excluded from consideration (Beersheba, Arad, Tell Beit Mirsim and the Isaiah 10 list if it can be shown to relate to 701 and not an earlier conflict). This means of the 46 walled cities we can identify almost a third (14) fairly certainly. This leaves room for some exaggeration by the Assyrian annalist, but not as much as previously supposed. One could presume there were also some walled satellite towns dependent on the Philistine royal city (Gath?) and ruled directly by Hezekiah that also are a part of the 46 walled cities.

The number 46 is therefore exaggerated at the most by two or three times the actual number. Perhaps one could suggest something similar for the 200,150 figure. It is no doubt an exaggeration but not as great as previously thought by Ungnad and Olmstead. While the walled cities were no doubt not all of the same size and did not have the same number of dependent villages, one could suggest that the number of captives was in the thousands—more than the 2,150 figure of Ungnad—but how much more one cannot say. One should also take into consideration the 1500 dead found in a mass grave at Lachish (see below p. 166), a large administrative center. Since 1500 died at Lachish alone, it would appear doubtful that only 2,150 were taken captive from all the walled cities and dependent villages captured by Sennaherib.

What about those not deported at the end of the campaign but included in the reckoning as booty? Broshi has argued that the westward expansion of Jerusalem beyond its walls and the subsequent building of a new city wall to enclose this westward expansion toward the end of the

---

thinks this force was joined by one marching from the southwest from Lachish to conduct the siege of Jerusalem. Josephus (*Antiquities*, Book X ii) says Sennaherib took all the cities of the tribes of Judah and Benjamin by force. This would seem to indicate he thought the Isaiah 10 passage applied to the 701 campaign. However, the following prefer the Syro-Ephraimitic War as the setting for the oracle. Hallo regards Isaiah 6-39 as essentially chronological. Isa 10:24-32 would therefore refer to the Syro-Ephraimitic War, 734-32 B.C.E. (related to me in a private conversation, July, 1980). He cites Donner, *ZDPV* 84 (1968) 46-54. For an eschatological interpretation see D. L. Christensen, "The March of Conquest in Isaiah 10:27c-32," *VT* 26 (1976) 385-99. See also Markus Wäfler, *Nicht-Assyrer neuassyrischer Darstellungen* (*AOAT* 26 [Kevelaer: Butzon and Bercker; Neukirchen-Vluyn: Neukirchener Verlag, 1975] 48 n. 216). Ginsberg relates the oracle to Sargon's campaign against North Arabia in 715 (*The Book of Isaiah* [Philadelphia: The Jewish Publication Society of America, 1973] 16). Clements (*Isaiah*, 32, 111-12 note 5) prefers 713-711 but leaves the possibility open that it could be 701.

eighth century was due to an influx of refugees both from the northern kingdom of Israel after 721 and later from the refugees from Sennaherib's campaign of 701 who fled the territory of Judah conquered by Sennaherib and given to the Philistines at the end of the campaign.[41] Jerusalem tripled or quadrupled in size at this time. He estimates its population went from 6,000 to 8,000 to 24,000 based on a density of 40-50 people per dunam. Finally, Broshi indicates there was also an increase of population in the Judaean hills, Judaean desert and the Negev about the same time. New sites were occupied at the end of the 8th or beginning of the 7th century in these areas.[42] This would indicate that some of the population of the captured area became refugees and resettled in previously unoccupied areas after the 701 war. The fleeing of refugees from the enemy advance is mentioned in Isaiah 10, but again it is questionable that this refers to the 701 campaign. It does, however, indicate that refugees were common in warfare then as today.

Therefore, in addition to the exiles, there was also a substantial number of refugees who fled to that part of Judah not turned over to the Philistines. This partially explains the lack of mention of a subsequent resettlement of the conquered territory by the Assyrians. It is also likely that other Judaeans were turned over to the Philistine vassals who received Judaean territory. Finally, the Lachish excavators also found evidence of a small settlement at Lachish after the destruction of Level III (701) in the ruins of the city gate. This indicates even at Lachish some remained behind, though they were few in number.[43]

[41]Luckenbill (AR 2, 120). The annals say the land was given to Ashdod, Gaza, and Ekron, and a bull inscription written after the 6th campaign (p. 143) adds Ashkelon as well. M. Broshi, "The Expansion of Jerusalem in the reigns of Manasseh and Hezekiah," IEJ 24 (1974) 21-26. See also M. Avi-Yonah, "Excavations in Jerusalem—Review and Evaluation," in Jerusalem Revealed (ed. Yigael Yadin; New Haven: Yale University Press, 1976) 22: "There was an Israelite settlement on the western hill, at first unwalled and later fortified at least in part by a stout wall—from the 8th century B.C.E. on." See also in the same volume the article by N. Avigad, "Excavating the Jewish Quarter of the Old City," 41-51.

[42]Broshi (ibid.) cites 2 Chr 31:6 where a reference is made to refugees from the north living in the cities of Judah after 721. By the same author see also "Estimating the Population of Jerusalem," BARev 4 (1978) 10-15. The anonymous article, "Part of the Ten Lost Tribes Located" (BARev 1 [1975], 27 and 32) states the evidence for the population increase in the Negev, Judaean hills and Judaean desert comes from an archeological survey of 1967-68. Michael Eisman ("A Tale of Three Cities," BA 41 [1978] 47-60) follows Broshi's conclusions but omits his mention of refugees from Sennaherib's 701 campaign as being part of the reason for the population increase. That refugees were resettled in new areas at times is indicated in Sennaherib's annals, second campaign, in Bit-Kubatti and Hardishpi (Luckenbill, AR 2, 135).

[43]David Ussishkin, "Answers at Lachish," BARev 5 (1979) 16-39.

III. JUDAEANS IN THE LACHISH RELIEFS

R. D. Barnett has done extensive work on the Lachish relief from Sennaherib's palace and the other Assyrian imperial reliefs. He has demonstrated that the Judaeans depicted on the Lachish reliefs were also depicted on other reliefs of Sennaherib. These reliefs, then, tell us more about what happened to the Judaean exiles of 701. Barnett found two types of prisoners depicted on the Lachish relief. He argued they were distinguished by their dress. The long robed, curly headed captives he called the men of Hezekiah or Judaeans who had urged Lachish to resist. These are depicted begging for their lives before Sennaherib, being beheaded or being flayed. The second type Barnett called the natives of Lachish. They are shown with a distinctive turban or scarf wound round the head with a flap hanging down over the ear.[44] They are depicted going into exile with their wives, families and belongings. This second type Barnett also found in other reliefs depicted as workmen dragging a colossal bull into place for Sennaherib's palace in Nineveh. He also claimed to find them depicted in a procession scene from Sennaherib's palace to the temple of Ishtar. Here he regarded them as the royal bodyguard and called this scene "the earliest example in history of a Jewish regiment."[45] The distinctive feature that identifies them all as natives of Lachish is the turban or scarf with the pendant end.

Barnett's work was pioneering and definitely establishes an exile from Judah after 701. However, there are several comments to be made about his conclusions. First of all, one of the curly headed men Barnett called the men of Hezekiah is depicted on the Lachish relief going into exile leading a team of oxen pulling a wagon loaded with his family.[46]

---

[44]R. D. Barnett, "The Siege of Lachish," *IEJ* 8 (1958) 161-64. See also by the same author, *Assyrian Palace Reliefs and their Influence on the Sculpture of Babylonia and Persia* (London: Batchworth Press, Ltd., n.d.) 29 and pl. 79. For the Lachish reliefs see also Barnett and Lorenzini (*Assyrian Sculpture*) pls. 76-88; Ussishkin, "Answers," 16-39 and the covers for full color photographs. Cf. Archibald Paterson, *Assyrian Sculpture—Palace of Sennacherib* (The Hague: Martinus Nijhoff, 1915) Plates 68-77. For an excellent summary of the Neo-Assyrian palace reliefs see Pauline Albenda, "Syrian-Palestinian Cities on Stone," *BA* 49 (1980) 222-29. She summarizes the Lachish reliefs as follows: "The sculptured records of Sennacherib's campaign against Lachish were contained in one small chamber. The siege and capture of the city occupy 13 slabs that cover all the walls of the room (ca. 11.6 x 5.5m), relieved only by the entrance."

[45]Barnett, "The Siege," 164. Cf. Austin Henry Layard, *The Monuments of Nineveh* (Second Series; London: John Murray, 1853) Plates 11 and 13.

[46]See Barnett, *Assyrian Palace Reliefs*, Plate 45.

This means it is likely that all the captives had the same hairstyle but those with the scarves have their curly hair covered. Only clothing, not hairstyle, distinguishes the two types. They are all therefore Judaeans. In later works Barnett is somewhat unclear on what to call the second type of prisoner. In the *IEJ* article he calls them native Lachishites or a Jewish regiment. In two later works they are called "Philistines or Judaeans,"[47] or "a Philistine or Lachish regiment."[48] Perhaps he is assuming as he does elsewhere that the word "Philistine" meant Judaeans as well as Philistines to the Assyrians. A cylinder written after the 5th campaign mentions captives from Tyre and Philistia (i.e. the third campaign) as well as others from other campaigns working on the palace at Nineveh but does not mention Judaeans.[49] Here Barnett argued that the reason for the omission of the Judaeans was that they were included under the term Philistine by the Assyrians, because the Judaean territory conquered by Sennaherib had been turned over to the Philistines.[50]

That Sennaherib's bodyguard consisted of a Jewish regiment is questionable. In his *IEJ* article Barnett makes this claim on the basis of a plate formerly published by H. R. H. Hall. Barnett identifies this scene as coming from the ramp leading to the temple of Ishtar in Sennaherib's palace. Hall had identified the two soldiers depicted as Iranian bowmen from the time of Asshurbanipal. Was this because Sennaherib's palace was partially redone by Asshurbanipal? We are not told.[51]

In a later work Barnett prints two plates, the one from Hall (pl. 51) and the other (pl. 53) which he identifies as from the same procession

---

[47]Barnett, *Assyrian Scupture*, Pl. 83.

[48]Barnett, *Assyrian Palace Reliefs*, 28, though on 19 they are Lachishites again.

[49]Luckenbill, *AR* 2, 165-66. Also, Barnett, *Assyrian Palace Reliefs*, 19.

[50]Barnett, "The Siege," 164. Cf. Barnett, *Illustrations of Old Testament History* (London: British Museum Publications, 1977) 64-65. Judaeans are depicted in the following plates in Layard, *Monuments*:

Pl. 10 - about 15 towing with other captives a block of stone or boat?

Pl. 11 - about 35 towing a boat.

Pl. 13 - 9+ towing a colossal bull on a sledge.

Pl. 15 is the pl. to which Barnett refers in "The Siege," 164 n. 8; but here the workers are wearing a headband, not a scarf wrapped around the head and there is no pendant end.

Pl. 16 perhaps; though here the sash(?) hanging down below the skirt is missing.

Siege of Lachish pls. in Layard are the following: Pls. 21-24 and 36.

[51]H. R. H. Hall, *Babylonian and Assyrian Sculpture in the British Museum* (Paris: G. van Oest, 1928) Plate 38:1. Cf. Barnett, *Assyrian Palace Reliefs*, 19 and 28.

scene to the Ishtar temple.[52] The first plate shows one and a half or two bowmen (Hall's pl.). Pl. 53 depicts a bowman and a spearman, though here Barnett cuts off the spearman who, as we shall see, is the only clear Lachishite soldier. Of these four presumed Lachishite soldiers only one, the spearman, has the distinctive Lachishite headdress with pendant end. This is the one Barnett's plate cuts off, but he is shown on duplicate plates elsewhere (see n. 52), The bowman on pl. 53 with the Lachishite spearman is dressed similarly, but he has a headband with no pendant end. The hair on the top of his head is clearly visible. He does not appear to be Lachishite since he lacks the distinctive headdress. The two bowmen of pl. 51 also have a headband, this time with pendant end, but it is decorated, not plain as the headband of the bowman on pl. 53. These two bowmen are also dressed differently than the other two on pl. 53. Their quivers, sashes, and skirts are not the same as the bowman on pl. 53. They cannot be Lachishites, and we are left with Hall's original identification of them as Iranian.[53] Similarly dressed bowmen appear to be depicted fighting for the Assyrians on the relief fragment of the siege of . . . alammu. At least, the headbands and quivers appear to be the same.[54] So we have one and possibly a second Lachishite in the procession scene and two who are not. This is not therefore the earliest Jewish regiment in history.

Wäfler's work takes Barnett's a step further. In a work on non-Assyrians depicted in the Assyrian reliefs he devotes a full chapter to the Judaeans. He states that both types found on the Lachish reliefs are Judaeans. Type A (the ones with the scarves) are the inhabitants of Lachish. Type B (the long robed individuals) are Judaeans of a privileged class. They are distinguished from Type A by their dress and their treatment. Type A is also depicted on the Lachish relief wearing pointed helmets with the pendant end, a point Barnett had not mentioned.[55] It is

---

[52]Barnett, *Assyrian Palace Reliefs*, Pl. 51, depicts one bowman and half of another. This is the same scene as Hall's Pl. 38:1 (see note 51) and also is found in Barnett, *Assyrian Sculpture*, Pl. 83. Pl. 53 depicts a bowman (and spearman as we see from the other reproductions of this scene). This pl. is reproduced elsewhere in Barnett, "The Siege," Pl. 32b. It is also found in Paterson, *Assyrian Sculpture*, Pl. 99 and Markus Wäfler, *Nicht-Assyrer*, Tafel 3:2. In Hallo (*BA* 23 [1960]), it is on p. 45, Fig. 3. Hallo there correctly identifies only the spearman as a Lachishite soldier—not the bowman.

[53]Cf. Wäfler, *Nicht-Assyrer*, 60: ". . . ein Teil dieser Garde wurde nun offensichtlich von Judäern gestellt, unverkennbar trotz assyrischierter Kleidung und Barttracht an ihren charackteristisch gewickelten Turbanen." Note he says *a part* (ein Teil) of the guard.

[54]S. Smith, *Assyrian Sculptures in the British Museum* (London: British Museum, 1938) pls. XLII, LXIV and LXII.

[55]Wäfler, *Nicht-Assyrer*, 52-53.

type A which is found working on Sennaherib's palace and as part of the royal guard. Wäfler describes the characteristic scarf with pendant end that identifies the Judaeans in Sennaherib's relief as follows: "Kreuzförmig sich überschneidende Kalottenwindungen und das unter der Stirnwindung durchgezogene und lose herabfallende Ende."[56]

To the previous finds of Barnett he adds several other depictions of Judaeans. First, a scene of three musicians—the one on the left curly-headed and the other two having the scarf but without a pendant end. All three are long robed. Wäfler thinks they are some of Hezekiah's musicians sent as tribute to Nineveh.[57] A relief from Til Barsip shows a row of lance-bearing soldiers wearing the Lachish headdress. However, the date appears to be from the time of Shalmaneser V, a point Wäfler is unable to explain.[58] A fragment depicts a single man wearing a Lachish headdress previously published separately by Barnett.[59] Also, another relief fragment depicts a single man wearing the characteristic headdress.[60]

Therefore the Lachish reliefs and other reliefs from Sennaherib's palace indicate there was a Judaean exile after 701 B.C.E. It was an exile of a significant number of people. Some of the exiles according to the reliefs worked on building Sennaherib's palace at Nineveh. Others became a part of the Assyrian army, even of the royal bodyguard. They were incorporated into native Assyrian regiments, however, not a separate Jewish regiment.[61] The people of Lachish went into exile with their

---

[56]Ibid., 61.

[57]Ibid., Tafel 3:3. Cf. his note 292 for a discussion of the original location of this long known fragment. For a more complete picture see C. J. Gadd, *The Stones of Assyria* (London: Chatle and Windom, 1936) pl. 20. Barnett, *Assyrian Sculpture*, Plate 85, says it is from Room 36 which is the room from which the ramp came which led to the Ishtar temple in Sennaherib's southwest palace.

[58]Ibid., 55-56.

[59]Ibid., Tafel 2:4. Cf. Barnett *et al.*, "Altorientalische Altertümer in Museen und Privatsammlungen," *AfO* 20 (1963) 199-200 and Figure 15.

[60]Wäfler, *Nicht-Assyrer*, Tafel 2:3. Fragments of a relief depicting the siege of Lachish were also found in the throne hall of Sennaherib. The fragments are two meters high and photographs are found in Faisal El-Wailly, "Foreword, part 4. Nineveh" (*Sumer* 21 [1965], 6 and Figures 3 and 4). Nothing useful for our study can be obtained from the photographs.

[61]J. E. Reade's critique of Barnett's work is to be rejected ("The Neo-Assyrian Court and Army: Evidence from the sculptures," *Iraq* 34 [1972] 87-112). He rejected the idea of identifying Lachishites on the basis of the headscarf with earflaps (p. 105 n. 63), because he claimed that men wearing them appear in the Assyrian army at the siege of Lachish. Barnett's identification of Lachishites in Sennaherib's bodyguard, Reade thinks, is possible, but he seems to prefer to regard them as captives or descendants of captives from central Syria or Palestine taken by Sargon II (cf. 106). On the Assyrian army organization see H. W. F.

families and some of their possessions. The number of Judaeans on the reliefs indicates a substantial exile.[62]

IV. EVIDENCE FROM THE LACHISH EXCAVATIONS

We now turn to the archeological evidence from Lachish. The latest excavator of Lachish, David Ussishkin, thinks he has solved the long dispute about the date of Lachish Level III. He argues that the level is to be dated to 701 and not 597, because no other level appears to match the city depicted on the Assyrian relief and no other level matches the account of the 701 campaign.[63] Rainey agrees:

> Lachish III underwent a terrific destruction; signs of intense burning were everywhere; the brick walls were often seared red clear through. In short, Lachish in Stratum III was a mighty fortress, an important administrative center, and the city suffered total destruction by fire.[64]

Many iron arrowheads were also found in this level and a tomb associated with this level was found which contained the disarticulated skeletons of some 1500 people. The bones were buried with pottery fragments and animal bones (mostly pigs) thrown on top. Very few of the skeletons were of elderly people. It is thought the bones were buried in a mass grave during the cleanup after the fall of the city to Sennaherib. The pottery fragments found with the bones were dated to the late 8th or early 7th centuries.[65] Ussishkin thinks that Lachish was left in ruins for

---

Saggs, "Assyrian Warfare in the Sargonid Period," *Iraq* 25 (1963) 145-54; Yigael Yadin, *The Art of Warfare in Biblical Lands* 2 (New York: McGraw Hill Inc., 1963) 293-94. J. E. Reade (p. 102) notes that the provincial areas provided chariots, horsemen and foot soldiers to the army but that only the foot soldiers are depicted on the reliefs wearing native dress. Cf. *ANET*, 284-85, for Sargon's accounts of procuring chariots and horsemen from conquered Hamath for his army. See B. Parker, ("Administrative Tablets," 15) for the contingent from Bit-Yakin in Sargon's army.

[62]See Layard, *Monuments*, pls. 11 and 13 and n. 50.

[63]For a history of the controversy see Rainey ("The Fate of Lachish," 50-59). Also, David Ussishkin ("Answers," 25-26, 33; and "The Destruction of Lachish by Sennaherib and the dating of the royal Judaean storage jars," *Tel Aviv* 4 [1977] 30, n. 2). He argues that the Lachish evidence disproves Dougherty's theory. Cf. n. 25.

[64]Rainey, "The Fate of Lachish," 47.

[65]G. Ernest Wright, "Judean Lachish," *BAR* 2 (ed. Edward Campbell and David Noel Freedman; Missoula: Scholars Press, 1957) 304-5. Holladay, after examining the pottery of Lachish III and II in an earlier attempt to resolve the dispute, had concluded by saying, "Henceforth the burden of proof is on anyone who wants to argue an earlier date (i.e. anyone who wants to argue for 701) and

much of the 7th century, aside from a poor habitation on the ruins of the city gate. About the time of Josiah it was rebuilt (Level II).[66]

The archeological evidence therefore indicates the thorough destruction of Lachish in Sennaherib's 701 campaign. Only a few remained living at the site after the destruction. The site was probably turned over to the Philistines after the war. The total destruction of Lachish indicated by archeology disproves Dougherty's theory as does the new join mentioning the destruction of Azekah.[67]

V. ONOMASTIC EVIDENCE

Before turning to the Biblical evidence, several comments are in order on the onomastic evidence. A Hebrew inscription has been found on an ivory from Nimrud dating from the 8th century, but there is no way of telling how it got to Nimrud (as tribute from Menahem, Hezekiah, or booty from Samaria,[68] or even from Ahaz we could add). Quite a few Hebrew names have turned up in various inscriptions of the 7th century B.C.E. in Mesopotamia, such as Menahem, Hosea, Neriah, Pelatiah and others.[69] Of those names which appear to be definitely Hebrew as opposed

---

the demonstration will have to assume as the first order of business the carrying back of the entire series of royal stamped jar handles into the 8th century." This Ussishkin and Rainey have done. Cf. John S. Holladay Jr., "Of Sherds and Strata: Contributions toward an Understanding of the Archeology of the Divided Monarchy," *Magnalia Dei* (Garden City: Doubleday, 1976) 266-67. See also note 66. For a similar mass grave at Ashdod of about 3000 skeletons probably from the assault of the Turtanu of Sargon II in 712-711, see M. Elat, "The Economic Relations of the Neo-Assyrian Empire with Egypt," *JAOS* 98 (1978) 33.

[66] Ussishkin, *BAR* 5, 34. The dating of Lachish Level III to 701 also means that the *lmlk* stamps are all to be assigned to Hezekiah's time, according to Ussishkin and Rainey. See note 65. Ussishkin, "The Destruction," 53 n. 14, rejects Elat's argument that a Philistine garrison and governor were located at Lachish after 701. See Elat, *Lachish* 5, 63-64. See also Na'aman, "Sennaherib's Campaign," and David Diringer, "Sennaherib's attack on Lachish: new epigraphic evidence," *VT* 1 (1951) 134-36, for further comments on the *lmlk* stamp controversy.

[67] See nn. 35 and 63. Ussishkin, "The Destruction," 53.

[68] A. R. Millard, "Alphabetic Inscriptions on Ivories from Nimrud," *Iraq* 24 (1962) 51.

[69] For a good summary of the onomastica see A. Malamat, "Exile, Assyrian," *EncJud* 6 (1972) 1034-35. Also, W. F. Albright, "An Ostracon from Calah and the North Israelite Diaspora," *BASOR* 149 (1958) 36; William Hallo, "From Qarqar to Carchemish," *BAR* 2, 176; J. D. Segal, "An Aramaic Ostracon from Nimrud," *Iraq* 19 (1957) 139-45. See Barnett, *Illustrations*, 62-64, for a discussion of the inscribed bronze bowls from Nimrud. Cf. Barnett, "Layard's Nimrud Bronzes and their Inscriptions," *Eretz Israel* 8 (1969) 1-7, and Yigael Yadin, "A Note on

to Northwest Semitic, there is no way to tell whether they are from Judah
or from Israel. Olmstead relates that a Judaean captive of 701 by the name
of Ahiyah was sold to the slave dealer Bahianu a year later. However, the
name he read as Ahiyah is probably to be read as Naṣir-yau. The text is
about the freeing of his son Mannu-ki-Arbaili from Bahianu.[70] Barbara
Parker discovered a Hilkiah in one of the Nimrud letters, a name which is
found in the Bible in 2 Kgs 18:37.[71] The onomastic evidence therefore
indicates Hebrews living in exile in Mesopotamia in various circumstances, but it doesn't provide us with any definite evidence for a
Judaean exile after 701.[72]

VI. BIBLICAL EVIDENCE

We turn now to the Biblical evidence for a Judaean exile after 701
B.C.E. One of the questions we asked at the beginning of this study was,
if there was a Judaean exile after 701, why is it not mentioned in the
Bible? There is no mention of an exile at this time in the account in
2 Kgs 18-20. The closest the Kings account gets is the speech of
Rabshakeh mentioned earlier in which he offers the people of Jerusalem
peace and promises to take them to a land like their own land. However,
Jerusalem was not captured and its inhabitants were not deported (except
for Hezekiah's wives, daughters, and musicians), and the speech relates
only to the people of Jerusalem. It says nothing about exiles from the
rest of Judah.[73]

---

the Nimrud Bronze Bowls," *Eretz Israel* 8 (1969) 6. [But see now J. Naveh, "The
Ostracon from Nimrud: an Ammonite Name-List," *Maarav* 2/2 (1979-80) 163-71.
Ed.]

[70]A. T. Olmstead, *History of Assyria* (New York: Charles Scribner's Sons,
1923) 305. Cf. C. H. W. Johns, *Assyrian Deeds and Documents* 3 (Cambridge:
Deighton, Bell & Co., Ltd., 1924) 404-5. Hallo indicates that Mannu-ki-Arbaili
probably means "Who is like (Ishtar) of Arbailu?" and calls it a notably
assimilationist name (from his critique of this paper).

[71]B. Parker, "Administrative Tablets," 27-28. ND2443 Col. 4, 1. 4 (no
date given).

[72]On Assyrian treatment of exiles cf. Hallo, *BAR* 2, 184. Cf. H. W. F. Saggs,
"The Nimrud Letters, 1952: Part III," *Iraq* 18 (1956) 40-56; "The Nimrud
Letters, 1952—Part IX," *Iraq* 36 (1974) 199-221; and Shalom Paul, "Sargon's
Administrative Diction in II Kings 17:27," *JBL* 88 (1969) 73-74. For a study of
Assyrian deportation see B. Oded, "Mass Deportation in the Neo-Assyrian
Empire—Facts and Figures." *Eretz Israel* 14 (1978) 62-68 (Hebrew), 124-25
(English summary). Also, B. Oded, "Assyrian rule in Transjordan," *JNES* 29
(1970) 177-86, "The Implementation of Mass Deportations in the Assyrian
Empire," *Shnaton* 2 (1977) xvi, and "Mass Deportations in the Neo-Assyrian
Empire—Aims and Objectives," *Shnaton* 3 (1978-79) xviii.

[73]2 Kgs 18:31-32 = Isa 36:16-17.

The Kings account is closely paralleled by the account in Isaiah 36-39.[74] In both accounts the emphasis is on Jerusalem's miraculous deliverance from the Assyrians by the Lord. The devastation of Judah is also emphasized.[75] Both accounts emphasize the surviving remnant which would come out of Jerusalem and take root. Finally, both accounts focus on the promise that Jerusalem would not be taken. These accounts therefore emphasize the fate of Jerusalem in the 701 campaign. They find the continuation of the national existence in the remnant which survived in the land, especially in Jerusalem. The king, the temple and the city remained in existence. Both the 8th century Israelite exile and the 6th century Judaean exile marked the end of national entities. The 8th century Judaean exile did not. That fact, together with these accounts' emphasis on the national existence continuing through the remnant in the land, led to the ignoring of the exiles from Judah after 701. The growth of the remnant in the land after the devastation was seen as fulfillment of prophecy at this time and not the fate of the exiles. They are not mentioned because they did not fit the author's purpose and theme.

The 2 Kings account closes with the story of Hezekiah's illness, the embassy from Babylon and Isaiah's comment on Hezekiah's reception of that embassy. In this Isaiah speech (2 Kgs 20:16-19) we get a promise of an exile from Judah which could be applied to the 8th century Judaean exile (since the story is obviously out of chronological order, the envoys

[74] 2 Kgs 18:14-16 is not included in Isaiah. This section is the closest to the account in Sennaherib's annals. 2 Kgs 18:17-19:35 = Isa 36:1-37:38 except for a few minor differences in style for which see Leo L. Honor, *Sennacherib's Invasion of Palestine* (New York: Columbia University Press, 1926) 36 and Brevard Childs, *Isaiah and the Assyrian Crisis* (SBT 3; Naperville, Ill.: Alec R. Allenson Inc., 1967) 73. 2 Kgs 20:1-19 = Isaiah 38-39 except 38:9-22, the letter prayer of Hezekiah, is not in Kings. For a discussion of this literary type see W. Hallo, "Royal Correspondence of Larsa I," *AOAT* 25 (1976) 209-24. 2 Kgs 20:7-11 is abridged in Isa 38:7-8. See Honor, *Sennacherib's Invasion*, 69 n. 6. For a thorough discussion of the nature of the sources and for an evaluation of the various hypotheses, see Honor, *Sennacherib's Invasion*, 13-25, 42-44, 61-62; Childs, "Isaiah," 119-20; and Clements, "Isaiah," 28-30. Clements regards 2 Kgs 18:17-19:37 as a theological embellishment of a circle of writers from the time of Josiah who were elaborating on Isaiah 10:5-15. The mention of the destruction of the Assyrian army by the angel of the Lord he regards as an editorial addition to dramatize God's deliverance of Jerusalem in 701. The age of Josiah saw a special theological significance in Jerusalem's being spared from the Assyrians. This optimistic picture of God's favor for Jerusalem was modified by the addition of the stories in 2 Kings 20 after the fall of Jerusalem in 598 but before 587 (pp. 61-62, 68-69, 90-92).

[75] 2 Kgs 18:13 = Isa 36:1 and 2 Kgs 19:25-26 = Isa 37:26-27.

having been sent sometime before 701),[76] but the passage refers to *sons* of Hezekiah becoming eunuchs in the palace of the king of *Babylon*. The purpose of the account in the narrative is to set the stage for the Babylonian exile. The rest of Kings tells us how this was fulfilled: Hezekiah's descendants and treasures were taken to Babylon. So it refers to the 6th century exile, not the 8th century exile from Judah. One could argue that the mention of Babylon is a later insertion in place of an original Assyria, but there is no evidence for such a substitution.[77]

The Chronicles account (2 Chronicles 32) emphasizes even more the miraculous deliverance of Jerusalem and Hezekiah than the Kings-Isaiah account. It omits Hezekiah's surrender, his tribute, and his reliance on Egypt for help. Even the mention of the taking of all the fortified cities of Judah is changed to an intention by Sennaherib to take them. What is recounted is mainly taken from the Kings-Isaiah account except for vv 2-8 of chap. 32.[78] Again there is no mention of an exile at this time. Even the devastation of Judah is almost totally removed from the account except for a rather vague reference to "wrath that came upon Judah and Jerusalem."[79]

There is a reference to an exile at the beginning of the Chronicles account of Hezekiah's reign in chapter 29. Hezekiah is speaking to the people of Jerusalem in the first year of his reign and says, "For lo, our fathers have fallen by the sword, and our sons and our daughters and our wives are in captivity for this" (v 9). This refers not to the Judaean exile of 701, but to the previous chapter's account of captives taken in the reign of Ahaz by the Edomites (v 16) and Damascus (v 5) and Israel (v 8). The captives taken by Israel were returned to Jericho (v 15). This therefore tells us nothing about the exile we are discussing, but it does hint at the beginnings of a dispersion from Judah already in the latter

[76]Hallo, *BAR* 2, 182.

[77]H. R. Hall (*The Ancient History of the Near East*; London: Methuen and Co. Ltd., [1913] 485) proposes this switch. The text does say Hezekiah's own son born to him would be taken away. However, the annals of Sennaherib mention only daughters of Hezekiah taken to Nineveh, not sons. Secondly, Hezekiah's comment obviously indicates he thought he would escape the threat of Isaiah. Another possibility is to connect this oracle with 2 Chr 33:11-13 which states Hezekiah's son Manasseh was bound and taken as a prisoner to Babylon but later returned to Jerusalem.

[78]Honor, *Sennacherib's Invasion*, 63. Rowley, *Men of God*, 107. Childs (*Isaiah*, 106-7) calls the story in Chronicles a midrash whose purpose is to present Hezekiah as a model of faith throughout. On the Babylonian embassy account see Brinkman, "Merodach-baladan II," 32.

[79]2 Chr 32:25-26.

part of the eighth century before Hezekiah.[80] Therefore Chronicles also ignores the 701 exile like the Kings-Isaiah account.

Finally we turn to the eighth century prophets. Here we find for the first time a few references to this exile. The reason for the few references in Isaiah is to be explained by the fact that "the prophet's whole preaching is permeated from its very beginning by the theme of Zion threatened but finally redeemed."[81] As in Kings, the emphasis in Isaiah falls on the remnant who survived "a campaign whose aim was their total destruction."[82] Rowley summarizes the message of Isaiah by saying that he prophesied that the land would be devastated but Jerusalem would be spared. And this is what happened.[83]

Isaiah described the devastation of Judah in the eighth century in several ways: as a booth in a vineyard or a lodge in a cucumber field— almost like Sodom and Gomorrah (1:4-9), as the toppling of a forest with an ax (10:33-34), as the shaving with a razor the hair of the beard and the hair of the feet (7:20), and as a vineyard about to be destroyed (5:5-6), so that the cities would lie waste (6:11-12). Assyria was viewed by Isaiah as the rod of Yahweh's anger (10:5-11), but Assyria had gone too far. Therefore it also would be punished by Israel's God (10:12-19) and be broken in the land of Judah (14:25). Before this happened, destruction for Judah was decreed (10:22), because of its covenant with death (28:18) and reliance on Egypt for help (30:1-5) so that only a few survivors would be left (1:9).[84]

Despite this emphasis there do seem to be a few passages in Isaiah which relate to an exile after 701 B.C.E. either in a general way or in a very specific way. "Therefore my people go into exile for lack of knowledge" (5:13) comes soon after the song of the vineyard. It is part of

[80]For an opposing view see Ernest Nicholson, "The Centralization of the Cult in Deuteronomy," *VT* 13 (1963) 385. He argues this refers to Hezekiah's wives and daughters taken into exile by Sennaherib. Since the speech is said to come from the first year of Hezekiah and due to the exiles just previously mentioned in chapter 28 in the reign of Ahaz, this seems unlikely.

[81]G. von Rad, *The Message of the Prophets* (New York: Harper and Row, 1962) 136.

[82]Ibid., 135. Honor (*Sennacherib's Invasion*, 79) says Isaiah prophesied on two themes during 705-701: 1. The anticipated destruction and 2. the great deliverance. Clements rejects the second point as not a part of Isaiah's message (*Isaiah*, 51). He argues the message of the overthrow of Assyria in Isaiah was added by Josianic editors who themselves were not referring to the events of 701. Instead, they were referring to the imminent downfall of Assyria in the time of Josiah.

[83]Rowley, *Men of God*, 123-24.

[84]See also Isa 32:9-14, 30:16-17, 4:2-3, 2:22-3:4.

an announcement of punishment against the people of the land and the nobility of Jerusalem whose content is closely related to the song of the vineyard. At the end of Isaiah's call-vision is a general reference to dispersal from the land (6:12 "and the Lord removes men far away"). This is connected with the desolation of the cities of Judah and the land. Both of these passages are probably from the early part of Isaiah's career and so speak in a general way of the 701 exile but also include the devastation and captives taken during the Syro-Ephraemite war. They apply to the whole of Isaiah's ministry, not just to the period 705-701. Yet they do indicate Isaiah expected an exile from Judah towards the end of the 8th century.

11:12-16 is an oracle promising a return from the exile in Assyria for the exiles of both Judah and Israel. It is preceded by a verse which promises a return from Assyria and several nations scattered throughout the ancient world. Because of v 11 and the mention of the highway in the desert (v 16) (found elsewhere only in 40:3-4, 42:16 and 57:14), the oracle is usually dated to the 6th century Babylonian exile. However, if one assumes a terrible devastation of Judah in 701 and an exile soon thereafter to Assyria of many of Judah's people, then the promise of a return from Assyria of both Judah and Israel fits the 8th century very well. One could assume that the reference in v. 11 to the other nations besides Assyria was a later updating for the 6th century situation of an original 8th century oracle promising a return to the 8th century exiles.[85] A promise of a return from Assyria in the 6th century, and not Babylon, for exiles from both Judah and Israel makes little sense unless one presumes something like the above suggestion.

The last passage in Isaiah comes from another section usually dated to the 6th century Babylonian exile: "by exile thou didst contend with them (Isa 27:8)." This mention of an exile is closely connected with a mention of deserted fortified cities (v 10) and with a promise of a return (v 12-13). This promise of a return is for exiles found in three places, within the borders of Syria-Palestine, in Assyria, and in Egypt. This fits best the 8th century situation given an 8th century Judaean exile and captives taken earlier by Judah's neighbors in the Syro-Ephraemite war. The mention of Egypt is a problem as there is no other specific reference to Judaeans fleeing to Egypt at this time or being driven there. However, it is an even greater difficulty if assigned to the 6th century because then

---

[85]Otto Kaiser, *Isaiah 1-12* (OTL; Philadelphia: Westminster Press, 1972) 164. Bezalel Porten would date this to the 8th century B.C.E. See his *Archives from Elephantine* (Los Angeles: University of California Press, 1968) 7-8. Something similar occurs in Amos 5:27 and Stephen's quotation of it in Acts 7:42-43. The Amos text reads "I will exile you beyond Damascus," but Damascus is replaced by Babylon in the Acts passage.

it directly opposes the several prophecies of Jeremiah which predict the destruction of the remnant of Judah which went to Egypt after 587.[86] What helps even more to place this promise of a return and mention of an exile in the 8th century is that a similar promise of a return from Assyria and Egypt is found in an earlier 8th century prophet (Hos 11:11 "They shall come trembling like birds from Egypt and like doves from the land of Assyria").[87] Isaiah did therefore refer to the exile after 701 from Judah and promised a return from that exile to the exiles of Judah and the exiles from Israel from the earlier Assyrian campaigns. This type of promise is also found in Hosea and Micah.[88]

The clearest reference to this exile from Judah after 701, however, is found in Mic 1:16 "For they shall go forth from you into exile." This is the concluding verse to the oracle describing the Assyrian advance through the Shephelah from Gath to Lachish.[89] The verse opens with a call to mourn "for the children of your delight" who are about to go into exile. Given the context, it is impossible to understand how this could be interpreted as a "later application of Micah's saying to Jerusalem after the city has fallen to the Babylonians."[90] Other references to the campaign of 701 in Micah are probably to be found in 2:4-5 which speaks of the giving of the ruined portion of Judah to the Philistines at the end of the campaign. 4:6 contains a promise of the Lord that he will gather those who have been driven away and those whom he has afflicted. This could be related to the Assyrian practice of bringing out and reckoning as booty after the conquest of a city. It could refer to refugees or exiles and, given the situation in the 8th century, there is no need to assign this automatically to the 6th century. 4:10 speaks of going forth from the city and dwelling in the open country which sounds similar to the passage from the speech of Rabshakeh cited earlier (2 Kgs 18:31-32). "You shall go to Babylon" could then be seen as a 6th century updating of an 8th century oracle. Or it is conceivable that Micah may have even thought some of the 701 exiles were going to Babylon. Babylonia had been devastated in Sennaherib's first campaign and over 200,000 people deported from that area. It was Assyrian practice to bring

---

[86]H. L. Ginsberg ("Gleanings in First Isaiah," *Jubilee Volume Mordecai Kaplan* [New York: Jewish Theological Seminary, 1953] 250) thinks that 27:8f comes from late in Isaiah's career. See also Jeremiah 42-44.

[87]Cf. Hosea 8:13, 9:3, 6, 11:5 and Micah 7:11.

[88]See notes 85, 86, and 87.

[89]See Na'aman, "Sennacherib's Campaign," 67-68 and 83 for a discussion of this section in Micah.

[90]Mays, *Micah*, 60. He says this despite referring to Sennaherib's deportation of the outlying population in the previous sentence.

in exiles from other conquered areas to provinces from which deportations had taken place.[91] There is also in Micah as in Isaiah an emphasis on the devastation coming on the land as the result of the Assyrian attack: destruction of the cities and chariots as well as idolatries (1:10-16, 5:10-14), and the earthwork Sennaherib claims to have set up around the city of Jerusalem (5:1).[92] Finally in 7:11 a promise of a return from Assyria and Egypt is found similar to those from Hosea and Isaiah cited above (pp. 171-72).

Therefore the biblical narrative accounts concentrate on the devastation of Judah, the deliverance of Jerusalem by the Lord, and the remnant which would survive the destruction and remain in the land. However, the 8th century prophets do refer to the 701 exile.[93] The references in Isaiah and Micah to this exile have often been overlooked or assigned to the 6th century Babylonian exile. The prophets did not emphasize this 8th century exile, and it was overshadowed by the later 6th century one, but they did not ignore it either.

VII. CONCLUSION

There was an exile from Judah at the end of the 8th century, indicated by Assyrian and Biblical sources. How many captives were actually deported we cannot estimate, but it must have been a sizeable number, certainly in the thousands. Certainly it was a number comparable to the 8th century Israelite exile to Assyria and the 6th century Judaean exile to Babylon. According to the Rassam cylinder those who were deported from Judah in 701 were divided among the Assyrian army, the governors of the provinces and the inhabitants of the large cities. We know of deportees from Lachish (reliefs), from Azekah (the new join) and Jerusalem (the annals—Hezekiah's tribute). Some of the exiles worked as slaves on Sennaherib's building projects at Nineveh. Some were incorporated as auxiliaries into the Assyrian army. Other Judaeans reckoned as booty became refugees and moved into the territory of Judah not given to the Philistines at the end of the campaign. Here they

---

[91] See Luckenbill, *AR* 2, 133, and my discussion of Sennaherib's second campaign on pp. 150-51. Also see notes 31 and 32 above.

[92] Mays (*Micah*, 113) again thinks this refers to the Babylonian siege of the city of Jerusalem. For the opposite view see H. L. Ginsberg, "Judah and the Transjordan States from 734 to 582 B.C.E.," (*Alexander Marx; Jubilee Volume on the occasion of his seventieth birthday*. [New York: Jewish Theological Seminary, 1950] 259). See also Sennaherib's annals quoted earlier on pp. 149-51.

[93] Hallo suggests, "The fact that the prophets refer to the exile of 701 but 2 Kings does not may be because this exile did not fit the Deuteronomic view of history—Hezekiah being reckoned as a good king." [Quoted from his critique of this paper.]

became part of that remnant which took root and ate the first year what grew of itself, and the second year what sprang up of the same. In the third year they sowed and reaped and planted vineyards and ate of their fruit (2 Kgs 19:29).

The 8th century prophets saw Judah's future in that remnant in the land. They did not, however, forget the Judaean exiles of 701. To those exiles in Assyria and possibly also in Egypt,[94] the 8th century prophets spoke a word of hope—a promise of a return. It did not come for them but for others a century and a half later. Despite this, the promise of the return still held and was renewed and adapted to the 6th century Babylonian exile by the later prophets. The seed for the promise of the return in the 6th century was sown with the promise of the return to the 8th century exiles from both Israel and Judah. This 8th century Judaean exile did not become a chronological turning point in the prophetic view of Israel's history, but it did happen. It influenced the thought about and interpretation of the later climactic Babylonian exile.

The dispersion of the exiles from Israel and Judah in the latter part of the 8th century and beginning of the 7th century sowed the seed for the understanding of the later dispersion after the sixth century exile and return. The 8th century Judaean exile is important, therefore, because it marks the beginning of those necessary changes in the prophetic understanding of Israel's covenant relationship with her God which were caused by the later Babylonian exile. Without the seed sown by the 8th century prophets, the fruit produced in the later prophets regarding the Babylonian exile would not have been possible.

[94]Ginsberg ("Judah and," 250) states that some of the Ephraimites went to Egypt after 721. Perhaps some of the Judaeans did as well. See Porten, *Archives*, 7-8.

REALPOLITIK IN JUDAH (687-609 B.C.E.)

RICHARD NELSON

Lutheran Theological Seminary

I. JUSTIFYING A NEW LOOK AT THIS PERIOD

Reconstructions of the history of the reigns of Manasseh, Amon, and Josiah tend to share certain characteristics:

1. Critical events in Judah, such as the murder of Amon or Josiah's twelfth year, are coordinated with significant Assyrian happenings.

2. Religious apostasy and reformation are linked to loyalty and disloyalty to Assyria.

3. Manasseh and Amon are characterized as pro-Assyrian in foreign policy, Josiah as anti-Assyrian.

4. There is an often unstated judgment that Manasseh was a yielding and unpatriotic weakling who was willing to sell out his heritage because of his pro-Assyrian position.

5. There is, conversely, the explicit opinion that Josiah's loyalty to Yahweh and solidarity with Judah's past traditions of greatness made him so rigidly anti-Assyrian that he was willing to risk his life, his nation's army, indeed Judah's very existence as a nation, to prevent aid from reaching Assyria in its final hour.

The time for a re-evaluation has come. Apparently we can be certain now that Assyria did not demand the adoption of its religion as a condition of vassalage.[1] Manasseh's religious policies cannot automatically be taken as indications of subservient vassalage nor Josiah's reformation as a declaration of political independence from Assyria. The religious policies of these two kings can more reasonably be understood now as matters of internal struggle.[2] The troublesome *lmlk* jar handle stamps can no longer be used to deny any substantive expansion of

---

[1]J. McKay, *Religion in Judah under the Assyrians* (SBT 2/26; Naperville: Allenson, 1973); "Further Light on the Horses and Chariots of the Sun in the Jerusalem Temple (2 Kings 23:11)," *PEQ* 105 (1973) 167-69; M. Cogan, *Imperialism and Religion: Assyria, Judah and Israel in the Eighth and Seventh Centuries B.C.E.* (SBLMS 19; Missoula: Scholars Press, 1974) 20-88, 112-14.

[2]M. Smith, *Palestinian Parties and Politics That Shaped the Old Testament* (New York: Columbia University, 1971) 15-56.

Josiah to the north.[3] New light has been thrown on the last decades of Assyrian history in matters of chronology[4] and by redaction-critical studies of the source material.[5]

There is also today a more general appreciation of the complexity of the primary historiographic sources from both Judah and Mesopotamia. The Deuteronomistic history was written for a political and religious purpose and underwent at least one major editorial reworking.[6] The Assyrian and neo-Babylonian materials were also created for political and even religious purposes. They too sometimes underwent redaction, as in the case of the sources for the reign of Assurbanipal.

Let us begin by reflecting on the terminology "anti-Assyrian" and "pro-Assyrian." To modern ears these terms carry the implication of ideological loyalty, in the sense of "pro-Palestinian" or "pro-American." Of course no Lydian, Egyptian, or Judean was ever likely to be pro-Assyrian in that sense. Being pro-Assyrian could have meant nothing more than the belief that, in the ever-changing arena of international politics, this year at least the nation's best interests are served by subservience to Assyria. Are we to believe that any king of Judah was ever pro-Assyrian in the sense that he would go one single step beyond the national self-interest in supporting Assyrian policy?

Manasseh may have been the very model of the good vassal, but hardly for reasons of ideological attachment. He may have seen Assyria as a stabilizing element in Palestine which worked to Judah's advantage. He may have valued Assyrian trade contacts. He may have found in Assyrian suzerainty protection from hostile domestic elements. Nor could he forget that half a day's journey north of his capital was the Assyrian imperial border or that at about the age of seven he himself had lived through Sennaherib's siege of Jerusalem. He may have wished to avoid being flayed, impaled, or put in a dog collar to guard the gate of Nineveh. Yet to call him pro-Assyrian seems to invite misunderstanding.

---

[3]N. Na'aman, "Sennacherib's Campaign to Judah and the Date of the *LMLK* Stamps," *VT* 29 (1979) 61-86.

[4]J. Oates, "Assyrian Chronology, 631-612 BC," *Iraq* 27 (1965) 135-59; J. Reade, "The Accession of Sinsharishkun," *JCS* 23 (1970) 1-9; A. Spalinger, "The Date of the Death of Gyges and Its Historical Implications," *JAOS* 98 (1978) 400-9.

[5]M. Weippert, "Die Kämpfe des assyrischen Königs Assurbanipal gegen die Araber, Redaktionskritische Untersuchung des Berichts in Prisma A," *WO* 7 (1973) 39-85; A. Spalinger, "Assurbanipal and Egypt: A Source Study," *JAOS* 94 (1974) 316-28; M. Cogan and H. Tadmor, "Gyges and Ashurbanipal. A Study in Literary Transmission," *Or* 46 (1977) 65-85.

[6]F. M. Cross, "The Themes of the Book of Kings and the Structure of the Deuteronomistic History," *Canaanite Myth and Hebrew Epic* (Cambridge: Harvard University, 1973) 274-89.

Characterizing Josiah as anti-Assyrian is also unhelpful. He was able, thanks to the fortunes of history, to play a more independent game than his grandfather had. Yet since Assyria had never imposed Manasseh's syncretism on Judah to begin with, the reforming Josiah really had no reason to be ideologically anti-Assyrian at all. Doing what was best for the independence of Judah could mean siding with Egypt, Assyria, or even Babylon at any given time, but there is no reason to suppose that any of these options would have been more religiously distasteful than the others to Josiah.

II. MANASSEH'S FOREIGN POLICY

Manasseh achieved sole rulership in 687/686 after a ten year co-regency.[7] His only sensible course was loyal vassalage. Any hope of reversing the territorial loss dictated by Sennaherib and of preventing a recurrence of the 701 disaster demanded this. Assyrian architectural features in Stratum II of Lachish (after 701) suggest that it was garrisoned by Assyrian occupation forces and that Manasseh may have had a sort of Assyrian high commissioner watching over his shoulder.[8]

The murder of Sennaherib in 681 (*ANET*, 280) would have offered no temptation for "once burned, twice shy" Judah to revolt. The succession was decided in about six weeks in favor of Esarhaddon (*ANET*, 289-90). That he marched to Nineveh from the west without waiting to go through the procedure for provisioning his army is evidence of military activity not far from Palestine, a further deterrent to revolt.[9]

During the reign of Esarhaddon (680-669), Manasseh's wisest course continued to be that of the punctilious vassal. In spite of a growing threat from the north, Esarhaddon was militarily active in the west and in Egypt, providing a series of object lessons for his vassals.[10] Perhaps as early as 679, he campaigned in Philistia and plundered Arsa on the Egyptian border (*ANET*, 290). In 677, the rebellious city of Sidon was sacked and its king beheaded (*ANET*, 291, 302-3). To underscore the deterrent effect, Esarhaddon forced the vassal seacoast kings, Manasseh

[7]All Biblical dates are according to E. R. Thiele, *The Mysterious Numbers of the Hebrew Kings* (rev. ed.; Grand Rapids: Eerdmans, 1965).

[8]M. Elat, "The Political Status of the Kingdom of Judah within the Assyrian Empire in the 7th Century BCE," *Investigations at Lachish* V (Tel Aviv: Gateway, 1975) 61-70.

[9]H. W. F. Saggs, *The Greatness That Was Babylon* (London: Sidgwick & Jackson, 1962) 123.

[10]For these events, A. Spalinger, "Esarhaddon and Egypt: An Analysis of the First Invasion of Egypt," *Or* 43 (1974) 296-304.

included, to construct "Fortress Esarhaddon" nearby. War against rebellious Arabs the next year (676) brought Assyrian power west once more (*ANET*, 291-92). Although Ba'al of Tyre, secure in his island city, could get away with angering Esarhaddon and charting a relatively independent course, this was hardly an option open to Manasseh.

Esarhaddon's Egyptian adventure (*ANET*, 292-93, 302-3) began in 673. Even though the first expedition was a failure, success would come in 671 when, with Ba'al of Tyre subdued, the Assyrians captured Memphis. Once more Manasseh had but a single course open to him. With Assyrian military movements in his front yard using Aphek as a staging point, with Assyrian garrisons in places like Tell Jemmeh in south Philistia,[11] and with a permanent Assyrian military presence in Egypt, Manasseh must have been quite willing to pay his tribute (*ANET*, 291) and ignore the blandishments of Taharqa.

In 672, Esarhaddon moved to regularize the succession, requiring renewed vassal oaths from his subjects. There is Biblical evidence that Manasseh was one of those forced to pledge support for this plan of succession.[12] Esarhaddon died in 669 while campaigning against a newly resurgent Taharqa.

The Assyrian sources for the reign of Assurbanipal (*ANET*, 294-301) are characterized by scribal activity that sometimes scrambled the proper order of events, sometimes telescoped separate events into one. The process of retrieving some degree of chronological accuracy for this period is still underway.[13] After 649 (the end of the eponym list) and 643 (the approximate date of Prism A), the picture is even more confused until the Babylonian sources pick up again in 626.

It is clear, however, that Manasseh's options remained severely limited before the 650s. Assurbanipal was immediately obliged to deal with an Egyptian rebellion, which involved Ashkelon in some way. Manasseh was forced to provide military support and seems even to have joined the expedition personally (*ANET*, 294). Memphis was plundered in 669 as a stronghold of Taharqa. Assyrian power continued to be active in the west. There was a campaign against Arvad in this period (*ANET*, 296). Ba'al of Tyre rebelled, was besieged, and came to terms (*ANET*, 295-96). The Egyptian crisis came to a head in 664 when Tanatumun besieged the Assyrian garrison at Memphis. By 663, the

[11]G. W. Van Beek, *IEJ* 22 (1972) 245-46.

[12]M. Weinfeld, "Traces of Assyrian Treaty Formulae in Deuteronomy," *Bib* 46 (1965) 417-27; R. Frankena, "The Vassal Treaties of Esarhaddon and the Dating of Deuteronomy," *OTS* 14 (1965) 122-54.

[13]The table of the sequence of campaigns in Cogan and Tadmor, "Gyges and Ashurbanipal," 85, is helpful, along with Spalinger, "Assurbanipal and Egypt," 317-20.

Assyrian forces had succeeded in relieving Memphis, sacking Thebes, and driving Tanatumun into the Sudan. The fall of Thebes (No-Amon) made quite an impression on Judah (Nah 3:8-10), and it is probably no coincidence that Manasseh named his son born that year Amon,[14] presumably as a public witness to the vassal loyalty forced upon him by history. Egypt was reorganized under vassal rulers, the most powerful being Psamtik I (Psammetichus), and an Assyrian military presence was left behind.

The first quarter century of Manasseh's reign, therefore, was a period of almost unlimited Assyrian power. The wise policy, in fact the only policy open to him, was that of the loyal vassal. The fortification of Judah and Jerusalem reported in 2 Chr 33:14 was probably undertaken, not as a show of independence from Assyria, but to help Judah serve its expected role as a buffer against the unruly Egyptians. There is no reason to condemn Manasseh for doing what he had to do. Certainly Judah benefited from this period of stability. Judah's territorial security over against the Edomites or the Philistine states would have been assured. Jerusalem continued its population explosion throughout this period.[15] We know of no prophetic activity in Manasseh's reign, perhaps in part because there were no major crises nor any real options in foreign policy to preach about.[16]

In the 650s Assyria gradually relaxed its hold on Egypt. Psamtik, between 657 and 654, took over the country step by step with the aid of mercenaries from Asia Minor (Herodotus 2. 152) and perhaps Judah.[17] The opinion commonly held today is that this took place with Assyria's tacit permission or at least benign neglect. Assyria had not wished to control Egypt politically in the first place and was increasingly preoccupied with an Elamite threat which began in 654 and with rebellions among the Arab tribes. The Assyrian garrisons seem to have been withdrawn without fuss, and Psamtik is believed to have remained a vassal of sorts.[18]

---

[14]E. Nielsen, "Political Conditions and Cultural Developments in Israel and Judah During the Reign of Manasseh," *Fourth World Congress of Jewish Studies* (Jerusalem: World Union of Jewish Studies, 1967) 1. 103.

[15]M. Broshi, "The Expansion of Jerusalem in the Reigns of Hezekiah and Manasseh," *IEJ* 24 (1974) 21-26.

[16]Nielsen, "Political Conditions," 105.

[17]B. Porten, *Archives from Elephantine: The Life of a Jewish Military Colony* (Los Angeles: University of California, 1968) 8-13; Ep. Arist. 13.

[18]M. G. Gyles, *Pharaonic Policies and Administration, 663 to 323 BC* (James Sprunt Studies 41; Chapel Hill: University of North Carolina, 1959) 20-23; F. K. Kienitz, "Die Saïtische Renaissance," *Fischer Weltgeschichte* (Frankfort: Fischer Bücherei, 1967) 3. 258-60; K. A. Kitchen, *The Third Intermediate Period in*

Any temptation Manasseh may have had to use this as an opportunity for independent action would have been tempered by the apparently still cordial relations between Egypt and Assyria, to say nothing of the Assyrian police actions taken against the Arabs in the 650s (*ANET*, 297-301). These involved fighting in Edom, Moab, Ammon, and Zobah. Kamashaltu, king of Moab, took an active part on the Assyrian side. The punitive expeditions against Ushu (mainland Tyre) and Akko may also date from this period.[19]

Manasseh's only real chance to chart an independent foreign policy would have come with the rebellion of Shamash-shum-ukin between 651 and 648. This was Mesopotamia's first serious internal squabble since the death of Sennaherib thirty years before. The crisis was ended with the taking of Babylon in 648, the fiery death of Shamash-shum-ukin, and mopping up operations against the Arabs and in Elam, ending with the destruction of Susa in 646.[20]

We do not know whether Manasseh took this opportunity to withhold tribute or to give aid and comfort to Assyria's enemies.[21] Certainly our present understanding of Egypt's neutrality in this affair and the present dating of most of the Arab campaigns to before 651-48 make such a rebellion less likely than it may once have seemed. We may affirm, however, that Manasseh's decision, whatever it may have been, was conditioned by the realities of power politics and not by some unsubstantiated pro-Assyrian attitude.

Manasseh was succeeded by his enigmatic son, Amon, in 643/642, the victim of a palace revolt in his second year. Several attempts have been made to link the year 641/640 to some Assyrian or Egyptian event.[22]

Egypt (1100-650 BC) (Warminster: Aris & Phillips, 1973) 400-6; Spalinger, "Assurbanipal and Egypt," 323-25; "The Date of the Death of Gyges," 402-3; "Psammetichus, King of Egypt: I," *Journal of the American Research Center in Egypt* 13 (1976) 133-47.

[19]Weippert, 69-73.

[20]This date is based on the study of Prism F. Cf. Spalinger, "Psammetichus," 136.

[21]The Chronicler's report (2 Chr 33:11-13) is clearly tendentious. Although he does provide us with reliable information about military construction and organization, we should hesitate to trust him when his own theology is so strongly supported by an event he reports without outside support. The mention of Babylon may be a kernel of historical truth. Assurbanipal's gentle treatment of Neko I indicates a willingness to forgive a still useful vassal. The one solid historical clue is that Manasseh sacrificed his son sometime in his reign (2 Kgs 21:6), an action indicative of extreme national danger.

[22]H. Cazelles, "Sophonie, Jérémie et les Scythes en Palestine," *RB* 74 (1967) 42; Cogan, *Imperialism and Religion*, 70-71; A. Malamat, "The Historical Background of the Assassination of Amon King of Judah," *IEJ* 3 (1953) 26-29.

There were problems with northern barbarians in 640. The twenty-nine year siege of Ashdod by Psamtik (Herodotus 2. 157) may have begun that year. Yet there are plenty of possible internal motives for regicide as well: a power struggle between the "servants of the king" and the "people of the land," some sort of dynastic irregularity,[23] or the zeal of some reforming element. It is difficult to imagine where any potential rebels against Assyria would have intended to turn for help, given Psamtik's lack of hostility toward Assurbanipal.

III. JOSIAH'S ALLIANCE WITH ASSYRIA AND EGYPT

Josiah's reign has generally been reconstructed along the pattern of an increasingly anti-Assyrian foreign policy. In light of Assyria's indifference to the religious policies of its vassals, however, there is no reason to assume that Josiah's attitude towards Assyria was any more hostile than his grandfather's had been. Foreign policy surely remained a matter of political reality, not ideology.

The Chronicler (2 Chr 34:3) noted the eighth (633/632) and twelfth (629/628) years of Josiah as turning points in his internal religious reform. Since this reform was not an anti-Assyrian move, there is no reason to expect any correlation to Assyrian events.[24] In any case, there are no datable happenings until the death of Assurbanipal in 627, a year of major crisis. Apparently Sin-shar-ishkun and Sin-shum-lishir revolted against Assur-etel-ilani in that year. In 626, Sin-shar-ishkun and Nabopolassar seem to have recognized each other as kings of Assyria and Babylon respectively.[25] Clearly after 627 there was no likely prospect of Assyrian intervention in the west, given the continuing struggle with Nabopolassar, the Medes, and the Scythians. Assyria's last real penetration into Babylon was in 624, although a garrison would remain at Nippur somewhat longer. In 623 Der revolted.[26]

It has not been sufficiently appreciated by biblical historians that Egypt apparently continued to maintain good relations with Assyria throughout the 630s and 620s. Psamtik was able to enjoy the economic benefits of Syria-Palestine without conflict and could gradually move

---

[23]Was Manasseh's oldest son not born until he was forty-five? Thiele, *Mysterious Numbers*, 206.

[24]As attempted by F. M. Cross and D. N. Freedman, "Josiah's Revolt Against Assyria," *JNES* 12 (1953) 56-58. The reform of Josiah's eighteenth year was triggered by a purely internal discovery (2 Kgs 22:8-10).

[25]Reade, "Accession of Sinsharishkun," 1-9.

[26]For these events, R. Borger, "Der Aufstieg des neubabylonischen Reiches," *JCS* 19 (1965) 59-78, esp. 68-76; Oates, "Assyrian Chronology," 147-53; D. J. Wiseman, *Chronicles of Chaldean Kings (626-556 B.C.)* (London: British Museum, 1956) 7-10.

into the power vacuum left in Philistia.[27] When the witness of the Babylonian Chronicle picks up in 616 (*ANET*, 303-5), Egypt is a full-fledged Assyrian ally, and there is apparently no reason to see this as a change of long-standing policy. Josiah would have had very limited foreign policy options in this situation. As Jeremiah put it, he had to drink from both the Nile and the Euphrates (i.e. Assyria; Jer 2:18) and ally himself with both nations.

The most obscure factor in this political equation is the enigmatic Scythian invasion (Herodotus 1. 105), which is supposed to have reached the Egyptian border, only to be bought off by Psamtik.[28] The fear of another Scythian incursion would have further cemented the natural Egyptian and Judean alliance with Assyria, the best bulwark against these northern hordes.[29]

As Assyria continued its slide towards disaster, Egypt must have realized the danger of a new Babylonian world empire. The obvious policy for Psamtik, and for Josiah as well, would be to support Assyria as the weaker party in order to prevent a concentration of power in Asia. It is not unreasonable to suppose that Josiah remained a nominal Assyrian vassal right up to the end. His penetration into the Assyrian provinces to the north, without opposition from either Egypt or Assyria, is evidence for this.[30]

There is Biblical evidence for an Egypt-Judah-Assyria alliance as well. We have already referred to Jer 2:15-18, 36, oracles which decry trust in Egypt and Assyria and must date between 627 and 622.[31] A change from one nation to the other, as is usually assumed, is not necessarily implied. It would be just as natural to conclude that Judah has added an alliance with Egypt to an earlier one with Assyria:

[27]Spalinger, "Egypt and Babylonia," 222-23.

[28]Cazelles, "Sophonie," 25-27. No universal domination of Asia was meant by Herodotus 1. 104, 106, according to R. P. Vaggione, "Over All Asia? The Extent of the Scythian Domination in Herodotus," *JBL* 92 (1973) 532-30. A. Spalinger has dated this to 622-20, "Psammetichus, King of Egypt: II," *Journal of the American Research Center in Egypt* 15 (1978) 49-57. Zeph. 1:18 may refer to Psamtik's policy of the purse in regard to the Scythians.

[29]Saggs, *Greatness That Was Babylon*, 136. For other indications of good relations between Josiah and Psamtik, see Spalinger, "Psammetichus, King of Egypt: II," 52.

[30]W. F. Albright, *The Biblical Period from Abraham to Ezra* (New York: Harper Torchbooks, 1963) 80; H. L. Ginsberg, "Judah and the Transjordan States from 743 to 582 BCE," *Alexander Marx Jubilee Volume* (New York: Jewish Theological Seminary, 1950) 353.

[31]J. Milgrom, "The Date of Jeremiah, Chapter 2," *JNES* 14 (1955) 66-69. J. Bright, *Jeremiah* (AB 21; Garden City: Doubleday, 1965) 17-18.

And now what do you gain by going to Egypt,
to drink the waters of the Nile?
Or what do you gain by going to Assyria,
to drink the waters of the Euphrates? — Jer 2:18

* * *

How lightly you repeat[32] your way.
You shall be put to shame by Egypt
as you were put to shame by Assyria. — Jer 2:36

Isa 19:16-25 describes an Assyrian-Egyptian alliance with Judah as its religious center. A highway connects Egypt with Assyria, Israel is the third partner in the axis, and God announces:

Blessed be Egypt my people, and Assyria
the work of my hands, and Israel my heritage. — Isa 19:25

Gottwald convincingly dates this oracle between 660 and 609.[33] Certainly if it has any more historical grounding than a utopian vision of some eschatological universalism[34] or a third century reference to the diaspora of the Seleucid and Ptolemaic kingdoms,[35] it gives strong support for the idea of an alliance of Josiah with both Egypt and Assyria.

The Deuteronomistic historian, writing during Josiah's reign (see n. 6) and speaking through Moses, clearly excludes Edom, Moab, and Ammon from the land of promise (Deut 2:5, 9, 11). Even though David's imperialism in Syria is taken as the model for Israelite hegemony (Deut 1:7; Josh 1:4), these trans-Jordanian elements of his empire are explicitly eliminated. In other words, the historian is looking forward to Judah's rule in the Assyrian provincial system to the north to an extent that has not yet taken place under Josiah, but excludes the territories of the vassal states outside the provincial system. This is exactly what we would expect if Josiah has expanded northward as a nominal Assyrian vassal, but still must respect the territory of his fellow vassals.

[32]This understands *šnh* as "repeat" rather than "change" (cf. the LXX). This requires a repointing of the infinitive construct from Pi^cel to Qal.

[33]N. W. Gottwald, *All the Kingdoms of the Earth* (New York: Harper & Row, 1964) 224-27. The origin and dates for the foreign nation oracles of Isaiah 13-23 is a complex question. The unit 19:16-25 has been gathered with other oracles concerning Egypt (chaps. 18-20) on the basis of geography. Nothing certain about either the date or the authorship of this unit can be derived from its present position in the book of Isaiah.

[34]R. Feuillet, "Un sommet religieux de l'Ancien Testament. L'oracle d'Isaïe XIX (vv. 16-25) sur la conversion de l'Egypte," *RSR* 39 (1951) 65-87; W. Vogels, "Egypte mon peuple, l'universalisme d'Is. 19:16-25," *Bib* 57 (1976) 494-514.

[35]O. Kaiser, *Isaiah 13-39: A Commentary* (OTL; Philadelphia: Westminster, 1974) 105-10.

Along with a bloc of other Isaiah prophet legends (2 Kgs 18:17-20:19), the Deuteronomistic historian has included the visit of the envoys of Merodach-baladan to Hezekiah (2 Kgs 20:12-19). Although often understood as a *vaticinium ex eventu* of the Babylonian exile, no exile is actually in view. There is only a rather general mention of a transfer of national treasure and of the selection of members of the royal family as courtiers in Babylon. Military defeat is neither mentioned nor implied. The unit's only obvious point is to speak of the dangers involved in an alliance with Babylon. This would mean merely trading one suzerain for another, even more rapacious one. Leaving aside the quetion of the origin and transmission of this unit, we must ask why the Deuteronomistic historian felt a need to include it. Advice on the folly of accepting an alliance with Babylon would make sense in the Josianic period only if Josiah were still a nominal Assyrian vassal but the possibility of a switch was being discussed. If by the time of the Deuteronomistic history's composition (certainly after 622), Josiah had already come to an understanding with Nabopolassar, there would have been no motive for including such a warning.

IV. NEKO'S TREACHERY

If we accept an alliance of Egypt, Judah, and Assyria, what sense can be made of the Megiddo incident of 2 Kgs 23:29-30?[36] The events of 616 through 609 are well-documented and need no review here. In 616 and again in 610, Egypt had joined first Sin-shar-ishkun and then Assur-uballit in moves to prop up Assyria as a buffer against the Medes and Babylonians. Judah's interests must have corresponded to Egypt's in this. Josiah's control of the former Assyrian provinces would be short-lived indeed unless some sort of rump Assyrian state could be maintained

[36]The literature is extensive. B. Alfrink, "Die Schlacht bei Megiddo und der Tod des Josias (609)," *Bib* 15 (1934) 173-84; J. Boehmer, "König Josias Tod," *ARW* 30 (1933) 199-203; Cross and Freedman, "Josiah's Revolt," 56-58; S. B. Frost, "The Death of Josiah: A Conspiracy of Silence," *JBL* 87 (1968) 369-82; A. Hjelt, "Die Chronik Nebopolassars und der syrische Feldzug Nechos," *Vom Alten Testament: Karl Marti zum 70. Geburtstage* (BZAW 41; Giessen: Töpelmann, 1925) 142-47; A. Malamat, "The Historical Setting of Two Biblical Prophecies on the Nations," *IEJ* 1 (1950-51) 149-59; "The Last Wars of the Kingdom of Judah," *JNES* 9 (1950) 218-27; "Josiah's Bid for Armageddon," *JANESCU* 5 (1973) 267-79; "The Last Years of the Kingdom of Judah," *The Age of the Monarchies: Political History* (*World History of the Jewish People* 4/1; Jerusalem: Masada Press, 1979) 205-6; G. Pfeifer, "Die Begegnung zwischen Pharao Necho und König Josia bei Megiddo," *Mitteilungen des Instituts für Orientforschung* 15 (1969) 297-307; M. B. Rowton, "Jeremiah and the Death of Josiah," *JNES* 10 (1952) 128-30; A. C. Welch, "The Death of Josiah," *ZAW* 43 (1925) 255-60.

across the northern approaches to Palestine. After the fall of Nineveh (612) and the loss of Harran (610; *ANET*, 304-5), the situation became critical. Neko II, who had just succeeded his father and would be eager for military glory, prepared to move north to join Assur-uballit in an assault on Harran.

Across his route lay the fortress of Megiddo. The cubit measure used to construct it indicates it was built either by Egypt or Judah, but in the absence of any definite archeological indication, there is controversy as to whether Josiah or the Egyptians controlled it.[37] Yet because Josiah did control Meṣad Ḥashavyahu, 13 km. north of Ashdod, a permanent Egyptian presence so much farther north seems unlikely. If Josiah had taken over the Assyrian province of Magidu as a vassal, the provincial capital would have presumably gone with it.

Josiah had not hindered his Egyptian allies on their march through the Megiddo pass in 616 or 610. About the 609 campaign, however, 2 Kgs 23:29 reports: "King Josiah went to meet him; and he killed him in Megiddo when he saw him." Did Josiah go out to oppose Neko as is generally assumed? Much effort has been expended to provide him with a reason for such a drastic step (see n. 36), a good deal of which can be reduced to the assumption that Josiah was anti-Assyrian. Yet an attack by Josiah on Neko is actually very hard to accept,[38] even apart from the probability that Josiah was an ally of both Neko and Assur-uballit. The Egyptian line of march would not have directly threatened Judah. Josiah would have had no reason to take any risks in order to give Assyria its *coup de grace* when matters were going so poorly for Assur-uballit anyway. It is hard to see what Josiah would have had to lose by simply waiting for the outcome of Neko's rescue attempt, but he would have everything to lose by opposing Neko's "great Egyptian army"[39] with his mercenaries and militia.

The realities of the situation left Josiah with two options, neither of which was an attack on a friendly Egyptian army. He could wait out the result of the rescue attempt and then come to terms with the victor. Or he could actively aid Neko in his attempt to fragment the Mesopotamian threat.

---

[37]Malamat, "Josiah's Bid," 268-69 (Egypt); Y. Aharoni, *The Land of the Bible* (rev. ed.; Philadelphia: Westminster, 1979) 403 (Judah).

[38]The only scholar to see this clearly, as far as I am aware, is Pfeifer, "Begegnung zwischen Necho und Josia," 297-306, whose reconstruction of the events of 609 shares certain points with this one.

[39]*ummāni* ^{kur}*Mi-ṣir ma-at-tú*. A. K. Grayson, *Assyrian and Babylonian Chronicles* (Texts from Cuneiform Sources 5; Locust Valley, NY: Augustin, 1975) 96, line 66.

What really happened at Megiddo? It is important to note that 2 Kgs 23:29 says nothing about a Judean army and nothing about a battle.[40] What probably happened is that Josiah went out from Megiddo to welcome his ally Neko, not to oppose him. They would probably be meeting as fellow kings for the first time.[41] Josiah intended to throw open the pass to the Egyptian advance[42] and re-establish the understanding he had had with Psamtik. Instead, Neko double-crossed him.

Neko wanted to re-establish Egypt's former hegemony in Palestine. His father had already conquered Ashdod as a first step in this direction. Furthermore, Neko was unwilling to leave his escape route under the control of an independently-minded ally who might switch sides and block his retreat before a victorious Babylonian army. He wanted Megiddo as part of a chain of cities from Ashdod through Riblah to Carchemish. The cheapest way to gain Megiddo was by treachery. He murdered Josiah at the onset of their negotiations in or near Megiddo. The fortress received an Egyptian garrison. Neko hurried north to his rendezvous with destiny, leaving behind a Judah shattered and demoralized by its encounter with *Realpolitik* in its most cynical form.[43]

This reconstruction runs directly counter to the generally accepted view that Josiah marched out to stop Neko in order to prevent him from supporting Assur-uballit and that Josiah was killed in battle. It may be objected that we know too little about Josiah's situation to understand whatever motives and whatever optimism could have led him to attack Neko. Yet this reconstruction is not as outrageous as it might seem at first. Josiah had no reason to be anti-Assyrian in an ideological sense.

---

[40]It is from the Chronicler that we hear of a battle, constructed out of the report of Ahab's death (1 Kgs 22:29-38). The purpose of this narrative, made clear by Neko's sermon to Josiah, was to provide a reason for Josiah's early and violent death.

[41]Psamtik died one to four months before the Harran conflict of 610. K. S. Freedy and D. B. Redford, "The Dates in Ezekiel in Relation to Biblical, Babylonian, and Egyptian Sources," *JAOS* 90 (1970) 475.

[42]Do we have a copy of a letter from Assur-uballit to Josiah asking him to permit the Egyptian forces to pass? Y. Yadin, "The Historical Significance of Inscription 88 from Arad: A Suggestion," *IEJ* 26 (1976) 9-14.

[43]For treacherous murder as a foreign policy tool, see Herodotus 1. 106. Neko's later behavior is consistent with this reconstruction. Jehoahaz was placed on his father's throne by the "people of the land," who thus passed over his older brother, Eliakim. One possible reason for this could be that, as heir apparent, Eliakim had become too closely identified with his father's Egyptian alliance, now completely discredited by Neko's treachery. After three months, Jehoahaz was summoned to Riblah by Neko and deposed in favor of Eliakim, who was willing to collaborate with his father's murderer, something not out of character with what little we know of him (Jer 22:13-17; 36:21-25).

There is Biblical evidence that he remained a nominal Assyrian vassal (Deut 2:5, 9, 11; 2 Kgs 20:12-19) and that he was part of the Egyptian-Assyrian alliance (Jer 2:15-18, 36; Isa 19:16-25). Such a policy would have made sense, given what we do know of the international situation.

It was the Chronicler who first led us astray with his tale of a battle. If Josiah had been friendly to both Assyria and Egypt, only treachery can explain his death at Neko's hand. And treachery, too, is the best explanation for the narrator's reticence in describing the event itself: "King Josiah went to meet him, and he killed him in Megiddo when he saw him" (2 Kgs 23:29). How embarrassing that the noble Josiah should have died as a fool dies (cf. 2 Sam 3:33-34). Yet the very ambiguity of Josiah's end meant that his life and death could be viewed in a strangely positive way by those who reflected on them (cf. 2 Kgs 22:20; Jer 22:10, 15a-16a).

THE BIBLICAL BOOK OF LAMENTATIONS IN THE CONTEXT OF NEAR EASTERN LAMENT LITERATURE

W. C. GWALTNEY JR.

Milligan College

I. INTRODUCTION

The biblical book of Lamentations has enjoyed a surprising renewal of interest in recent years. In extensive studies over the past twenty years the text, philology, and theology of Lamentations have received the lion's share of attention.[1] Other questions remain unanswered, however. What are we to make of the five compositions comprising Lamentations in terms of poetic analysis? May we reconstruct

---

[1] Several studies must be highlighted as bringing scholarly criticism up to date on Lamentations. Delbert Hiller's volume, *Lamentations*, in the Anchor Bible series (Garden City: Doubleday, 1972) is a good starting point because of its clear statement of the critical problems relating to Lamentations, its selective bibliography, and its informative and balanced notes. Hillers made good use of several noteworthy studies from the 1960s which applied the best of available scholarship to questions of text, philology, higher criticism, theology, and form analysis. Those leading commentaries were A. Weiser's *Klagelieder* (ATD 16; Göttingen: Vandenhoeck and Ruprecht, 1962) pp. 297-370, W. Rudolph's *Das Buch Ruth—Das Hohe Lied—Die Klagelieder* (KAT 17/1-3; Gütersloh: Gütersloher Verlagshaus Gerd Mohn, 1962), and Hans-Joachim Kraus's *Klagelieder* (BKAT 20; 3d ed.; Neukirchen-Vluyn: Neukirchener Verlag, 1968). These three German commentaries provide exhaustive bibliographies as well. Norman Gottwald's chief contribution, *Studies in the Book of Lamentations* (SBT 1/14, 2d ed.; London: SCM, 1962), lies in his perceptive treatment of Lamentations' theology. Specific texts within Lamentations have been elucidated by numerous detailed studies. Bertil Albrektson (*Studies in the Text and Theology of the Book of Lamentations* [Lund: CWK Gleerup, 1963]) has communicated an extremely valuable tool, a critical Syriac text of Lamentations, and has made a detailed study of the MT in the light of LXX, Peshitta, and Latin versions. Gottlieb's shorter study (*A Study on the Text of Lamentations* [Århus: Det Laerde Selskab, 1978] = Acta Jutlandica 48, Theolgy Series 12) discusses textual matters either not treated by Albrektson or those where Gottlieb wishes to take issue with Albrektson or others. The essay of Lanahan, ("Speaking Voice in the Book of Lamentations, *JBL* 93 [1974] 41-49) draws attention to the literary and dramatic effect of the change of speaker in Lamentations.

these compositions in a metrical pattern as *Biblica Hebraica* did? Is
Freedman's syllable-count method[2] to be preferred to the older system of
counting stresses? May we even use the concept of meter in regard to
Hebrew and Near Eastern poetry? What are the characteristics of Near
Eastern poetry anyway? The question of poetry, metrics, and the use of
acrostics is far from settled.

Another matter of serious note has been treated in the commentaries
in a somewhat cavalier manner. What are the Near Eastern antecedents
of the kind of literature we find in the biblical book of Lamentations?
To date only one serious attempt (that of McDaniel[3]) has appeared in
print to explore the claim of Kramer:

> There is little doubt that it was the Sumerian poets who originated and
> developed the "lamentation" genre—there are Sumerian examples dating
> possibly from as early as the Third Dynasty of Ur . . . and as late as the
> Parthian period . . . and that the Biblical Book of Lamentations, as well as
> the "burden" laments of the prophets, represent a profoundly moving
> transformation of the more formal and conventional Mesopotamian proto-
> types.[4]

Ten years later Kramer wrote:

> But there is little doubt that the biblical *Book of Lamentations* owes no
> little of its form and content to its Mesopotamian forerunners, and that the
> modern orthodox Jew who utters his mournful lament at the "western
> wall" of "Solomon's" long-destroyed Temple, is carrying on a tradition
> begun in Sumer some 4,000 years ago, where "By its (Ur's) walls as far as
> they extended in circumference, laments were uttered."[5]

Because of advances in the realm of Sumerian and Akkadian literary
analysis during the 1970s, a reappraisal of Thomas F. McDaniel's
pioneer critique is imperative to investigate this question of possible
Sumerian antecedents. This paper will argue that McDaniel's conclusions can no longer be maintained and that Kramer's views are more
defensible now than when he made them in 1959 and 1969.

---

[2]D. N. Freedman, "Acrostics and Metrics in Hebrew Poetry," *HTR* 65
(1972) 367-92.

[3]Thomas F. McDaniel, "The Alleged Sumerian Influence upon Lamentations," *VT* 18 (1968) 198-209.

[4]S. N. Kramer, "Sumerian Literature and the Bible," AnBib 12 (Studia
Biblica et Orientalia 3 [1959]) 201, n. 1.

[5]S. N. Kramer, "Lamentation over the Destruction of Nippur: A Preliminary
Report," *Eretz Israel* 9 (1969) 90.

McDaniel begins by pitting Kramer,[6] Gadd,[7] and Kraus[8] against Rudolph[9] and Eissfeldt[10] to demonstrate that scholarly opinion is divided on the question of Sumerian influence on the biblical Lamentations (pp. 199f.). He then proceeds to "present and evaluate the parallel motifs appearing in both the Hebrew and Sumerian works . . ." (p. 200). These "parallel motifs" number fourteen and represent terms, concepts, and choices in wording. McDaniel then judges, "All of the motifs cited from Lamentations are either attested otherwise in biblical literature or have a prototype in the literary motifs current in Syria-Palestine."[11] Furthermore McDaniel affirms that

> certain dominant themes of the Sumerian lamentations find no parallel at all in this Hebrew lament. For example, one would expect to find the motif of the "evil storm" . . . somewhere in the biblical lamentation if there were any real literary dependency.[12]

Next McDaniel questions how a second millennium Mesopotamian genre could have influenced a first millennium Palestinian work. He argues that evidence is lacking to demonstrate the survival of an eastern cuneiform tradition in Iron-age Syro-Palestine. The only possible means he sees to bridge this spatial and temporal chasm is the intervening Canaanite, Hurrian, and Hittite literature whose remains have failed to provide us with exemplars of the lament genre. He also disagrees with Gadd's contention that exiled Judeans adopted this genre in Babylon.

[6]McDaniel draws from Kramer's published work as of 1968 including "The Oldest Literary Catalogue: A Sumerian List of Literary Compositions Compiled about 2000 B.C.," *BASOR* 88 (1942) 10-19; "New Literary Catalogue from Ur," *RA* 55 (1961) 169-76; *Sumerian Literary Texts from Nippur in the Museum of the Ancient Orient at Istanbul* (AASOR 23; New Haven: American Schools of Oriental Research, 1943-44) 32-35; *Lamentation over the Destruction of Ur* (Assyriological Studies 12; Chicago: University of Chicago, 1940); "Lamentation over the Destruction of Ur," *ANET*[2] 455-63; "Sumerian Literature, A General Survey," *The Bible and the Ancient Near East* (Albright Anniversary Volume; Garden City: Doubleday, 1961) 249-66.

[7]McDaniel cites C. J. Gadd, "The Second Lamentation for Ur," *Hebrew and Semitic Studies Presented to Godfrey Rolles Driver* (ed. D. W. Thomas and W. D. McHardy; Oxford: Oxford University, 1963) 59-71.

[8]McDaniel cites Hans-Joachim Kraus, *Klagelieder (Threni)* (BKAT 20; 2d ed.; Neukirchen-Vluyn: Neukirchener Verlag, 1960) 10.

[9]McDaniel cites Wilhelm Rudolph, *Das Buch Ruth— Das Hohe Lied— Die Klagelieder*, p. 9.

[10]McDaniel cites Otto Eissfeldt, *Einleitung in das Alte Testament* (3d ed.; Tübingen: Mohr, 1964) 683.

[11]McDaniel, "Sumerian Influence," 207.

[12]Ibid.

He reasons that exiled Israelites would not have been in any mood to adopt a literary form of their captors, especially since they had "their own rich local literary traditions" (p. 209). "At most the indebtedness would be the *idea* of a lamentation over a beloved city."[13] Of his arguments, the most crippling to Kramer's, Gadd's, and Kraus's position is the spatial and temporal gap separating Lamentations from the Sumerian city-laments. This paper will summarize the history of the Mesopotamian lament genre, give a brief analysis of the later evolved lament form, and show that there no longer exists a significant spatial and temporal gap between the Mesopotamian congregational lament form and the biblical book.

II. MESOPOTAMIAN LAMENTS

Early Mesopotamian Lamentations

Following the pioneering publications of Kramer [14] and Jacobsen[15] in the 1940s and 1950s a younger group of scholars (W. W. Hallo,[16] Mark E. Cohen,[17] Raphael Kutscher,[18] Joachim Krecher,[19] and Margaret

[13]McDaniel, "Sumerian Influence," 209.

[14]See above, n. 6. Add to the Kramer bibliography: "Literary Texts from Ur VI, Part II," *Iraq* 25 (1963) 171-76; "Lamentation over the Destruction of Sumer and Ur," *ANET*[3] 611-19; and "Two British Museum iršemma 'Catalogues,'" StudOr 46 (1975) 141-66.

[15]See T. Jacobsen in his review of Kramer, *Lamentation over the Destruction of Ur* in *AJSL* 58 (1941) 219-24; *Proceedings of the American Philosophical Society* 107 (1963) 479-82.

[16]See especially W. W. Hallo, "Individual Prayer in Sumerian: The Continuity of a Tradition," *JAOS* 88 (Speiser Anniversary Volume, 1968) 71-89, where he traced the development of the individual lament from the older letter-prayer genre. Other articles of W. W. Hallo relating to Sumerian literary genre history include: "The Coronation of Ur-Nammu," *JCS* 20 (1966) 133-41; "The Cultic Setting of Sumerian Poetry," *Actes de la XVIIᵉ Rencontre assyriologique internationale* (Ham-sur-Heure: Universite Libre de Bruxelles, 1970) 116-34; "Another Sumerian Literary Catalogue?" StudOr 46 (1975) 77-80 with additions in StudOr 48:3; and "Toward a History of Sumerian Literature," *Sumerological Studies in Honor of Thorkild Jacobsen on His Seventieth Birthday* (Assyriological Studies 20; Chicago: University of Chicago, 1975) 181-203.

[17]Mark E. Cohen, *Balag-compositions: Sumerian Lamentation Liturgies of the Second and First Millennium* B.C. (Sources from the Ancient Near East, vol. 1, fasc. 2; Malibu: Undena, 1974) and *The eršemma in the Second and First Millennia* B.C. (Unpublished doctoral dissertation at the University of Pennsylvania, n.d.). [See Addendum.]

[18]Raphael Kutscher, *Oh Angry Sea (a-ab-ba ḫu-luḫ-ḫa): The History of a Sumerian Congregational Lament* (Yale Near Eastern Researches 6; New Haven: Yale University, 1975).

[19]Joachim Krecher, *Sumerische Kultlyrik* (Wiesbaden: Otto Harrassowitz, 1966).

Green[20]) has delineated and analyzed the Sumero-Akkadian genre of laments in dissertations, articles, and monographs. Although it is still premature to attempt a definitive treatment of the genre, the broad outline of the development of laments in Mesopotamian culture can be shown to span nearly two millennia.

Kramer remarked as early as 1969 that the "incipient germ [of the lament genre] may be traced as far back as the days of Urukagina, in the 24th century B.C."[21] He cited a list of temples and shrines of Lagash which had been burned, looted, or otherwise defiled by Lugalzagessi as being the first step in the creation of the lament genre. No laments are extant for the Akkadian, Gutian, or Ur III eras. Laments were invented as a literary response to the calamity suffered throughout Sumer about 2000 B.C.E. immediately after the sack of Ur in the days of Ibbi-Sin, the last of the Third Dynasty rulers of Ur.

At present five Old Babylonian Sumerian city-laments form the earliest stage of the lament genre. They are the "Lamentation over the Destruction of Ur"[22] which has received the greatest amount of attention, the "Lamentation over the Destruction of Sumer and Ur,"[23] the "Nippur Lament" to be published by Å. Sjöberg,[24] the "Uruk Lament," edition in preparation by M. Civil and M. W. Green,[25] and the "Eridu Lament," critical edition by M. W. Green.[26] The so-called "Second Lamentation for Ur," the "Ibbi-Sin Lamentation," and the "Lamentation over the Destruction of Sumer and Akkad" have all turned out to be parts of the "Lamentation over the Destruction of Sumer and Ur."[27] Nor are we including here the so-called "Curse of Agade" even though it employs lament or complaint language.[28] The usually accepted *terminus*

---

[20]Margaret W. Green, *Eridu in Sumerian Literature* (Unpublished doctoral dissertation at the University of Chicago, 1975), chap. 9: "Sumerian Lamentations" and chap. 10: "The Eridu Lament." See also M. W. Green, "The Eridu Lament," *JCS* 30 (1978) 127-67.

[21]Kramer, *Eretz Israel* 9 (1969) 89.

[22]See Kramer's treatments cited in n. 4.

[23]See Kramer, "Lamentation over the Destruction of Sumer and Ur," *ANET*³ 611-19.

[24]Green, *Eridu*, 279. See also D. O. Edzard, *Die "Zweite Zwischenzeit" Babyloniens* (Wiesbaden: Otto Harrasowitz, 1957) 86-90.

[25]Ibid.

[26]Green, *Eridu*, chap. 10, 326-74 and Green, "Eridu Lament," 127-67.

[27]See Kramer, *ANET*³ 612 and n. 9 as well as C. J. Gadd and S. N. Kramer, *Literary and Religious Texts, Ur Excavation Texts, 6, Part 2* (London: British Museum, 1966) 1 for the joins of tablets to show the unity of these fragments.

[28]See Kramer's comments in "The Curse of Agade: The Ekur Avenged," *ANET*³ 646f. See also M. W. Green's remarks in Green, *Eridu*, 279f. and Kutscher's in *Oh Angry Sea*, 1.

ante quem for the five major city-laments is 1925 B.C.E.[29]

The city-laments describe one event,[30] were written largely in the Emesal dialect of Sumerian[31] by *gala*-priests, and were composed to be recited in ceremonies for razing Ur and Nippur sanctuaries in preparation for proper restoration.[32] They were not reused in later rituals and did not become a part of the priests' ritual stock of available religious poetry for liturgical use. In the Old Babylonian scribal schools they became a part of the scribal curriculum but ceased to be copied during the First Millennium. Kutscher, remarking about the literary merit of these city-laments, writes, "From a literary point of view these laments display a masterful use of the classical Sumerian language, freshness of style and a sincere creative effort."[33]

The Old Babylonian Eršemma

The second stage in the history of the Mesopotamian lament genre occurred in the Old Babylonian era with the nearly simultaneous creation of the *eršemma*-composition and the *balag*-lament. Cohen suspects that the *eršemma*, a liturgical composition of the *gala*-priests in Emesal dialect, may have preceded the *balag* slightly on the grounds that the *eršemma* had a more compact form while the *balag* appears to have had a more composite nature.[34] Unfortunately, clear textual evidence is lacking for us to fix priority within the Old Babylonian period.

Although the term *eršemma* means "wail of the *šèm*-([Akkadian] *ḫalḫallatu*-) drum," not all *eršemmas* are completely mournful since at points the subject matter served to praise a god.[35] However, a large percentage of *eršemma*-subject matter centered on catastrophes or the dying-rising myth of Inanna, Dumuzi, or Geshtinanna.[36] Kramer as recently as 1975 published two Old Babylonian *eršemma*-incipit catalogs from the British Museum from which he isolated no less than 109

---

[29]Cohen, *balag*, 9. M. W. Green ("Eridu Lament," 129f.) raises the possibility of finding the origin of the Eridu lament in the reign of Nur-Adad of Larsa (1865-50 B.C.E.) but prefers an earlier date in the reign of Išme-Dagan of Isin (1953-35).

[30]Cohen, *balag*, 11.

[31]Kutscher (*Oh Angry Sea*, 3) claims that city-laments were written in the standard Emegir dialect, while Cohen (*balag*, 11 and 32) claims they were Emesal compositions.

[32]See Cohen, *balag*, 11.

[33]Kutscher, *Oh Angry Sea*, 3.

[34]Cohen, *eršemma*, 24.

[35]Cohen, *eršemma*, 9.

[36]Ibid.

*eršemma*s.[37] Of these, about 100 are unknown to us at this time. Cohen has demonstrated that in general the Old Babylonian *eršemma*s are characterized as being a single, compact unit addressed to a single deity.[38] Cohen has also contended that the *gala*-priests, when called upon repeatedly to provide more liturgical compositions to be chanted on the occasion of rebuilding cities and temples, borrowed *eršemma* material to create new *eršemma*s and appropriated hymnic Emegir material for insertion into new *eršemma*s.[39] Also Old Babylonian *eršemma*s and *balag*s occasionally shared lines of text.[40] Cohen was not able to determine the direction of this borrowing.[41] The exact Old Babylonian cultic use of the *eršemma* remains a mystery, although we may speculate that they were intoned in a liturgical context similar to that of the *balag*-laments.[42]

The Old Babylonian Balag

The *balag* was created as a lamentation form about 1900 B.C.E. as a literary outgrowth of the older city-lament. In support of this thesis Cohen has established a "high probability of direct relationship between the city-laments and the *balag*-lamentations"[43] by examining four factors: 1) the structure and form of city-laments and Old Babylonian *balag*s,[44] 2) their content,[45] 3) their ritual use,[46] and 4) whether there was sufficient opportunity for development to occur.[47] Even though we may conclude there was a close association between the *balag*-lament and its older city-lament predecessor, we must note several differences between the two. City-laments were composed for one specific "performance" to be retired afterwards to the scribal academy as a classical work;[48] *balag*s were adopted for further liturgical use and were copied over and over down into the Seleucid era. City-lament subject matter concentrated on one specific disaster in detailed description; *balag*s were more general in

---

[37]Kramer, "Two British Museum iršemma 'Catalogues,'" StudOr 46 (1975) 141-66.
[38]Cohen, *eršemma*, 9f., 12.
[39]Cohen, *eršemma*, 22-24.
[40]Cohen, *eršemma*, 24.
[41]Ibid.
[42]Cohen, *eršemma*, 27f.
[43]Cohen, *balag*, 11.
[44]Cohen, *balag*, 9f.
[45]Cohen, *balag*, 10f.
[46]Cohen, *balag*, 11.
[47]Ibid.
[48]Ibid.

their description of disaster and could be borrowed from city to city. City-laments were used in a narrow setting of temple demolition and reconstruction; *balag*s were recited in broader contexts apparently as "congregational laments."

Although most compositions of this genre were not called by the title "*balag*" in the Old Babylonian era, five examples in which such was the case have been recovered.[49] One of these five, a *balag* to Dumuzi (CT 42, 15), was composed in the Larsa period about 1870 B.C.E.[50] Kutscher has explained this low number of labeled examples as arising from the fact that the term "*balag*" in Babylonian times designated function, not generic title. The composition was to be intoned to the accompaniment of the *balag*-instrument,[51] in all likelihood a drum.[52] Cohen observed that the unusual length of the *balag*s caused them to be written on large tablets or in series of smaller tablets so that the final lines with their colophons were lost in many cases with the result that the designation "*balag*" is missing.[53] The form of the general all-purpose lament had already emerged in the Old Babylonian era even though the label "*balag*" was not always attached to the extant Old Babylonian recensions.

Kutscher's publication of YBC 4659[54] which preserves stanzas IV-XIII of the *balag*, a-ab-ba ḫu-luḫ-ḫa (Oh Angry Sea), makes clear that even in its Old Babylonian form this particular *balag* may be roughly divided in half.[55] The first half was devoted to lamentation presumably to be chanted during ceremonies at the demolition of an old temple. The second half (a hymn and prayer to Enlil) was probably "recited during the ceremonies marking the laying of the foundation to the new temple."[56] Cohen points to the concluding line in some Old Babylonian *balag*s, "This supplication . . . return the 'x-temple' to place," as indicating the use of the *balag* in temple-restoration ceremonies.[57] The Old Babylonian *balag*s also appear to have been included in liturgies for various festivals and for certain days of the month.[58]

---

[49]Cohen, *balag*, 6.

[50]Cohen, *balag*, 12.

[51]Kutscher, *Oh Angry Sea*, 3.

[52]Cohen, *balag*, 31 (Excursus on the *balag*-instrument).

[53]Cohen, *balag*, 6.

[54]Kutscher, *Oh Angry Sea*, 25-27 (history of YBC 4659), 52-54 (transliteration of YBC 4659), 143-53 (translation of the composite text), plates 6 and 7 (copies of YBC 4659 [*sic*! Captions inadvertently interchanged with those of Plates 1 and 2. Ed.]).

[55]See Kutscher, *Oh Angry Sea*, 6f., for this interpretation.

[56]Kutscher, *Oh Angry Sea*, 7.

[57]Cohen, *balag*, 11.

[58]Cohen, *balag*, 13, 15.

The First Millennium Balag *and* Eršemma

The Middle Babylonian period marked an advance in the lament genre although documentary evidence for it is meager. In fact, none of the main Emesal hymnic types of the first millennium—the *balag*, the *eršemma*, the *šuilla*, and the *eršaḫunga*—are attested in Middle Babylonian times.[59] Several *eršemma*s were possibly composed during Kassite times, however. Cohen somewhat tentatively suggests that the joining of *balag*-laments with *eršemma*-compositions to form a new composite genre occurred at some point during the Kassite era (ca. 1600-1160 B.C.E.).

During the Middle Babylonian period the two genres [*balag* and *eršemma*] had apparently been so closely identified with each other, presumably on the basis of ritual function, that each *balag* was assigned one *eršemma* as its new conclusion. The *eršemma* was then reworked, adopting a second concluding unit which contained the plea to the heart of the god and the concommitant [*sic*] list of deities, although this list was drastically reduced in size from the final *kirugu* of the Old Babylonian lamentation.[60]

Interestingly, Kutscher was able to amass exemplars of the Old Babylonian *balag* titled *a-ab-ba ḫu-luḫ-ḫa* (Oh Angry Sea) for the Old Babylonian, Neo-Assyrian, Neo-Babylonian, and Seleucid periods but could not locate even a one-line scrap of Kassite origin.[61] Even the Middle Assyrian era provided two scraps consisting of eight lines of text.[62] A Middle Babylonian catalog may, however, list Kutscher's *balag* under the title *a-ab-ba ḫu-luḫ-ḫa* *ᵈen-líl-lá*.[63]

---

[59]See E. Sollberger's remarks in his review of J. Krecher, *Kultlyrik*, which was published in *BO* 25 (1968) 47a.

This hiatus in documentation is probably caused by the fact that following the fall of Babylon about 1600 B.C.E. the scribal schools of Nippur and Babylon closed, and their scholars, taking their texts with them, fled southward to the Sealand. Under the Kassites, however, new scribal schools were established to perpetuate the classical literary tradition. In this corpus, which Hallo calls "Post-Sumerian" and "Bilingual," cultic texts and especially laments dominated. In fact, this bilingual collection survived as the canon for the remainder of the history of classical Mesopotamian literature through the Seleucid era into the Arsacid period. See W. W. Hallo, "Problems in Sumerian Hermeneutics," *Perspectives in Jewish Learning* 5 (1973) 6f. and "Toward a History of Sumerian Literature," 189-91, 198, 201, on bilinguals in the history of the canons.

[60]Cohen, *balag*, 9.

[61]See Kutscher, *Oh Angry Sea*, 9f., for a chart of the texts he was able to combine to reconstruct this *balag*.

[62]Kutscher, *Oh Angry Sea*, 11. Kutscher's Ca (=VAT 8243, 11. 32-37) and Db (=VAT 8243, 11. 142 and 143).

[63]Kutscher, *Oh Angry Sea*, 17 (TMHnF 53:21).

Precisely how the text of earlier *balag*s and *eršemma*s passed into the first millennium from their Old Babylonian point of origin is not totally clear. We may postulate, however, that these compositions had become essential ingredients in liturgies and were, therefore, preserved by the clergy. At any rate, from the Neo-Assyrian period through the Seleucid, *balag-eršemma* laments are exceptionally well documented from three major sources: 1) incipit catalogs, 2) ritual calendar tablets, and 3) copies of the laments themselves together with their colophons indicating *inter alia* the nature of the genre.

During the first millennium older lament material from both *balag*s and *eršemma*s became somewhat interchangeable. Cohen was able to produce two *eršemma*s of this era which had been created from earlier *balag* material with some modification.[64] The more general term *ér* = "lament," came to be used for the wide range of lamentations in keeping with the broadening of both the form and its function.

The ritual use of the *balag-eršemma* in the first millennium was even broader than in the Old Babylonian era. Numerous texts detailing the cultic performance of *gala*-(Akkadian *kalû*-)priests reveal how the *balag-eršemma* laments were integrated into complex rituals for a variety of situations.[65] Furthermore, the *balag-eršemma*s provided the ritual wording for ceremonies conducted on certain days of the month as noted in numerous calendar texts.[66] Often on such occasions a lament was recited while offerings and libations were being presented to a deity. The *balag-eršemma* continued to be sung on the occasion of razing an old building.[67] Caplice has given us a case of a lament's being chanted as a part of a *namburbi*-ritual for warding off a portended evil.[68] Cohen has also presented other examples when an evil portent prompted a *namburbi*-ritual which included a god-appeasing lament.[69] Thus the lament served the purpose of tranquilizing the potentially destructive god so that catastrophe could be prevented. The ritual for covering the sacred kettledrum involved the singing of a *balag* with its *eršemma* accompanied by the newly covered kettledrum later on in the rite.[70] Libations and offerings were not presented on this occasion. Cohen interpreted the occasion as a formal testing of the drum.

---

[64]Cohen, *eršemma*, 25f.
[65]See, for example, Kutscher, *Oh Angry Sea*, 5; Cohen, *balag*, 13-15.
[66]Cohen, *balag*, 13-15.
[67]Cohen, *balag*, 13.
[68]Caplice, "Namburbi Texts in the British Museum, IV," *Or* 39 (1970) 118f.
[69]Cohen, *balag*, 14f.
[70]Ibid.

III. ANALYSIS OF LAMENTATION FORM

City-Laments

On its most superficial level of organization the city-laments were divided into "songs" called *kirugu*, usually equated with Akkadian *šēru* = Hebrew *šîr*.[71] The number and length of these stanzas were seemingly at the composers' discretion. Each stanza, except the last, was followed by a one or two line unit called *gišgigal*, usually interpreted as "antiphon."[72] The *gišgigal* summarized the content of its *kirugu* or repeated a key line or two from the *kirugu*. Beyond these divisions the city-laments seem not to have had further formal external structure.[73]

Margaret Green in an unpublished Chicago dissertation[74] has discussed the poetic devices used in the city-laments.[75] Significant among these devices are: 1) the use of couplets, triplets, and even longer units of lines in which only one element is changed from line to line, 2) parallelism, 3) repeating units of a part of a line or a whole line or several lines, 4) complex interweaving of two or more refrains, and 5) use of lists. All these devices appear in Sumerian poetry of various genres and are not restricted to laments. Beyond these structural techniques two other characteristics appear to a greater or lesser extent in all five city-laments. For one thing, the composition alternates between first, second, and third persons. Such change in speaker possibly reflects the dramatic function of the city-laments. Furthermore, the dialect alternates between Emesal and standard Emegir Sumerian. This alternation has provoked a minor debate over whether the city-laments were "Emesal compositions" or "Emegir compositions."[76] Without entering the technicalities of this

---

[71]On *kirugu* see A. Falkenstein, "Sumerische religiöse Texte," *ZA* 49 (1950) 104f. where he interpreted the term as meaning "to bow to the ground." *Šēru* is probably related to Sumerian *šîr*, a generic title for poetry and/or song; see *AHW* 1219a. See also Green, *Eridu*, 283-85.

[72]On *gišgigal* see A. Falkenstein, "Sumerische religiöse Texte," 92, 93, 97f., 101. Falkenstein interpreted the term simply as "antiphon." See also Green, *Eridu*, 285f. See *AHW* 641a, sub *me/iḫru*, 3) where *giš-gál* = *mi-ḫir za-ma-ri* = antiphonal song and *giš-gi₄-gál* = *me-eḫ-ru/rù*.

[73]See Cohen, *balag*, 8 and Green, *Eridu*, 283-86 on structural matters.

[74]See n. 20 above.

[75]See Green, *Eridu*, 286-89. For a fuller analysis of Sumerian poetic form, see C. Wilcke, "Formale Gesichtspunkte in der sumerischen Literatur," *Assyriological Studies* 20 (Chicago: University of Chicago, 1975) 205-316.

[76]See n. 31 above.

question, we may observe that whenever a goddess speaks the Emesal dialect is used. In spite of Green's argument, however,[77] we are not yet entitled to judge that every occurrence of Emesal implies a female speaker. *Gala*-priests intoned a wide range of liturgies in the Emesal dialect even when a female speaker is not implied.[78]

Although the five preserved city-laments are quite individualized in theme and theme development as well as in style and structure, they have certain underlying themes in common.[79] The most prominent theme is destruction of the total city: walls, gates, temples, citizens, royalty, nobility, army, clergy, commoners, food, crops, herds, flocks, villages, canals, roads, customs, and rites. Life has ceased. A second common theme lies in the concept that the end has come upon Sumer by virtue of a conscious decision of the gods in assembly. The invading hordes, whether Subarians, Elamites, Amorites, or Gutians, "storm" the land by the "word" of the gods. A third theme centers around the necessary abandonment of the city by the suzerain-god, his consort, and their entourage. The lament may scold the god for his callous abandonment. The goddess in longer or shorter monologues pleads with either her divine spouse or Enlil or the council of gods to show mercy and relent. In the fourth place, the city-laments either specifically mention, or at least presume, restoration of the city or sanctuary. As a fifth common element, the chief god eventually returns to his city with his entire company. The five laments do not all handle this theme in identical fashion, but in every case the gods' return is indispensable to the plot. The final common thematic element is a concluding prayer to the

---

[77]Green, *Eridu*, 288f.

[78]Kutscher (*Oh Angry Sea*, 5) takes the position that *gala*-priests "specialized in Emesal" and that when they composed or recited compositions in worship settings, they employed the Emesal dialect. Krecher (*Kultlyrik*, 27f.), however, maintains that other cult personnel, namely the *nārū*-singer, also sang the Emesal compositions. Krecher, however, admits that the Emesal songs were almost exclusively sung by the *kalû*-(=*gala*)priests. Cohen (*balag*, 11) attributes the composition of the city-laments, as well as *balag*s and *eršemma*s, to the *kalû*-priests. See also Cohen, *balag*, 13, 15, and 32 as well as Cohen, *eršemma*, 9, 11, 17, and 24. Hallo ("Individual Prayer in Sumerian: The Continuity of a Tradition," *JAOS* 88 [1968] 81b) shows that "the later penitent commissioned the gala-singer to recite his prayer orally." Such *eršaḫunga*-prayers were also composed in Emesal (see Krecher, *Kultlyrik*, 25 and Hallo, "Individual Prayer," 80-82) and were recited, at least on occasions, to the accompaniment of the *halhallatu*-drum (Cohen, *eršemma*, 27). For a discussion of the *gala*-priests as Old Babylonian cult personnel, see J. Renger, "Untersuchungen zum Priestertum der altbabylonischen Zeit," *ZA* 59 (1969) 189-95.

[79]In outlining these six common themes I am following Green, *Eridu*, 295-310.

concerned god involving either praise, plea, imprecation against the enemy, self-abasement, or a combination of these elements.

The exact cultic circumstances for the recitation of the city-laments is not totally agreed upon. Jacobsen proposed that their "Sitz im Kultus" was the demolition of the ruins of a temple and its rebuilding.[80] Hallo[81] and Cohen[82] have followed this line of thinking. Green, however, offers the alternative that the lament was performed by the king in his priestly function at the installation ceremony when the god's statue returned to its refurbished shrine.[83] The god's leaving may not always have been caused by foreign devastation but may have been forced by needed renovations of the temple in peacetime.[84] That the five major city-laments arose from something more serious than a renovation in peacetime appears evident from the extreme violence they depict. Perhaps Green's suggestion has merit in explaining the function of Old Babylonian *balag*s and *eršemma*s. As for the king's reciting the lament before the cult image, we may question the king's acumen and literacy to read and recite both Emesal and Emegir dialects in complex poetry.

First Millennium Balag-Eršemmas

The first millennium composite lament form, the *balag-eršemma*, has been clarified by Kutscher in his study of the history of the long-lived *balag* called *a-ab-ba ḫu-luḫ-ḫa* (Oh Angry Sea). He shows that this *balag* originated in Old Babylonian times but was expanded for public ritual use during Neo-Assyrian, Neo-Babylonian, and Seleucid times in at least nine recensions.[85]

In terms of poetic devices this *balag* in Emesal makes use of the usual techniques: repetition, refrain, parallelism, listing, division into stanzas (unlabeled in some recensions), use of divine epithets, and apparent antiphonal performance. The *gišgigal*-unit (antiphon) is absent.

The later form of this lament may be outlined as follows:[86]
A. "Prayerful Lament," lines 1-152 (stanzas II-X)
   1. Enlil's epithets, lines 1-12 (stanza II)
   2. Nippur's and Babylon's ruin, lines 13-27 (stanza II)
   3. "How long?" plea to Enlil, lines 28-40 (stanza III)
   4. Wailing and mourning, lines 41-48 (stanza IV)

---

[80]Jacobsen, *AJSL* 58 (1941) 219-24.
[81]Hallo, "Cultic Setting," 119.
[82]Cohen, *balag*, 11.
[83]Green, *Eridu*, 309f.
[84]Green, *Eridu*, 311f.
[85]Kutscher, *Oh Angry Sea*, 21.
[86]Translation in Kutscher, *Oh Angry Sea*, 143-53.

5. Enlil's power, lines 49-72 (stanza V)
6. Enlil's dignity, lines 73-98 (stanzas VI-VII)
7. "How long?" plea with "return to the land!", lines 99-118 (stanza VIII)
8. Enlil's dignity, lines 119-25 (stanza IX)
9. Plea to Enlil to "restore (your) heart," lines 126-52 (stanza X)
B. Hymn to Enlil, lines 153-236 (stanzas XI-XVII)
1. Enlil sleeps, lines 153-59 (stanza XI)
2. List of devastated areas of the city, lines 160-71 (stanza XI)
3. Let Enlil arise!, lines 172-84 (stanza XII)
4. Enlil sees the devastation, lines 185-91 (stanza XIII)
5. Enlil caused the destruction, lines 192-212 (stanzas XIV-XV)
6. The exalted Enlil, lines 213-24 (stanza XVI)
7. Lines 225-36 (stanza XVII) broken
C. *Eršemma*, lines 237-96
1. Plea for Enlil to "turn around and look at your city!", lines 237-53
2. Plea for Enlil to "turn around and look at your city!" from various locations, lines 254-72
3. The flooded cities in couplets, lines 273-80
4. The gluttonous man starves, lines 281-82
5. The fractured family, lines 283-87
6. The population rages, lines 288-91
7. Death in the city streets, lines 292-96

We may observe that section A (stanzas II-X) calls attention to Enlil's destructive power as evidenced by the devastation. Section B (stanzas XI-XVII) concentrates on awakening Enlil in hopes of encouraging his return so that the city may regain its lost glory. The *eršemma* seeks to inspire some spark of pity within Enlil.

Cohen demonstrates that the *balag* exhibited a certain development within its history.[87] In its Old Babylonian form the *balag* like the city-lament had a rather formal external structure of *kirugu*-divisions in which each stanza was followed by "first, second, etc. *kirugu*."[88] In some cases there followed a one-line *gišgigal* (antiphon) as in the city-lament. Many scribes set the *kirugu* and *gišgigal* off by horizontal lines across the text both above and below these labels. As time passed, the labels tended to drop out leaving only the horizontal lines to mark stanzas. Another Old Babylonian convention of *balag* construction was the "heart pacification-unit" in the concluding stanza of older Enlil-*balags*.[89] *Balags* to other divinities omit this plea that the wrathful god's heart

[87]Cohen, *balag*, 8, 11f.
[88]Cohen, *balag*, 8.
[89]Cohen, *eršemma*, 17.

and liver might be pacified. Following this unit comes the formula expressing the wish that x-temple should return to its place, then the rubric *kišubim* which means something like "coda."

Modification in *balag* structural organization became necessary, however, following the later joining of *balag* and *eršemma*. Each first millennium *balag*-lament had an *eršemma* attached to its end. In its new function as last stanza the *eršemma* had to be redesigned.[90] For one thing, even though their first millennium counterparts always were one-unit compositions, the first millennium *eršemma*s often consist of two or three units each.[91] In these cases the last unit either begins with or contains a "heart pacification-unit" which seems to have originated in Old Babylonian Enlil *balag*s. The "heart pacification" is followed by a list of gods who were to add their pleas to those of the priests and worshipers. In this composite form the *balag-eršemma* continued to serve as liturgical material during hundreds of years through the Seleucid era.

When comparing these later laments with their ancient ancestors, the city-laments, the modern literary critic may think of them as grossly inferior. Kutscher,[92] for example, uses such descriptions as "repetitive," "unimaginative," "composed to a large extent of clichés, and devoid of poetic rhythm," "stereotyped," and we may add boring. Their longevity and broad range of use suggest to us, however, that the ancients found great merit in them.

IV. THE FIRST MILLENNIUM MESOPOTAMIAN LAMENT AND BIBLICAL LAMENTATIONS

In order to draw meaningful comparisons between the book of Lamentations and Mesopotamian laments we will create a typology in summary form for the first millennium Mesopotamian lament genre under four major headings: Ritual Occasions, Form/Structure, Poetic Techniques, and Theology. Then we will compare the book of Lamentations with this typology to formulate a hypothesis regarding the relationship of the two.

In the present state of cuneiform scholarship[93] we find four categories of religious circumstances when lamentations were employed in the cults of Mesopotamia. They are: 1) before, during, or after daily sacrifices and libations to a wide range of deities, 2) special services,

---

[90]Cohen, *eršemma*, 28.

[91]Cohen, *eršemma*, 12.

[92]Kutscher, *Oh Angry Sea*, 4.

[93]Cohen, *eršemma*, 9f., 27f.; Cohen, *balag*, 11, 13-15; Kutscher, *Oh Angry Sea*, 6f.; Krecher, *Kultlyrik*, 18-25, 34.

feasts, or rituals like the Akitu festival or the ritual for covering the sacral kettledrum, 3) *namburbi* incantation rites to forestall impending doom, and 4) especially those circumstances of pulling down sacred buildings to prepare the site for rebuilding.

The structure of first millennium laments was flexible but usually followed a broad pattern as follows:

1) praise to the god of destruction, usually Enlil
2) description of the destruction
3) lamenting the destruction ("How long?")
4) plea to the destructive god to be pacified
5) plea to the god to gaze upon the destruction
6) plea to other deities (often a goddess) to intercede
7) further description of the ruin.

Those poetic techniques employed by lament composers may be outlined under the following captions:

1) interchange of speaker (third, second, first person) involving description (third person), direct address (second person), monologue (first person), dialogue (first, second, and third persons)
2) use of woe-cries and various interjections
3) use of Emesal dialect apparently to simulate high-pitched cries of distress and pleading
4) heavy use of couplets, repeating lines with one word changed from line to line, and other devices of parallelism
5) antiphonal responses
6) tendency to list or catalog (gods, cities, temples, epithets, victims, etc.)
7) use of theme word or phrase which serves as a cord to tie lines together, or whole stanzas.

We may outline the underlying ideas under three major captions: divinity, humanity, and causality.

A. Divinity

1) The god of wrathful destruction, usually Enlil, abandons the city, a signal for devastation, often called a "storm," to begin.
2) This chief god may bring the havoc himself or may order another deity to attack the city or sanctuary.
3) In any case, Enlil's will is irresistible; he has the backing of the council of gods.
4) Enlil is described and addressed in anthropomorphic terms:
    a) a warrior
    b) the shepherd of the people
    c) his word destroys
    d) his "heart" and "liver" must be soothed
    e) he must be roused from sleep
    f) he must inspect the ruins to see what has occurred
    g) he must be cajoled to change his mind.

5) Yet there is an unknowable quality to Enlil; he is unreachable.

6) Lesser deities must intercede with the chief god to bring an end to the ruin.

B. Humanity

Surprisingly, humans are of little significance in the laments. The gods occupy the limelight. The following ideas about the place of human beings do emerge, however:

1) Human tragedy is described in terms of
   a) death
   b) exile
   c) madness
   d) disruption of families
   e) demolishing the buildings associated with the general population.

2) Mesopotamian society placed great emphasis on job definition; it is a tragedy when people cannot fulfill their jobs.

3) The citizens were seen as Enlil's flock but were "trampled" by Enlil.

4) The only response the population can make to the disaster is to mourn and offer sacrifices and libations. There seems to be a pervading sense of helplessness before the gods' power.

5) A gap separates the citizens and the gods. People must keep their distance. A sign of the tragedy is that the temple is demolished and people can see into the holy sanctuary.

C. Causality

In Mesopotamian experience ultimate causation lies in the largely unseen world of the gods. Storms of barbarians may crash upon the city, but they were called upon the scene by a decision of Enlil in consultation with the council of the gods. The emphasis of the laments is upon the power of the divine, not upon the rightness of the decision. There appears no resort to the justness of the gods. The humans have committed no particular crime or sin which moves the gods to their decision. The devastation is not judgment on evil humans. In fact the Eridu lament says, "The storm, which possesses neither kindness nor malice, does not distinguish between good and evil."[94] There does appear to be a primitive magical use made of the laments, however. To recount the havoc and recite the appeasement of the god is the same as experiencing the disaster physically. The lament becomes a means of avoidance of ruin, in other words, a means of controlling the causality which resides with the gods.

When we look at the biblical Lamentations in the light of this typology, we are impressed with both similarities and differences. In order to move from the clearest to the least clear category, we begin with

---

[94]Green, *Eridu*, 342, 1. 1:20.

some observations relative to the theology of Lamentations. Those points of similarity and difference are:

1) God's majesty and irresistible power, 5:19 (but Lamentations goes beyond Mesopotamian laments by insisting on God's righteousness in 1:18, 3:22, 26, 32)

2) God was the cause of the city's fall, 1:5, 12-15, 17; 2:1-8, 17; 3:1-16 (God brings misery on the "man"), 32-38, 43-45; 4:11, 16; 5:22

3) God abandoned his city, 2:1 (refused to remember), 6 (spurned), 7 (spurned and rejected), 8 (thought to destroy); 5:20-22

4) God as a mighty warrior, 2:2-8, 20-22; 3:4-13, 16, 34; 4:11

5) God's wrath, 2:1-4, 6, 21, 22; 3:1, 43, 65-66; 4:11

6) God caused the destruction by his word, 2:17; 3:37, 38

7) God called upon to look at the havoc, 1:9, 11; 2:20; 3:61 (God is to hear the enemy's plots), 63; 4:16 (God refuses to look); 5:1 (God is to remember)

8) a goddess wanders about the destroyed city and bemoans its sad plight (Of course, Israelite theology could not tolerate such an idea, but the city Jerusalem fulfills this role especially in 1:12-17)

9) God to be aroused from sleep is totally lacking in biblical Lamentations

10) God's heart to be soothed and his liver pacified is likewise missing

11) God called upon to return to his abandoned city is missing

12) The theme of lesser gods called upon to intercede with the destroyer god is obviously lacking.

More space is devoted to humans and their plight in biblical Lamentations than in Mesopotamian laments. In both, the personified city occupies much of the description. Social grouping appears in rather general terms: king, princes, and elders; priests, prophets, and Nazirites; army men, pilgrims, and citizens; old men, mothers, young men, virgins, children, and infants; orphans and widows. Skilled craftsmen are not enumerated. The description of the horrors of war suffered by the population is in some ways a bit more gruesome in the biblical Lamentations. For example, young and old dying in the streets of thirst and hunger, the lethargic march of the priests, mothers eating their children, cruel enslavement of one-time nobles, the shame of ridicule and exposure—all are expressed in poignant detail.

As in the Mesopotamian laments the biblical Lamentations clearly placed ultimate causation with God, but God is justified in the decision since the citizenry of Jerusalem was guilty of numerous crimes (1:5, 8, 18, 20; 4:6). The prophets (2:14; 4:13), priests (4:13), and fathers (5:7) must bear a large portion of the guilt for their failure to correct the evils which prompted God to take his angry action. God's extreme action in warring against Jerusalem has produced repentance on the part of the survivors, however. Now the mercy and love of God are being sought to change the fortunes of the people and, especially, the city.

In comparing poetic techniques, we find the interchange of speaker involving first, second, and third persons with accompanying change in perspective reminiscent of dramatic or liturgical performance. Likewise woe-cries and interjections occur to intensify dramatic effect. Parallelism of various orders runs throughout the five Lamentations poems. Only the Mesopotamian predilection for cataloging is lacking in biblical Lamentations.

In addition, other strategies utilized by Mesopotamian laments appear in biblical Lamentations either directly or with modification. Among these devices are: the poet addresses God (1:10 and the whole of chapter 5), but God never answers; the poet addresses or questions Jerusalem who seems to function in Lamentations much as the goddess functions in Mesopotamian laments (2:13-16, 18-19; 4:21, 22); invective against the enemy (1:21, 22; 3:55-66; 4:21, 22), the city which weeps or speaks (1:1-3, 8, 9, 11-15, 16, 18-20, 22; 2:11, 20-22; 3:48-51, 55-66; 5:17), the city ridiculed or embarrassed (1:7, 8, 17, 19, 21; 2:15-17; 3:14 (the "man"), 30 (the "man"), 45 (the citizens), 46, 63; 4:12, 15), detailed description of the carnage (1:4, 5, 18-20; 2:2, 5-12, 20-22; 3:4-16 [the "man" is a prisoner]; 4:1-10, 14-15, 17-19; 5:1-18). The stock-in-trade woe-cry "How long?" does not occur in biblical Lamentations. Neither is restoration stated though we may infer that the total work envisions Jerusalem's rebuilding as do several statements which recall God's mercy (3:22-27, 31-33; 4:21, 22; 5:20-22).[95]

When we come to a comparison of structure and organization, we find a decided lack of similarity. God is not honored by reciting a long list of epithets. The simple order of movement perceivable in Mesopotamian laments does not occur (abandonment, invasion by the "storm," plea to the god to awake, rouse himself, and gaze upon the ruins, lesser gods involved to add weight to the pleas, further recalling the ruination). Each of the five poems does show "poetic development" especially discernable in change of speaker, but not a plot type of movement.

We come finally to the question of cultic context. On this question we are without documentation to inform us. Of the four cultic occasions when first millennium Mesopotamian laments were recited, the most likely candidate for the biblical is that of temple restoration.

Jer 41:5 informs us that some 80 mourners of Shechem, Shiloh, and Samaria brought offerings and incense to the "House of Yahweh"

---

[95]See Gottwald's discussion of the interplay of doom and hope in Lamentations in his chap. 3 ("The Key to the Theology of Lamentations"), chap. 4 ("The Theology of Doom") and chap. 5 ("The Theology of Hope") in *Studies in the Book of Lamentations*.

during the Gedaliah days following the temple's destruction at the hands of the Babylonians. The signs of their mourning were shaved off beards, ripped clothing, and gashed skin. Zech 7:3-5 refers to mournful fasts at Jerusalem in the fifth and seventh months which have been observed "these 70 years." Apparently a commemoration of the sack of Jerusalem and the burning of the Temple occurred in the fifth month and a memorial to the slain Gedaliah in the seventh month. Zech 8:19 adds to the fifth and seventh month fasts by citing fasts in the fourth month (the breaching of the walls) and in the tenth month (the onset of Nebuchadnezzar's final siege). We may assume from the statement in Jer 41:5 that some form of religious practice continued on the site of the largely demolished Temple. The other fasts likewise focused on the ruined city, walls, and Temple. Finally the time came for rebuilding the Temple immediately following the Persian conquest of Babylon and Cyrus's edict of toleration in 539. Exiles, including priests from Babylonia familiar with long practiced Mesopotamian liturgies for rebuilding demolished shrines, joined with their brothers who had been left behind "these 70 years" to live within sight of the ruins and to fast and mourn among the Temple's ruins. Together they bewailed the fallen sanctuary as clearing the site began in preparation for reconstruction. Such an occasion would provide a fit setting for the recitation of Lamentations and could have provided the impetus for writing or editing these five lament-poems for the performance.

V. CONCLUSION

McDaniel rejected direct Sumerian influence on the biblical Lamentations on the grounds that there was too great a gap between them in terms of both time and space.[96] Furthermore he argued that there were no distinctively Mesopotamian elements in the biblical book.[97] On the basis of the discoveries of the 1970s we can now fill the gap in time between the city-laments and biblical Lamentations with the lineal liturgical descendants of the city-laments, the *balag-eršemma*s. Gadd's suggestion [98] that the Babylonian Exile provided the opportunity for the Jewish clergy to encounter the laments has proved correct. We may add that the exiles of the Northern Kingdom also had similar opportunities in the cities of Assyria to observe or participate in these rituals. Thus the spatial gap has been closed also. Beyond these considerations, we have demonstrated strong analogies between the Mesopotamian lament

[96]McDaniel, "Sumerian Influence," 207f.

[97]McDaniel, "Sumerian Influence," 207.

[98]Gadd, "Second Lamentation," 61, cited in McDaniel, "Sumerian Influence," 209.

[99]McDaniel, "Sumerian Influence," 209.

typology and that of the biblical book of Lamentations though there were dissimilarities also. Because of the polytheistic theology underlying the Mesopotamian laments and their ritual observance, they could not be taken over without thorough modification in theology and language. Still the biblical book of Lamentations was more closely associated with the Near Eastern lament genre than simply borrowing the "idea" of a lament over the destruction of a city as McDaniel conceded.

[Addendum:
Mark E. Cohen's significant study, *Sumerian Hymnology: The Eršemma* (*HUCA Supplement* 2 [Cincinnati: Hebrew Union College-Jewish Institute of Religion, 1981]), appeared while this study was in press, and consequently, could not be incorporated into the body of this essay. Although most of Cohen's later conclusions were anticipated in the earlier form of his dissertation, one major refinement requires a modification in the discussion of the first millennium *eršemma* offered above.

On pages 27, 41, and 42 Cohen calls attention to *eršemmas* labeled *kidudû* which appear in incipit lists unrelated to any *balag*. These independent *eršemmas* were recited in various ceremonies such as those relating to the covering of the sacred building. Thus the *eršemma* enjoyed two forms of usage in the first millennium, that is, as a separate work and as the last section of the composite *balag-eršemma*, The recognition of this independent status of the *eršemma* does not alter the conclusions drawn concerning the composite *balag-eršemma*, however.]

JOB AND ANCIENT NEAR EASTERN WISDOM LITERATURE

R. G. ALBERTSON
University of Puget Sound

I. INTRODUCTION

The book of Job is not easily classified or neatly described. Its forms are various and its themes are complex. Features of it are very old while its final editors are among the most recent in Old Testament literature. Marvin Pope calls it "an oft' told tale"[1] and Robert Gordis describes it as "sui generis, literally unlike any other book, incomparable."[2] Yet there is a long history of frequently spun yarns with what Samuel Noah Kramer calls "the Job motif."[3] It is from them, their contexts, and from what contemporary scholars have written about them that this paper inquires as to a literary history developing around Job and its Near Eastern antecedents from which one can find fresh clues to unity in a fragmented text and a dubious genre.

"Clearly the book is not a literary unity as it stands," R. B. Y. Scott concluded.[4] He noted the disarrangement of the third cycle of dialogues, the intrusion of Wisdom Songs and of Elihu's speeches, the seeming irrelevance of the message of the voice out of the storm, and the difficulty in dating the canonized collection. He concluded that Job must have followed the rise to influence of the Deuteronomic point of view of which it is so profoundly critical, that linguistic similarities with Jeremiah place it in the early 7th century, and that the "shocking death in 609 B.C. of the reforming King Josiah" must have initiated a debate "out of which the book of Job was written."

Manuscripts associated with the timeless theme of the suffering of the righteous extend from the earliest Job text discovered at Qumran and

---

[1] M. Pope, *The Book of Job* (AB 15; Garden City, NY: Doubleday, 1965) xxix.

[2] R. Gordis, *The Book of God and Man—A Study of Job* (Chicago: University of Chicago, 1965) 4.

[3] S. N. Kramer, "Man and His God," *ANET*[3] (1976) 589.

[4] R. B. Y. Scott, *Proverbs and Ecclesiastes* (AB 18; Garden City, NY: Doubleday, 1965) xx.

dated in the last hundred and fifty years before the Christian era[5] back to a Sumerian account of an innocent victim written in 1700 B.C.E. from an original composition dated by Kramer at least three hundred years earlier.[6] It is no wonder that Elie Wiesel was struck by the irony of a figure out of the distant past who cursed the day he was born, wanted to die, and has lived almost forever.[7]

William W. Hallo and others have sought and established a criterion of basic linguistic unity for Sumerian literature including the distinctive features, "antiquity, longevity and continuity."[8] The classification, Wisdom literature, and subclassification, the Job motif, may well be informed by features of that search and by establishing the position of each work in a tradition, by approaching the history of genres and the development of a type morphologically, and by identifying major periods of creativity, adaptation and consolidation.

The thesis of this study of the Job motif in the context of its own Biblical setting and in that of Ancient Near Eastern Wisdom Literature is that similarities and differences, continuity and creative variation, contribute to the discovery of an integrity in the Biblical book.

Attempts to impose unified interpretations on Job have been made by disciples of the doctrine of retribution, by advocates of theodicy, and by theistic apologists. Yet each mistakes a fragment for the whole, or excludes fragments that do not fit the favored view. Job has resisted unification by retribution, justice, and theophany. The alternative is to examine the work in the larger contexts of other biblical literature and of selected Near Eastern texts.[9]

II. JOB, NOAH AND DANIEL IN EZEKIEL

The first contribution to a sense of unity in Job derived from biblical scholarship is in reference to the name itself and to parallel situations. Shalom Spiegel and Martin Noth traced the mention of Job with Noah and Daniel in the book of Ezekiel.[10]

---

[5]B. Zuckerman, "Job, Book of," IDBSup (Nashville: Abingdon, 1976) 479-81.

[6]S. N. Kramer, ANET.

[7]E. Wiesel, "Job: Our Contemporary," Messengers of God (New York: Random House, 1976) 212.

[8]W. W. Hallo, "Toward a History of Sumerian Literature," Sumerological Studies in Honor of Thorkild Jacobsen (=AS 20; Chicago: University of Chicago, 1974) 181-203.

[9]M. Pope, Job, 1-lxvi.

[10]S. Spiegel, "Noah, Danel, and Job, Touching on Canaanite Relics in the Legends of the Jews," Louis Ginzberg Jubilee Volume (New York: AAJR, 1945) 303-55; M. Noth, "Noah, Daniel, and Hiob in Ezechiel XIV," VT 1 (1951) 251-60.

> Even though these three men, Noah, Daniel, and Job, were in it (the land), they would by their righteousness deliver only their own lives, says the Lord God (Ezek 14:14).

And again.

> Even though Noah, Daniel, and Job were in it, as I live, says the Lord God, they would save neither son nor daughter; they, by their righteousness, would save but themselves (14:20).

If Daniel was the biblical Daniel, Spiegel pondered, why were the names out of chronological synchronization? If the three were listed as ancient and righteous deliverers of sons and daughters perhaps another hero with the same name as Job was meant.

It is useful to learn that an Ugaritic hero, Dan³el (compare $dn^{\jmath}l$ in Ezek 14 and $dny^{\jmath}l$ in Ezek 28:3 to $dny^{\jmath}l$ in the book of Daniel and $dny^{\jmath}l$ in the Ugaritic) was the king of a region near Mt. Hermon. His palace and court and his harness of silver and saddle of gold marked him as "one whom the gods prospered." He had a dutiful wife, generous in entertaining, but, alas, barren. The king, conscious of their advanced age, stormed heaven with supplications and sacrifices, offerings and oblations for seven days and seven nights, all the time "weeping tears like quarter shekels." Baal, Dan³el's personal god, was moved to mercy and took the petitioner's case to the head of the Ugaritic pantheon, kindly El, who heard and heeded the request, promised a male heir, and sent the king home with joy. There he fed with a generous hand all the goddesses-of-the-new-born and the givers-of-all-good-bounty for seven days and sent them on their way. In due time a son was born and was named Aqhat (a name according to Spiegel that could mean "obedience or filial piety," a central theme in the story). As the lad grew to manhood he incurred the jealousy of Anath the war goddess who had him killed. King Dan³el roared with grief and raged and prayed for the gods to scorch the earth for seven years of drought. He cursed the cities near his slain son and gathered the boy's bones for careful burial (a prerequisite for resurrection). It began to rain and Anath breathed the breath of life into the nostrils of Aqhat. The lad was revived and restored to Dan³el. The broken text then lists four (originally seven?) repetitions of what a dutiful son does for his father. Hearing the recital of filial faithfulness the king broke free from his sorrow and laughed, resting his foot on a footstool and singing a song of praise and thankfulness for the restored family, for what a son means to a father, and for the manner in which a pious and righteous father can deliver and redeem his children.

Spiegel was aware of the double connectedness of the three righteous family restorers. Noah was a just man and perfect in his generation; it was his righteousness that rescued all his house from the flood, his wife and sons and his sons' wives (daughters). Job was a man "perfect and upright" who regained his children, or replacements for them.

The precise date of the passage in Ezekiel coincides with the prophet's grim warnings about hopeless rebellion, the horrors of family separation, the perils to sons and daughters. Not even the righteousness of Noah, Dan²el and Job could save them from the pending judgment. What unites the three narratives besides their international (gentile) witness to righteousness and shared roles in restoring families is the fact that "each survives the wreckage of an old order, sees the world reborn." Spiegel holds that the author of Job utilized such a folktale to say "yes" to Job's innocence, that there is such a thing as "unselfish virtue," and "yes" to the suspicion left in the wake of the damaged Deuteronomic doctrine of retribution, "there is such a thing as undeserved suffering."[11]

III. PARALLELS IN THE JOSEPH STORY

But what good is such suffering? In literature the difference between pathos and tragedy turns on the answer. In Donald B. Redford's discussion of the Joseph story as literature and as a *Märchen-Novelle* rather than Wisdom, the use of reversals plays an important, if ironic, part. The cloak of Joseph is evidence to clear the brothers of guilt in the hands of Jacob, but his coat in the hands of Potiphar's wife condemns innocent Joseph in his master's eyes. The dreams he interpreted at home put him in trouble with his brothers, but the interpretation of the Pharoah's dreams in Egypt got him out of trouble and put him in a position to aid his brothers. The special affection of the father for Joseph and for Benjamin caused them suffering and terror and forced the other brothers to plan and execute evil deeds, but the story concludes that what they meant for evil God used for good. All these reversals are cited as evidence of the storyteller's art in what Redford describes as a "masterpiece . . . perhaps unequalled in Biblical literature." That Redford refuses to see Joseph as an idealized Wise Man of the court, and perceives the moralistic editing of the retribution reversal as a miscellaneous parallel imposed by someone under the influence of such a court, does not detract from the power of the reversals to "subvert a hearer's expectation and to reveal a teller's intention."[12]

It is to the possibility of "classical recognition" and the shudder that accompanies it that Gerhard von Rad points in his description of Joseph and of Job as "didactic narratives." Von Rad calls the reader's attention to the intention of the narrator in linking innocence and affection, envy and terror, and providence and family restoration in a causal chain. The plot invites sensitivity to the awful implications of righteousness, of envy (brothers, or the Satan in the divine council), of

[11]S. Spiegel, "Noah, Danel, and Job," 305.
[12]D. B. Redford, *A Study of the Biblical Story of Joseph* (VTSup 20; Leiden: E. J. Brill, 1970) 67-74.

undeserved suffering (Egypt or Edom, prison or dung heap), of the meeting of accuser and accused (actualized between Joseph and his brothers, invited by Promethean Job), of the moment of recognition and dramatic resolution (in revealing himself to his brothers, Joseph witnesses to the way in which intended evil has worked for good, and in recognition Job sees and knows "beyond good and evil"). In both stories the family is restored even at the expense of unanswered questions: could God's goodness to righteous Job have caused the wager that occasioned the suffering that initiated the new relationship between Job and his Sovereign and the restoration of the family?

For von Rad the most important factor in the stories is that "in all the calamity and confusion, miraculously, a beneficent divine plan was at work. . . . Not only did God have an overall hand in the situation, but in the evil a divine guiding force succeeded in bringing about deliverance."[13]

IV. PARALLELS IN THE STORY OF ABRAHAM

The story of Abraham has provided a third source of comparison within the Biblical context for contemporary scholarship, not so much for themes in the Genesis account as for the structure itself. The manner in which a self-contained story unit is analyzed by John Van Seters is as suggestive for the study of Job as the role of reversal and recognition just described. The problem of the relationship between Abraham and Sarah on entering Egypt had remained unsolved even after E. A. Speiser's application of Hurrian marriage customs to the thrice told tale (Genesis 12, 20, and 26). Van Seters followed a lead from the ten "epic laws" of A. Olrik to create from a "relatively simple and straightforward" tradition a structure consisting of five elements:

a) a situation of need, problem or crisis
b) a plan to deal with the problem (wise or foolish)
c) the execution of the plan with some complication
d) an unexpected outside intervention
e) fortunate or unfortunate consequences

In Genesis 12:10-20 there is a crisis (a) in that the famine in Canaan has forced Abraham and Sarah to travel temporarily to a foreign and potentially hostile region, Egypt. Because Sarah is very beautiful such a situation could endanger the life of her husband, Abraham. So the patriarch devises a plan (b) that they act as brother and sister. This means that Abraham, as her guardian, will be well-treated for her sake. It may also suggest that Abraham could forestall any suitors for the duration of the famine. The plan is put into effect (c) and is successful as far as Abraham's life is concerned, but with a complication. Sarah is taken into the royal harem.

[13]G. von Rad, *Wisdom in Israel* (Nashville/New York: Abingdon, 1972) 200.

There is, however, an unexpected intervention by God (d) who plagues Pharoah, and thereby the inadvertent act of adultery is disclosed. Yet since Pharaoh is as threatened by the circumstances as is Abraham, the danger to the Patriarch is neutralized and Pharoah merely expels the man and his wife from the land (e). In the end Abraham is greatly enriched by the whole turn of events.[14]

More important than the line by line application of the structure to the story is the manner in which the exercise indicates the tenacity of the tradition in its repetition and the function of basic elements. In comparing Genesis 12, 20, and 26 the similarities and differences are clear; those elements that constitute the tradition are readily distinguished from other features of the story that contribute to its entertainment value, but then are secondary to the essential structure.

Van Seters notes the "fine balance" between the plan, as set forth in vv 11-13, the execution/complication, in 14-16, and the divine intervention and consequences, vv 17-20. What was a troublesome problem becomes incorporated into the unity of the narrative, a feature of a significant text.

In such a manner the structure of the story of Job may cease to be a problem, and a canonized collection of sometimes disparate fragments may reflect its literary integrity and religious meaning.

V. PROVERBS: BASIC UNIT AND NARRATIVE STRUCTURE

In Wisdom Literature the proverb is the basic unit. Common moral sense expressed succinctly constitutes the tenacious tradition. J. L. Crenshaw refers to the proverb as the "constitutive element" and asserts that it serves as the vehicle for the doctrine of retribution and the handmaiden of Deuteronomic history.[15] The proverb is practical, international, universal, brief and to the point, ordinary, traditional, ancient, simple, active rather than reflective, collected rather than created, preserved rather than revised, and defended rather than examined. It is the key to success. Fathers and mothers (older sisters, teachers and wise kings) pass proverbs along to siblings, students and subjects. When all else fails, the proverb endures. Like the drone of an Indian raga, the proverb contributes to the unity and the harmony of the cosmos. It holds the world together. It gives Wisdom its generic quality, its didactic mission, and its cynical potential.

In the structure of the Joban motif two elements accompany the basic unit: righteous innocence and suffering. Obedience introduces the former while experience assures the latter.

[14]J. Van Seters, *Abraham in History and Tradition* (New Haven: Yale University, 1975) 168.
[15]J. L. Crenshaw, "Prologomenon," *Studies in Ancient Israelite Wisdom* (New York: KTAV, 1976) 15.

J. J. A. Van Dijk translated and classified ancient wisdom and created an inclusive list of sub-genres that has freed scholars from the narrowness of notions of Wisdom limited to expressions of retribution and theodicy. His eleven sub-genres began with proverbs and concluded with righteous-sufferer poems. Between the extremes were fables and parables, folk-tales and miniature essays, letters to gods and men, school (*edubba*) compositions and wisdom disputations (*tensons*), maxims and practical instructions and precepts.[16]

By following Van Seters and the search for unity in the Abraham and Sarah story, and von Rad and Redford in the application of reversal and recognition to the story of Joseph, one perceives the relevance of a narrative structure. Now two elements are added to the basic unit (retribution's proverb) of the genre: innocence and suffering. If what the hearer or reader receives from a story is a moral lesson including proverb, obedience, and reward, then the structure is simple and there are no surprises. And even if one recognizes from experience a reversal and instead of a reward obedience results in suffering, still the reflexes of the audience accommodate what has become an extended proverb. The righteous sufferer will practise patience, express pain and (unfounded) penitence and the reward, though delayed, will be forthcoming. The reversal may even be doubled to include the immediate rewarding of disobedience, but ultimately retribution will adjust and renewal will come to the righteous. In Job, however, a genre that provides only proverb, retribution, innocence, and immediate or delayed reward is inadequate to carry the weight of the narrative or give integrity to the text. Van Dijk's extended list of sub-genres incorporates the needed addition: wisdom disputations. An important motif is added to the search for unity in Job. S. Talmon defines its significance as follows:

A literary motif is a representative complex theme which recurs within the framework of the Old Testament in variable forms and connections . . . (it) gives expression to ideas and experiences inherent in the original situation, and is employed to reactualize in the audience the reactions of the participants in that original situation. . . .[17]

VI. THE CONTROVERSY PATTERN

Van Dijk's wisdom disputations (*tensons*) constitute such a representative complex form and theme. Both G. Ernest Wright and George E. Mendenhall have written on it as the *rîb* or controversy pattern in

---

[16]J. J. A. Van Dijk, "Les Justes Souffrants," *La Sagesse Suméro-Accadienne: Recherches sur les Genres Litteraires des Textes Sapitiaux* (Leiden: E. J. Brill, 1953) 119-34.

[17]S. Talmon, "The Desert Motif in the Bible and in Qumran Literature," *Biblical Motifs* (ed. A. Altmann; Cambridge, MA: Harvard University, 1966) 39.

Deuteronomy 32, the Song of Moses. Wright interprets the passage against the basic form of a divine lawsuit with the heavenly assembly serving as a court of law. He traces a three-part pattern for the lawsuit, including the summons to witnesses, the indictment, and the verdict of the judge and delivery of sentence. Heaven and earth are the judges, Yahweh is the plaintiff, and Israel the accused. Such a heavenly lawsuit implies a suzerain who claims authority over all the powers on earth and presides over the highest tribunal in the universe. Furthermore, a covenant is implied which the suzerain has granted a vassal and that the vassal has broken. Wright compares the form of the Mosaic Covenant Renewal with that of the Covenant Lawsuit and concludes that the latter is a reformulation of the former and thus a covenant-renewal confession, a hymn of hope and faith for resolving tensions, and a didactic device in the period between 900 and 600 B.C.E. Wright suggests that the rîb was used in Job to provide Yahweh (the voice out of the whirlwind) with an occasion to recite his providential goodness as well as to warn and threaten Israel. Consistent with Deuteronomic determinism, Israel rebelled and was punished. The rîb in the Song of Moses, Wright concluded, had both a Deuteronomic and a Prophetic dimension. The writer or final editor of Job must have known the implications of such a prophecy for a rebellious individual as well as for a nation.[18]

Mendenhall minimized the significance of Wright's supreme court covenant renewal and covenant lawsuit setting. He saw the rîb as a much more familiar phenomenon in Palestine, a village court procedure used metaphorically in the realm of religion and historical thought. He reduced the text to a proverb, a moral story, "Whatsoever a man sows, that shall he also reap," and neither a covenant renewal nor a lawsuit at all.[19]

Where some see the dialogues between Job and his friends as a rîb in the formal sense, R. N. Whybray and others minimize the dimension of disputation appropriate to logical discourse. The alternation between questions and answers and between Job and his friends is not a dispute since points raised are seldom refuted. Rather than a proper debate the dialogues are no more than people taking turns talking. The friends frequently and consistently recite proverbial retribution doctrine. Job speaks redundantly of innocence and suffering. Only Elihu, in his three orderly refutations, seems to know how to debate. Should a knowledgeable editor have inserted Elihu's three summary statements, one between

[18]G. E. Wright, "The Lawsuit of God: A Form Critical Study of Deuteronomy 32," *Israel's Prophetic Heritage* (ed. B. W. Anderson and W. Harrelson; New York: Harper and Row, 1962) 22-68.

[19]G. E. Mendenhall, "Samuel's 'Broken Rîb': Deuteronomy 32," *No Famine in the Land* (Festschrift John L. McKenzie; Missoula: Scholars Press, 1975) 63-74.

each of the three rounds, an appropriate symmetry would have been preserved and a model formal disputation approached.[20]

The most thorough treatment of the *rîb* as controversy pattern comes from B. Gemser. He believes that it is to be found throughout the Bible both in the courtroom and in the family, between Yahweh and Israel, and as a persistent feature of the Hebrew mentality (or human nature) expressed in contentiousness. Gemser traces the semantics of *rîb*, its use in the legal clauses of the Book of the Covenant, of Deuteronomy, of Prophetic literature, and in specific court procedures such as bringing a matter into court, laying the case before the assembly of judges, calling witnesses and adversaries (Job 9:19, 13:18, 23:4). The accusation, mostly brought orally before the court, could also be handed in in writing ("O that I had the indictment written by my adversary!" Job 31:35). Also the defense could be presented in writing ("Here is my signature!" Job 31:35). Gemser indicates the relationship between *hokmâ* (wisdom) and *rîb* by identifying 26 occurrences in Proverbs and 19 in Job in which derivatives of the verb *hôkîah* are applied to actions of different actors in a dispute including mediators, arbiters, umpires ("Would that there were an umpire between us who might lay his hands upon us both!" Job 9:33).

Gemser cites Jeremiah (as well as Moses) as a parallel to Job, a contender with Almighty God, "soft, sensitive, peace-loving, not at all quarrelsome by nature, but characterized by himself as a 'man of strife and contention to the whole world.'" Jeremiah's dialogues with God contain accusations, questions, declarations of innocence, divine answers, rebukes, vindications; they are full of judicial phraseology, and are characterized by the prophet as *rîb* and *mišpāṭîm* (cases presented for judgment). So with Job; the audacious religious individualism is carried still further, according to Gemser.

> . . . not a prophet, but an individual as such, albeit a blameless servant who enters into judgment with his God on account of his personal experiences and sufferings. The book not only abounds in judicial phraseology, but formally it cannot be better understood than as the record of the proceedings of a *rîb* between Job and God Almighty in which Job is the plaintiff and prosecutor, the friends of Job are witnesses as well as co-defendants and judges, while God is the accused and defendant.[21]

Yet in the background and in the final analysis Gemser perceives God as the ultimate judge of both Job and his friends, and their restorer.

[20]R. N. Whybray, *The Intellectual Tradition in the Old Testament* (BZAW 136; Berlin/New York: Walter de Gruyter, 1974) 61-67.

[21]B. Gemser, "The Rib—or Controversy Pattern—in Hebrew Mentality," VTSup 3 (Leiden: E. J. Brill, 1960) 120-37.

Further, Van Dijk holds that the traditional prize in the formal *rîb*, a piece of money, is bestowed on the winner.[22]

> The Lord gave a turn to the fortunes of Job when he interceded for his friends; and the Lord doubled all his previous possessions. Then came to him all his brothers and sisters and all his former acquaintances and ate bread with him in his house; they also bemoaned him and comforted him for all the affliction, which the Lord had brought upon him, and every one gave him a piece of money and a gold ring (42:10-11).

The genre and sub-genres appropriate to Job are given fullest expression by including the classifications of Van Dijk. Proverbs, righteous sufferer poems, and wisdom disputations extend retribution, righteousness and suffering to include contention and controversy. Van Dijk equates the sub-genre, *tensons*, with a Sumerian phrase, *adaman-duga* (duels with words). Edmund Gordon heralded Van Dijk's 1953 publication of Akkadian and Sumerian wisdom literature "including a new and more precise classification of the known wisdom literature into eleven genres" by describing the event as "the turning point in the study of the wisdom literature of ancient Mesopotamia."[23] He might have added, "and of Job in both its Biblical and Near Eastern contexts as well."

VII. "MAN AND HIS GOD"

The first of the Near Eastern texts to be considered is that which Kramer identified as "Man and his God" from the tablets excavated at Nippur and inscribed about 1700 B.C.E. as a copy of an original composition from the beginning of the second millennium. Its author was a sage of the *edubba* or Sumerian academy. The piece, consisting of five tablets and fragments, was written to prescribe "the proper attitude and conduct for a victim of cruel and seemingly undeserved misfortune." Kramer confirms the basic assumption of such wisdom literature, the doctrine that misfortunes result from misdeeds, that no man is without guilt, and that there are therefore no instances of injustice, of undeserved suffering. Man may think of himself as innocent until the gods quicken his consciousness to realize the truth of the line from the Sumerian version of the righteous sufferer: "Never was a sinless child born to its mother." Because of the temptation of the uninitiated to challenge the justice of the gods and to contend with them in a blasphemous manner the "school composition" was written. The five parts of the poem are:

[22] J. J. A. Van Dijk, *La Sagesse*, 40 n. 48. [See in greater detail *idem, Orientalia et Biblica Lovaniensia* 1 (1957) 15f. Ed.]

[23] E. I. Gordon, "A New Look at the Wisdom of Sumer and Akkad," *BiOr* 17 (1960) 122-52.

1) instructions for praising the god and soothing him with lamentations
2) introduction of the hero who describes his miserable condition
3) petition of the sufferer, description of mistreatment by friends and foes, request for their help in singing his woes
4) confession of guilt and final plea for deliverance
5) deliverance and doxology.

It is of special interest that the first parts of the poem to be published, before all of it was found and identified, were thought to be proverbs (basic units); the work was only identified as a righteous sufferer poem when more of the fragments were joined and the essay could be read in its entirety. Kramer acknowledges that the poem contains no philosophical speculation, but limits itself to a direct working out of the situation by remaining within the conservative dimensions of the common morality and the established form for coming before the god. The wise and righteous hero blessed with family and friends loses his health, wealth, and respect, but not his patience or temper. Humbly he approaches his personal god with tears and prayerful petitions. His god is pleased and compassionate, heeds his prayer and restores him, turning his sorrow to joy. The Sumerian Job "was not to argue and complain in face of seemingly unjustifiable misfortunes, but to plead and wail, lament and confess his inevitable sins and failings to his personal god."[24]

Thorkild Jacobsen classifies "Man and his God" as a Penitential Psalm. In that sub-genre as in "Letters to Gods" Jacobsen perceives the notion of an appeal to a personal god rather than to an abstract sovereign. The appeal of the young hero to such a deity is apparent in the following translation by Kramer:[25]

My companion says not a true word to me,
My friend gives the lie to my righteous word.
The man of deceit has conspired against me,
(And) you, my god, do not thwart him.
You carry off my understanding . . .

The man—his bitter weeping was heard by his god,
When the lamentation and wailing that filled him had soothed the heart of his god for the young man,
The righteous words uttered by him, his god accepted,
The words which the young man prayerfully confessed,
Pleased the . . . , the flesh of his god, (and) his god withdrew his hand from the evil word,
. . . which oppresses the heart.

[24]S. N. Kramer, *The Sumerians* (Chicago: University of Chicago, 1963) 125-29, esp. p. 126.
[25]Ibid., 127.

Jacobsen, noting that the god still cares "deeply and personally about him and his fortunes," notes the paradox in such personal religion between the holiness (divine distance) of god and the singular worth to him of an individual.[26]

In the piece discussed above the basic proverbial unit dominates, the single reversal is the expected one: an innocent man suffers. There is no contention or rebellion but dialogue on a highly personal level and a predictable resolution—renewal. The ascending parallel structure embellishes the basic unit.

VIII. THE BABYLONIAN JOB AND THE BABYLONIAN THEODICY

In the introductory essay to W. G. Lambert's collection of Babylonian Wisdom Literature the author indicates the failure of such counsel as that of the school's wise man to repress controversy. The growth of law codes from the time of Ur III (2100-2000 B.C.E.) onwards accentuated the problem of felt injustice. "If, in the microcosm, a matter could be taken to law and redress secured, why, in the macrocosm, should one not take up a matter with the gods?" With the Deuteronomists of fourteen centuries later yet to come the most common complaint in the relationship between men and gods, as between nations, or between men, would be over broken contracts. "A man served his god faithfully, but did not secure health and prosperity in return. The problem of the righteous sufferer was certainly implied from the time of Third Dynasty of Ur. An Akkadian name of this period was *Mina-arni*, 'What-is-my-guilt?' "[27]

Lambert compares two religious texts written during the second half of the second millennium B.C.E., both of which imply the line of reasoning: I have suffered, I must have done wrong; what can it be? The first text, a Babylonian dialogue between a man and his god, incorporates the plaintive cry, "The crime which I did I know not." Marduk is addressed by one Šubši-mešre-Šakkan, formerly a man of influence and authority who had occupied high positions, owned slaves and fields, had a family, and was a model of piety to gods and to the king. The poem of the righteous sufferer begins with the line, "I will praise the Lord of Wisdom," and has sometimes been referred to as "The Babylonian Job." The second text, in which the speaker says, "I have been treated as one who has committed a sin against his god," is written as an acrostic perhaps a little later than the first (c. 1000 B.C.E.) and has been identified as "The Babylonian Theodicy."

---

[26]T. Jacobsen, *Treasures of Darkness* (New Haven/London: Yale University, 1975) 147-64, esp. p. 150.

[27]W. G. Lambert, *Babylonian Wisdom Literature* (Oxford: Clarendon Press, 1960) 10.

"I Will Praise the Lord of Wisdom" is a monologue asking the standard question of Marduk's reason for allowing his servant to suffer.[27a] The responsibility is placed squarely on the god, not on human persecutors or devils or even personal gods. Men do not make or maintain moral standards; they are invested with the gods. In time sufferings end and bliss will follow, but until then, despair. The outline includes

a) introduction
b) complaint that the hero is forsaken by gods
c) humans, from slaves to the king, have turned on him
d) the hero is afflicted by all kinds of diseases
e) deliverance is promised in three dreams
f) health is restored.

Again, the theme of ultimate restoration dominates the poem. Little space is given for reflection on reasons for suffering righteousness. Lambert notes the "blasphemous implications" of such probing and the willingness of the hero to wait, to hope. "Though it be the Lord who has smitten, yet it is the Lord who will heal."

In the "Babylonian Theodicy" a dialogue is supported by a symmetrical pattern of eleven-line alternate contributions from the hero and the friend. In each the hero, "Saggil-kinam-ubbib, the exorcist, an adorant of the god and king," is given the first and last word. Unlike the above, this poem pays much attention to the oppressors and thereby becomes a document of social history. The friend repeats again and again his conviction that "piety brings prosperity"; yet, he never accuses the sufferer and, unlike Job's counsellors, maintains friendly respect for his unfortunate friend, a feeling that is reciprocated. Evils of the society are pointed out by the sufferer, and life's experiences with unexplainable injustices are rehearsed, even agreed with, but no answers are forthcoming. The doctine of retribution is never questioned, only asserted. Lambert notes the similarity in form between this poem and Psalm 119 and is complimentary to the author and his "consummate learning" and careful literary workmanship as evidenced in the following three passages:

(1) Mankind is deaf and knows nothing.
    What knowledge has anyone at all?
    He knows not whether he had done a good or a bad deed.
(2) Where is the wise man who has not transgressed and (committed) an abomination?
    Where is he who has checked himself and not ba(ckslided?).
(3) Who is there who has (checked) himself and not done an abomination?
    People do not know their(..) which is not fit to be seen.

[27a][Cf. now also D. J. Wiseman, "A New Text of the Babylonian Poem of the Righteous Sufferer," *Anatolian Studies* 30 (1980) 101-7. Ed.]

A god reveals what is fair and what is foul.
He who has his god—his sons are warded off.
He who has no god—his iniquities are many.[28]

In all of these poems the mentality of the proverb, wisdom's basic
unit, dominates as the only appropriate response to life's reversals. If
there was knowledge of this literature by biblical writers it must surely
have supported the conviction that patience was the proper price to pay
for restoration. But how unlike Job's strident attestation of innocence is
the soft acceptance by the hero of the "Babylonian Theodicy."

I have gone about the square of my city unobtrusively,
My voice was not raised, my speech was kept low.
I did not raise my head, but looked at the ground.

May the god who has abandoned me give help,
May the goddess who has (forsaken me) show mercy.[29]

IX. JOB AND THE "TALE OF APPU"

There are indications that the name of Job is a clue to the history of
the literature. Execration texts from Egypt (ca 2000 B.C.E.) refer to a
Palestinian chief, ꜣybm, ꜣAyyabum. Akkadian documents from Mari,
Alalakh, and Amarna (Letter #256) describe a Prince of Ashteroth in
Bashan, Ay(y)ab, (a-ya-bu)—names translated by Albright as meaning,
"where is my father?"[30]

H. A. Hoffner, translating the "Tale of Appu" from Hittite mythol-
ogy, indicates that there is a slight resemblance in the two men's names,
but even greater similarity in their lives. Both were wealthy men living
in the East; each had an unsympathetic wife; each knew acute suffering.
Appu always lacked children, was always wealthy; Job lost both children
and wealth. Each contended with god. Appu became the father of twin
sons, and the folk tale continues as a moral story of family renewal.[31]

Tur-Sinai, in his commentary on Job, points to the authenticity and
antiquity of the name. He claims that ꜣAyyab>ꜣIyyob is a well-attested
common name borne by a number of Semites in the 2nd millennium. He
notes the strong Aramaic coloring in the book of Job, intertwined with
Hebrew, and holds that Job is more Aramaic than any other biblical
book, that the original Aramaic is Babylonian, not later than the
6th century. He concludes that the author of Job was a Jew writing in

---

[28]*Babylonian Wisdom Literature*, 16.
[29]Ibid., 89.
[30]B. Zuckerman, "Job," *IDBSup* 479.
[31]H. A. Hoffner, "Some Contributions of Hittitology to Old Testament
Study," *TynBul* 20 (1969) 27-55.

the early days of the Exile; later the book was translated in Palestine. But the name Job has double roots: Hebrew (ʾyb) and Arabic (ʾwb). The latter means "return, repent, the penitent or submissive one." But the former means "enmity, hostility, the inveterate foe." Tur-Sinai adds that the tension between the two roots might indicate one's ambiguity to seemingly senseless suffering.[32]

X. DISCONTINUITY

In developing a literary history the task to this point has been to develop a history of the genre within the biblical tradition and to examine evidences of it in the Ancient Near East, thus establishing a context in which continuity and change are apparent and in which periods of creativity, adaptation, and consolidation of the literary material appear.

It is to the differences rather than the parallels that we turn in conclusion: the changes, the creative elements in the book of Job that have threatened its own unity and raised problems for the genre itself as it has been stretched to include such texts as Proverbs and Ecclesiastes, Psalms and Esther, Genesis and Deutero-Isaiah.

The similarities have been recited. Job differs most dramatically in four ways:

a) although never denying the basic unit (the proverb and its use in defending the doctrine of retribution) the hero of Job moves away from it in his own utterances

b) the theodicy pattern (by means of which rewards are won: righteousness, suffering and penitence-lament) is broken

c) controversy (the rîb motif) is exaggerated

d) in relationship to other accounts, Job's rewards are overwhelming.

In the introduction to his collection of Babylonian Wisdom literature Lambert outlined a useful method for discerning change. He examined "two ends of the development" of an idea and "described them in broad terms in order to sketch the process of the development and to elaborate certain aspects of the later view as reflected in the earlier texts." For example, the "two ends" in the examination of the notion of the gods were Classical Sumerian/Neo-Sumerian (2500/1900) and Late Babylonian (600), periods that coincide roughly with the earliest stories of "Job" and the final writing of the biblical text. Lambert noted that the "most profound change" in the gods was their nature, for recalcitrant and immoral gods of the earlier period had become "responsible" by 1000. They would go to war with their respective city-states and would

---

[32]N. H. Tur-Sinai, *The Book of Job: a New Commentary* (Jerusalem: Kiryath Sepher, 1967) xxxvii-lxix.

share in the success or disaster, the guilt or credit. But an angered god could still forsake his city, leaving it vulnerable, even plot its downfall. The most common complaint of the later period was a broken contract. As gods ceased to personify aspects of nature and became gods in the rational image of man and man's purposes a new relationship emerged.[33]

In the wisdom texts with the Job motif the notion of the gods can be traced as well. First, a suffering hero would enlist the aid of a personal (lesser) god or goddess in getting the attention of and mercy from the high god. In "Ludlul Bel Nemeqi" lesser gods are present, but the hero takes his case directly to Marduk. In Job the personal god *is* the high God. When both an intercessor and one with whom to share the blame are gone, traditional theodicy is threatened, weakened. Jacobsen refers to the paradox of the Holy becoming the personal as a "tacit bridging of the cosmic world and the personal world" and the question it raises is, "How could such a union of contradictions in one attitude come to be; all that is highest, most awesome, and terrifying approached with such easy and close familiarity?"[34]

In tracing the historical evidence Jacobsen is led to the letter prayer and the penitential psalm as evidence of the accessibility of the divine. But Jacobsen sees Job as one who would write the letter prayer, but cannot know the address of the Sovereign . . . yet is addressed by Him in a way that re-establishes the distance. "The personal egocentric view of the sufferer is rejected. The self-importance which demands that the universe adjust to his needs, his righteousness, is cast aside, and the full stature of God as the majestic creator and ruler of the universe is reinstated."[35]

The inadequacy of man's notion of justice imposed on that kind of personal god requires a reformulation of wisdom itself. Uncommon sense rather than the proverbs of the ordinary is necessary. Albright sees a change in wisdom in the 6th century in the literature of Phoenicia and Ionia as well as Israel, new thinking that seems suddenly to appear, an active intellectual ferment which began with the foundation of Greek colonies all around the Eastern Mediterranean. He sees abundant evidence of Phoenician culture in Job and finds it significant that there is "not a single scriptural quotation in the whole of Job."[36]

R. B. Y. Scott anticipated the reformulation of wisdom in a manner that preserves its basic unit, the constitutive and conservative tradition, the continuity with the biblical context and with early Mesopotamia. He

---

[33]W. G. Lambert, *Babylonian Wisdom Literature*, 10.

[34]T. Jacobsen, *Treasures of Darkness*, 152.

[35]Ibid., 163.

[36]W. F. Albright, *Yahweh and the Gods of Canaan* (Garden City, NY: Doubleday, 1968) 258-60.

makes a distinction between levels of wisdom, between instructions for youth and assurances of their success, and the "speculative and radical, uncommon questioning" of Job. In Proverbs he notes ways to maintain morality, to predict prosperity, to encourage such standard values as modesty, decorum, obedience, goodness, self-control. But in Job he sees one sore-tested applying sapiential skill to Wisdom's ineffable mystery, to the riddle of the nature of man and god, to the possibility of relating without doctrinal aids-become-obstacles. He traces both levels of wisdom back into the Ancient Near East. In Egypt he found the emphasis on the conservative, practical, necessary, didactic common sense of Proverbs (with some exceptions), but in Mesopotamia he discovered evidence for both the tradition and the uncharted, the obedient and the speculative, the secure and the restive, the defensive and the critically offensive. The two levels of Wisdom were a necessary feature for the element of change: the one to maintain the tradition and assure its continuity, the other to recognize creative alternatives to adapt and survive.[37]

An illustration of the end of an era and the necessity of change, and perhaps the best evidence for dating Job no earlier than the Babylonian Exile (instead of the rise of Deuteronomic influence a century earlier), is found in Frank M. Cross's argument for dating Noth's Deuteronomic history (Dtr) in that period rather than with Josiah. The difference between the two editions of history is important to the unity of the literary material from Judges through Kings, but even more, for explaining the changes occurring in the life of the people and their hopes for the future. Cross points out that the retouching of the earlier Deuteronomic editing (his Dtr[1]) by the Exilic hand (Dtr[2]) contradicted the original theme of hope, denied the expectation of the restoration of the state, and muted the hope of repentance and possible return from Babylon. Such was the climate in which the author of Job wrote. The time for counseling patience was obviously past. The two wisdoms, the two histories (two doctrines of retribution) and the absence of the comforting compromise of two sovereigns explain if not justify the second pattern of contention, rîb, exaggerated controversy.[38]

The change, then, is from literature in which contention is repressed, sublimated, permitted to express itself only as lament, weeping and wailing, grovelling and confessing, a way to catch the attention and pity of the sovereign to affect renewal favorably . . . to Job. To read Job is to range through the full spectrum of the controversy pattern from sôd to rîb (from discussing with the elders at the city gate to challenging the Lord of History and the God of Nature to a duel with words), from seven

---

[37]R. B. Y. Scott, *Proverbs and Ecclesiastes*, xvii-xviii.
[38]F. M. Cross, *Canaanite Myth and Hebrew Epic* (Cambridge, MA/London: Harvard University, 1973) 287-89.

days of silence to twenty-six lines of lament, from eight of nine scheduled rounds of mounting maintenance of innocence against the accusations of friends to a scene in which Job stands up to the personal father Almighty God to recall his happiness, bewail his wretchedness, assert his integrity, hurl his challenge at the Deity without fear of indictment, approach his God as if he were a noble, a prince (though a farmer rather than a professional wise man), unbowed, unshattered, but not unheard.

The so-called insertion of Elihu at this point becomes an integral feature of a book-reclaiming-its-unity when it is seen in the structure of the *rîb* pattern. His three arguments are a reproof of Job, a justification of God, and a final defense of retribution (Dtr[1]) with Scott's "lesser wisdom." But Elihu illustrates the formal and proper use of disputation in debate, controlled controversy.

Three of the four changes in the book of Job compared to its counterparts have been accounted for. Retribution is not rejected, it is ignored. Theodicy is not repaired, it is replaced with higher level wisdom "beyond good and evil." The exaggerated controversy is understood in its historical context. But what about the renewal and the nature of the reward?

Perhaps, consistent with the literary structure of the folktale that not only accommodates reversals but creates them, the story of Job deliberately subverts the moral story once more, reverses the reader's expectation yet again. As with the reversals in the book of Ruth, or in Esther, or in the story of the prophet Jonah, the God of biblical literature needs room to act, to be God outside of the confines of pattern, expectation, comfortable and predictable symmetry. Job is a long parable. One does not expect a righteous servant to suffer, but he does. One expects the knowledgeable subject of similar tales to wait with patience, but he does not. Therefore one would hardly expect the reward of renewal to come since it is no longer necessary or expected by one "who had heard by the hearing of the ear, but whose eye now sees," but it does.[39]

This is not unique in the Job story. El and Marduk delight in turning sorrow to joy; it is their prerogative. In Job the reward seems irrelevant, the higher level wisdom that precedes it is overwhelming. So is the epilogue; it is unnecessary, unique, excessive, another epiphany.

---

[39] J. D. Crossan, *The Dark Interval* (Niles, IL: Argus, 1975) 121. This part of the paper draws heavily and gratefully on Crossan's discussion of the parable.

INDEX OF SUBJECTS

INDEX OF BIBLICAL REFERENCES

INDEX OF AUTHORS

970801   35.00 (17.47)